Eastern ⅄

M000214856

forthcoming

ECOLOGY CONTROL
& ECONOMIC DEVELOPMENT
IN EAST AFRICAN HISTORY

The Case of Tanganyika 1850–1950

ECOLOGY CONTROL
& ECONOMIC DEVELOPMENT
in East African History

The Case of Tanganyika
1850–1950

Second impression
with new Introduction
& additional Bibliography

HELGE KJEKSHUS

Formerly Senior Lecturer in Political Science
University of Dar es Salaam

James Currey
LONDON

Mkuki na Nyota
DAR ES SALAAM

EAEP
NAIROBI

Fountain Publishers
KAMPALA

Ohio University Press
ATHENS

James Currey
54b Thornhill Square
Islington
London N1 1BE

East African Educational Publishers
PO Box 45314
Nairobi

Mkuki na Nyota
PO Box 4246
Dar es Salaam

Fountain Publishers
PO Box 488
Kampala

Ohio University Press
Scott Quadrangle
Athens, Ohio 45701

© Helge Kjekshus 1977 & 1996

First published by Heinemann Educational Books
Second impression with new introduction 1996

2 3 4 5 6 00 99 98 97 96

British Library Cataloguing in Publication Data
Kjekshus, Helge.
    Ecology Control and Economic Development
    in East African History: Case of
    Tanganyika, 1850–1950. – 2Rev.ed. –
    (Eastern African Studies)
    I. Title   II. Series
    338.9678

ISBN 0-85255-728-0 (James Currey Paper)

Library of Congress Cataloging-in-Publication Data
Kjekshus, Helge.
    Ecology control and economic development in East African history/
Helge Kjekshus. -- 2nd ed.
        p.   cm.
    Originally published: London : Heinemann, 1977.
    Includes bibliographical references and index.
    ISBN 0-8214-1132-2 (pbk.)
    1. Tanzania--Economic conditions--To 1964.   2. Ecology--Tanzania-
-History.   3. Ecology--Africa, East--History.   I. Title.
HC885.K58   1995
338.9678--dc20   95-16144
                                                                      CIP

Typeset in 10/12 pt Baskerville
Printed and bound in Great Britain by Villiers Publications, London N3.

Contents

LIST OF MAPS

LIST OF FIGURES

LIST OF TABLES

Acknowledgements
to 1996 Impression

The suggestion made in the fall of 1993 by James Currey and Walter Bgoya to publish a second impression of *Ecology Control and Economic Development in East African History* has given me the privileged opportunity to revisit the subject after nearly 20 years. It has been an occasion to reflect on the study and relate it to the current discourse of the discipline in a new introductory chapter.

Research was carried out at the School of Oriental and African Studies (SOAS) at the University of London from January to February 1994. I am grateful to Dr David M. Anderson and Dr Richard Fardon for inviting me to SOAS and to the staff of the SOAS Library for excellent help and service.

I would also like to thank the authors of *Custodians of the Land: Ecology and Culture in the History of Tanzania* (Maddox, Giblin and Kimambo, eds, James Currey, London, 1996) for allowing me an advance view of their manuscript.

I have been fortunate to receive comments on the early drafts from David M. Anderson, Tore Linné Eriksen and Kjell Hødnebø, and I wish to thank them all for thoughtful criticism and suggestions.

The Norwegian Institute of International Affairs (NUPI) in Oslo has been helpful and supportive in the editorial work. Special thanks to Eilert Struksnes, and also Lynn Taylor at James Currey Publishers.

Finally, I want to thank the Royal Norwegian Ministry of Foreign Affairs and the Norwegian Agency for International Development (NORAD) for funding my research and travels.

Helge Kjekshus
London/ Oslo

Introduction
to 1996 Impression

The publication of *Ecology Control and Economic Development in East African History* (hereafter *Ecology Control*) in 1977 ended more than four years of data collection, applying novel paradigms and writing up my version of a historic past that had intrigued and puzzled me since my first encounter with Tanzania in 1966. Being a political scientist by training, the entry points chosen for ordering my queries were from the outset marked by some lack of historians' orthodoxies. This was, however, a deliberate choice that should be explained.

Taking as my starting point that people are the basis for their history, I initially sought to raise questions about assessments and quantifications of the early populations of the East African region. This led to my discovery of the writings of Rudolf Rene Kuczynski and his massive and learned study *Demographic Survey of the British Colonial Empire* (1949).[1]

Careful reading of Kuczynski's work convinced me that his thorough insights into demographic issues and the history of the East African populations had remained largely unnoticed by later historians. I felt that a reinterpretation of Tanzanian history should therefore commence with an effort to project the essentials of Kuczynski's work into the ongoing historical discourse.[2]

---

[1] Rudolf Rene Kuczynski (1876–1947) was a demographer and a statistician trained in some of the best European universities (Freiburg, Strasburg, Berlin and Munich) and with extensive experience from the USA (Brookings Institution in Washington) and England (London School of Economics and Political Science) where he made his home after leaving Germany in 1933. His many publications (Glass, 1948) leave no doubt that Kuczynski was a singular authority in his field, bringing rich historical insights and judicious common sense to his impeccable scholarship. His early interest in non-European population issues resulted in the book *Colonial Population* in 1937. He was named Demographic Adviser to the British Colonial Office in 1944. His life work is the study *Demographic Survey of the British Colonial Empire*, which was published in 1948–1953, after Kuczynski's death.

[2] I introduced my interpretation of Kuczynski's thinking on East African population history at a gathering of demographers and historians at Edinburgh University in 1977. Basil Davidson's summary of the discussion indicated a broad consensus among the participants about long-term population developments in Africa. See Fyfe, Christopher and David McMaster (eds.) (1977) *African Historical Demography* (Proceedings of a Seminar), University of Edinburgh, Centre of African Studies, and Wrigley, C.C. (1979) 'Population in African

The central work of another non-historian, the Danish economist Ester Boserup and her development models presented in *The Conditions of Agricultural Growth* (1965) was the second impulse for my understanding of economic initiatives in the Tanzanian past. Boserup's analysis was grounded in extensive field work in the Third World, notably in India and other Asian countries. Her well-argued model treated the population factor as an autonomous and dynamic element influencing changes in agricultural technology. In Boserup's observations, population growth led to increased and diversified food production. She noticed that agricultural change could be induced or imported and speeded up by ideas and practices borrowed from the outside. But she concluded that fundamental elements of dynamic change were inherent in traditional societies and were resting in the reproductive system itself.

The third impulse for *Ecology Control* came from a very personal experience. Sometime in 1973, as I recall it, I dropped in to listen to a lecture given at the University of Dar es Salaam by a visiting scholar, an entomologist and former Director of the East African Trypanosomiasis Research Organization. This person was John Ford, who talked about his work as a scientist dealing with the problem of tsetse flies in different places in Africa. I came away from the meeting with a compelling intuition that the speaker's ecological thesis put added meaning to my early drafts and research notes. I felt that I should re-examine my work in the light of Ford's thinking presented in the distinguished treatise *The Role of the Trypanosomiases in African Ecology* (1971).[3] This is a book which many find difficult and inaccessible. Others, with whom I agree, hold it to be 'the

---

[2] (cont.) History', *Journal of African History*, 20,1:127-131. The 'minimum population disruption thesis' from *Ecology Control* fitted well into the consensus on population development established at this time. As far as I can ascertain, there have been no major challenges to this consensus later. See Fyfe and McMaster (eds.) (1981) *African Historical Demography*. See also Hartwig, Gerald W. (1979) 'Demographic Considerations in East Africa During the Nineteenth Century', *International Journal of African Historical Studies*, 12,4:653-72 and Cordell, Dennis D. and Joel W. Gregory (eds.) (1987) *African Population and Capitalism: Historical Perspectives*, Boulder, Col.: Westview Press.

[3] John Ford (1910-1979) was educated at New College, Oxford before he was appointed Entomologist in the Department of Tsetse Research at Shinyanga, Tanganyika in 1938. At the outbreak of the Second World War, Ford enlisted in the colonial army. He was released with the rank of Captain in 1943 and rejoined the Tsetse Research Department in Shinyanga. In 1944 he was in charge of anti-tsetse work in Ankole, Uganda. He transferred to the East African Tsetse and Trypanosomiasis Research and Reclamation Organization in 1949 and became its Director in 1954. From 1957 Ford was the Director of the Tsetse and Trypanosomiasis Control Department of the Federation of Rhodesia and Nyasaland. In 1963 he served as FAO research officer on trypanosomiasis in Africa and continued research at the Agricultural Research Council of Central Africa in 1964. He returned to England in 1965 where he held an appointment at the University of London.

single most significant publication in the field of African human ecology in the last 25 years' (Richards, 1983:19).

. In summing up this sketchy genesis, I want to underline an important point about the book, namely its strong interdisciplinary character. It was the idea clustre of leading scientists in the fields of demography, economy and ecology that guided my understanding of the research material that eventually emerged as *Ecology Control.* These may have seemed unlikely historical impulses at the time. Nearly 20 years later, I am happy to note that the three mentors I have identified are included as standard references of African historians who continue to draw ideas and inspiration from them.

The book was very much part of the creative environment for historical studies at the University of Dar es Salaam in the 1960s and 1970s with its initial emphasis on indigenous agencies and initiatives following Terence Ranger's inspired formulation (1969). These were challenging themes that called for reassessment and rethinking of Tanzania's past from a dynamic African perspective. Ranger's ideas released a burst of interest that within a few years resulted in a series of important thematic studies and sub-national histories such as Abrahams (1981), Bennett (1971), Hartwig (1976), Ishumi (1980), Katoke (1975), Kimambo (1969, 1991), Knight (1974), Redmond (1985), Stirnman (1976) and Willis (1981), to mention only a few that have given voice and dignity to a number of ethnicities and cultures. In addition, major country-wide historical studies have been successfully attempted by Kimambo and Temu (eds.) (1967), Iliffe (1979) and Koponen (1988).

Research for *Ecology Control* commenced during my stay at the University of Dar es Salaam as a lecturer in political science. Early drafts (Kjekshus, 1974 and 1974a) were discussed with colleagues from various departments in what was at that time a small institution where research news was part of the campus commons. Some of the ideas from my research were reflected at the Conference of History Teachers at Morogoro in 1974 in the contributions of Temu, Rodney and Ferguson. The conference resulted in the book *Tanzania Under Colonial Rule* (Kaniki, 1980) which marked the shift among Dar es Salaam-based historians from Ranger's focus on indigenous agencies to the new ideas of political economy associated with Walter Rodney's famous work on the underdevelopment of Africa published in 1972. In this widely acclaimed work, Rodney introduced the research concepts of Latin American development economists (dependency, centre and periphery, and unequal exchange through trading relationships between the participants of the world capitalist system) to fellow historians. Rodney suggested that the world capitalist system should be seen as the dominant force of East African history circumscribing and foreclosing the range of indigenous choice and action during the last two centuries.

The Dar es Salaam-based historical debate was reviewed most recently by Henry Slater (1986). He traces the historians' move beyond the 'bourgeois limitations' of the 1960s into a post-nationalist phase to prepare intellectual craftsmen to interpret the past from the standpoint of workers and peasants. Slater describes a politicized research community that is conscious of its responsibilities as knowledge producers in the ongoing struggle with world economic forces. He insists that a great deal of important methodological refinement took place in this period as well as theoretical work on class formations at the periphery.

However, very little field-based historical research has come out from Tanzania to test the methodological advances and analytical reorientations that Slater discussed. This stagnation must of course be seen in the context of the country's accelerating economic hardships throughout the 1980s. Negative consequences soon followed for state-supported institutions like the University of Dar es Salaam. This made it extremely difficult to maintain a high level of academic research. Scarcity of printing facilities also caused delays and postponed publications. Important initiatives therefore seem to have slipped away from Dar es Salaam, at least temporarily, to external research communities that are funded, equipped and motivated to explore issues challenging to their disciplines.

In this overview, I have sought to place *Ecology Control* in the context of Dar es Salaam-based research. It was part of the milieu, yet it clearly represented a different research approach and it placed emphasis on novel dimensions of African agency and initiative. In a valuable historiographical review, Tore Linné Eriksen (1979) suggested that a new paradigm was breaking through in the late 1970s in what he called an ecological-historical approach to African history and development. Eriksen identified *Ecology Control* as an important example of this new approach characterized by a strong interest in material developments, changes in production systems and in interaction and conflict between man and his natural environment. He suggested that a growing number of historians (Willis, forthcoming work on Ufipa, Ström 1978, Ambler 1978 and Palmer 1977) were orienting themselves along this innovative approach to form the beginning of the ecological-historical paradigm.

Revisiting East African history during some hectic weeks in the beginning of 1994, I was struck first of all by the growth of literature and historical scholarship. In this context Tanzania's economic plight does not seem to have weakened the overall attraction of scholars to the study of the country's politics, development and history. The growth of various centres of African studies around the world has helped to sustain this interest. So has international research funding. This has inevitably been followed by a shift of leadership from Tanzania to overseas places of learning. A problematic current issue is therefore the continuing vitality of the Tanzanian knowledge base and its ability to define issues, to interact and grow in what now seems to be an externally supported intellectual thrust. But that is another story.

Along with a steady growth of research outputs there have been imaginative searches for new and better methodologies, stimulating cross-breedings to other fields of knowledge and academic disciplines and between narrow foci of research and larger paradigms. In the current multiplicity of approaches the environmental concerns have clearly become strengthened.

The reason for this lies in a number of developments way outside of the historians' own making. Important world events like the first United Nations' conference on the environment in Stockholm in 1972, the creation in the same year of the United Nations Environmental Programme (UNEP), which set up headquarters in Nairobi, and the World Commission on Environment and Development Report (Brundtland Commission Report) (1987) have all made significant impacts in favour of ecological awareness and concern. More directly, the African droughts of the 1980s dramatically called attention to ecological changes throughout the continent and to the appalling human suffering that followed. Through such events, different disciplines of learning have been sensitized to the environmental topics and caused new questions to be asked of and within the disciplines. New dominant themes and paradigms have emerged.

The result is that an ecological-historical trend is now strongly present in the field of African history where it seems to have made a lasting imprint on the profession. This becomes clear if one compares some of the latest major works on African history with earlier works of a similar scale. Thus, the prestigious *Cambridge History of Africa* (Vol.6:1985, Vol.7:1986), notably the contributions of Marcia Wright, John Lonsdale, Andrew Roberts and C.C. Wrigley, strongly convey ecological-historical awareness. The ecological collapse of the 1890s (which is a central theme in *Ecology Control*) is confirmed as a regional Eastern African catastrophe, not only impacting on Tanganyikan territories.[4]

Some influential scholarly journals have also responded to the current environmental awareness. I have taken note of special volumes on such issues in *Journal of Southern African Studies* (1989:15,2), *Review of African Political Economy* (1988:42) and *Social Science and Medicine* (1979:13B). In recent years

[4] Ecological themes are less evident in the UNESCO-sponsored *General History of Africa* (Vol.VII:1985). This work seems little aware of the growing interest in environmental issues and disease questions that took off among africanist historians in the mid-1970s.

these journals (others may have escaped me) have made special efforts to focus on ecological issues as important historical and contemporary themes.

In East Africa the ecological-historical theme was strengthened with John Iliffe's masterly synthesis *A Modern History of Tanganyika* (1979) and with Bethwell Ogot's important book *Ecology and History in East Africa* also published in 1979. This may have encouraged the very strong tradition notably of ecological-historical research that has developed on the basis of Kenyan field work. Some outstanding works in this tradition are the studies by Anderson and Grove (eds.) (1987) and Johnson and Anderson (eds.) (1988) with comparative lessons from wide Eastern African settings, and Ambler (1988), Spear and Waller (1992), and Waller (1988), with background in diverse Kenyan material. A similar approach was tried out by Lamphear (1976) in his study of cattle keeping in Kavirondo district in Uganda and further applied by Musere (1990) in his study of sleeping sickness in the same country.

The recent works by Giblin (1993) and Maddox, Giblin and Kimambo (eds.) (1996) are final indications of the enormous attraction of the ecological-historical line of analysis. The latter work integrates a dozen recent doctoral studies based on extensive field work in various Tanzanian locations into a powerful historical review of economic and ecological changes during the colonial period.

Ecology Control was written with time and budget constraints and subject to some self-imposed limitations. One regrettable casualty was the theme of social and political organization of economic activity or other action causing ecological impact.[5] Also, I drew my empirical evidence from written sources only, not from field research or oral history to follow up problematic material. However, I pointed out a number of interesting field situations where further investigations seemed likely to clear up perplexing questions left from my preliminary enquiry.

The book retained the local focus of my written sources. Their understanding of socio-political organization was the tribal unit. This has for some time been deemed to be a barren and a reactionary notion in African social science, but appears today to be re-emerging both as political reality and analytical concept. However, I treated the tribal concept as a vehicle for economic action rather than a static descent group and noted repeated

---

[5] The theme of political authority and ecological conditions has been developed in recent historical research on Tanzania, most notably in Feierman (1990) and Giblin (1993). The latter is a pathbreaking case study of Handeni District which in the late pre-colonial period experienced a remarkable spell of economic development under leadership of a lineage of entrepreneurial chiefs.

information about incorporation of kin and strangers into existing tribal units.[6]

Later research (and research that was not available to me at the time of writing) on Tanzanian and East African history amount to a number of thematic studies and community case studies that have strengthened and broadened the perspectives of *Ecology Control*. Since observation of process and interaction is one of the methodological strengths of the case study approach, these studies have demonstrated internal dynamics of local societies in a way that *Ecology Control* may not have adequately appreciated. Some of these studies have also given insights into unequal and exploitative features in traditional societies that for different periods of time were based on bondage and slavery.[7]

What follows is a selective review of some recent historical works that relate closely to the themes discussed in *Ecology Control*. I shall also address some misunderstandings that seem to have arisen from the book. But first I want to make a plea for further research into historical agencies and initiatives.

Restoring Indigenous Agencies

When I first wrote *Ecology Control* I was interested in the strength and diversity of indigenous initiatives and commenced a preliminary reconstruction of some that struck me as particularly important. I also became interested in developmental disruptions associated with the colonial takeover and pursued such evidence in various fields. Later research (see Cohen, 1983, and Chrétien, 1986) has broadened the picture beyond my exploratory findings for Tanzania and convinced me that the historical reconstruction of indigenous agencies should continue. I shall illustrate the point by some observations related to research on the regional trading networks of pre-colonial East Africa.

---

[6] As a case in point I suggest in *Ecology Control*, p. 21, that the basis of the Ngoni strength in Southern Tanzania was built on the ability to incorporate other local peoples into Ngoni organizational patterns. The practice of incorporation has been documented by Leroy Vail (1981) with respect to the Ngoni settlements in Northern Malawi where a small core of Ngoni migrants from Southern Africa gave ethnic title and identity to a much larger cluster of local peoples.

[7] *Ecology Control* did not consider the subject of slavery and slave production as part of the pre-colonial economy. The subject has been calling for further research since Sheriff (1971, 1987) demonstrated that in the final years of the legal slave trade most of the slaves were absorbed by labour demands from Zanzibar planters and slave-based settlements on the East (Swahili) Coast, the Mrima. Several important studies have analysed the closing days of slavery on the Kenyan coast (Cooper, 1977, 1980, and Morton, 1990). Also Tanzanian coastal slavery has been opened up for historical enquiry with Glassman's study (1991) with background in the plantation economy of the Pangani Valley, and with Sunseri's work (1993) from Mafia Island. No recent historical study has, as far as I am aware approached the subject of servitude in traditional societies.

Ecology Control emphasizes the indigenous nature of markets and trading relationships among Tanzanian peoples and suggests that long-distance trading organized from Zanzibar in the nineteenth century depended for its success on inter-tribal and regional trading networks already in existence. Although this perspective was novel in 1977, it based itself on the prevailing idea that human porterage was the sole transport technology available to support trading initiatives over long distances.

I have since realized that the situation was not that simple. A well-developed water-borne transport technology was available to East Africans as a complement to, or independent alternative to, human porterage. This technology was the basis of numerous trading networks throughout the entire region of East Africa. They interacted with and connected to the trading networks based on human porterage. To give an impression of the vast extent of the water-borne technology and its relevance to the Tanzanian situation, I shall summarize information on this transport initiative as observed by some of the early explorers.[8] Their information covers the great lakes of East Africa: Nyassa, Tanganyika, Kivu, Edward and Albert in addition to Victoria Nyanza and parts of several East African rivers.

The explorers' information is surprisingly uniform and rich and indicates a number of identical features throughout a vast geographical expanse. Canoes and boats were produced from different types of trees of sufficient size and quality, growing close enough to the navigable waterways to warrant exploitation. Lakes and rivers throughout East Africa displayed a great variety of crafts of various sizes and construction. They ranged from small canoes designed for one or two people to enormous crafts carrying upward to 60 boatsmen. These boats were either sewn together of bark slabs or wooden planks or they were dug out of single tree trunks. The boats were capable of freighting all standard trading commodities: iron, copper, salt, dried foodstuff (bananas, fish and meat), pottery, bark cloth and cotton products as well as livestock of various kinds.

The production of the bigger boats was a matter of trade specialization undertaken by skilled woodworkers. Specific locations are identified as the origin of boats of superior quality, while smaller crafts seem to have been constructed locally. The production of the largest boats was a complicated and expensive process involving many people, organizational and technical skills as well as the assistance of ritual. A heavy demand for manpower arose in connection with the hauling of half-finished crafts over considerable distances from timber forests to launching sites. The

---

[8] This summary is based on the extensive treatment of canoes, boats and water-borne transport found in Burton (1860), Junker (1891), Meyer (1916), Stanley (1880), Schweinfurth (1888), Wollaston (1908) and Young (1877).

good boats were highly priced and transfer of ownership took place against payment in tradable goods. Most boats seem to have been multi-purpose crafts utilized for the movement of people and goods as well as for fishing purposes and warfare.

The boats and canoes were propelled by punting and paddling. The boatsmen are sometimes reported to have preferred to stay near to the shore (coasting), but all the great lakes of East Africa, except Victoria Nyanza, were crossed by African crafts before the gradual and limited introduction of the dhow, the East Coast sailing vessel, on the inland lakes in the last half of the nineteenth century. The island peoples of the great lakes kept in contact with other islanders and with the mainland peoples with the help of boats. East African waterways facilitated transport and trade. Landing sites and market places were both foci for interchange of goods and products along and across East Africa's rivers and lakes.

Few East African historians have shown interest in this far-flung transport agency of the pre-colonial period. Michael Kenny (1979) pointed to the importance of canoes in the transport of salt from the Gulf of Kavirondo in Kenya to trading partners on the shores of Victoria Nyanza. Also Gerald Hartwig presented evidence for the importance of water-borne transport in his research on the Kerebe of Victoria Nyanza. His early contribution (1970) demonstrates the participation of canoes in long-distance trading connecting peoples from future Uganda to the Zanzibar network. In his later work (1976) Hartwig points to the role of canoes in the movement of goods among the various communities settled around Victoria Nyanza. He included altogether eight important population groups as partners to what may have been one of the largest of the pre-colonial trading networks of East Africa: Kerebe, Ganda, Ziba, Zinza, Sukuma, Kara, Ruri, and Luo.

The main theme of Hartwig's study is the survival of the Kerebe people. His information about water-borne transport in the regional (and long-distance) trading network is incidental to the tribal history. It seems to me, therefore, that the material warrants further investigation to complement our understanding of indigenous agencies and economic exchange.

The evidence seems to be that canoe transport serving commodity exchange was a widely shared experience among a number of peoples of East Africa. Canoe transport successfully took on the challenges of long-distance trading and was in many places an alternative to human porterage. Canoes served transport purposes either as specialized crafts or in addition to functions in warfare or fisheries. Such transport developments can be traced to all or most of the peoples surrounding the great lakes of East Africa and its navigable rivers.

Few systematic evaluations of trade and transport initiatives on East

African inland lakes and rivers are available today. The best examples of needed reconstruction are Newbury's great study (1991) of the trading system of Lake Kivu and Cohen's reconstruction (1983) of Uganda economies. Historical scholarship elsewhere has established that waterways generally have facilitated contact and interaction between peoples and cultures. While this perspective dominates in studies relating the Tanzanian coast, the Mrima, to the rest of the world, it has been lacking in historical reconstructions of the interior of the country which borders the great lakes and some major navigable rivers. I believe time is long overdue for researchers to look seriously into the historical role that water-borne transport played in the context of regional and local economic exchange along the many important waterways that came to define Tanzania's international borders.[9]

I also believe that we know too little about the demise of the water transport initiatives and that further historical research is needed to clarify this issue. We know that many of the Ganda canoes were destroyed in the civil wars in Uganda in the late 1880s and that the transport capacity of the central trading partner on Victoria Nyanza was crushed during these upheavals. We know less about the crippling effects that were undoubtedly suffered by the fleet operators resulting from the international boundaries that were introduced following colonial occupation of East Africa.

Extending the arguments I suggest that colonial organization and re-organization constituted repeated blows to all regional and local trade on the great lakes and rivers. Colonial borders divided integrated trading regions into artificial geographical units that were quickly and forcefully reoriented to colonially defined centres of administration and commerce. Old trading partners became separated by the borders of protectorates and *Schutzgebiete*, administrative districts and regions. What was once legitimate trade became subjected to custom and control and was in many cases hunted down as lawless contraband.

Old foci of initiative and interaction became isolated as restrictions on movement followed the colonial confines. Thus, a virtual closing of all the new international borders of East Africa followed the sleeping sickness epidemics which erupted from around 1900. Means of transportation, like boats and canoes, were seized and destroyed in frantic attempts

---

[9] Theuws (1992) contends that the Luba people of Zaire exported copper to East Africa and the coast before the westward thrust of the Zanzibar merchants. This information suggests early linkages between a Central African water transport system capable of delivering the metal at the eastern shores of Lake Tanganyika where East African porters would pick up the copper bars for distribution in local trading networks or for transport to distant destinations on the east coast where export might take place.

to control the spread of the disease. At roughly the same time, the demarcation of colonial forest reserves put timber for boat building out of reach to local craftsmen and prevented the renewal of the canoe fleets. On East African lakes and rivers traditional transport came to a temporary but decisive standstill.

Enough has been said to substantiate the plea for further research into the extent and viability of indigenous trading and transport networks in East Africa. Complementary investigations are needed into the economic effects of early colonial borders on the trading networks. In my opinion, too little attention has been paid to the overall disruption of functioning systems caused by boundaries and borders, restrictions, confinements etc. that were introduced by colonial occupation. Disruption visited most indigenous agencies, technologies and practices whether for trading and transportation or ecological control (grass burning, transhumant cattle herding or settlement patterns). Also, systems designed for human survival were negatively affected.

In *Ecology Control* I point to one crippling constraint imposed by German occupying forces on the Tanzanian Maasai when their transhumant grazing grounds were arbitrarily reduced to approximately one-seventh of their former extent (on the German side of the international border) in 1896. I show that even this so-called Maasai reserve was further restricted by government regulations responding to settler and wildlife interests. This was the beginning of the transformation from man-controlled terrain in the 1890s to wildlife domains in colonial times. Recent studies by Århem (1985) and Homewood and Rodgers (1991) have detailed this astounding development and given us insight into the current options for the Maasai people of Tanzania a century after their forced entry into a larger economic and political world.

Survival Strategies

The dynamism of indigenous economic activities is demonstrated throughout *Ecology Control*, and culminates with the documentation of markets and trading networks built on the underlying psychology of economic calculus permeating the minds of the actors. Implicit in this line of thinking is that crisis situations will follow when the normal functioning of market and trading networks fail through natural or man-made disasters. Needless to say, price fluctuations reflect supply and demand. Therefore, I am not at all surprised to learn from Hartwig (1976:107) that a particular scarcity situation is remembered in tribal legend as 'the famine of the profiteers' when prices had been driven to extortionate levels following shortfalls in the regional grain supply.

Research (by Johnson and Anderson (eds.) 1988) has demonstrated the existence of survival strategies carefully designed by pre-colonial Africans in anticipation of natural or man-made disasters. Thanks to the masterly reconstruction by these historians, we now have evidence of the dynamic practices through which East Africans sought to tackle disaster situations in the past. While trading networks required a certain scale of specialization, organization and resources, survival strategies seem to have been of household or clan character and may have involved women in a significant way.

I shall briefly call attention to *The Ecology of Survival* edited by Johnson and Anderson which adds significantly to our understanding of indigenous planning and adaptability in response to crisis situations. Such characteristics were undoubtedly shared also by the peoples of Tanzania. The argument is important because it indicates the existence of safety nets of regional-ecological character in the pre-colonial setting. These safety nets acted to alleviate the life-threatening potential of natural and man-made disasters. The argument also interacts in a meaningful way with the population thesis of *Ecology Control*.

The authors of *The Ecology of Survival* examine the responses of several local communities in Eastern Africa, the Sudan and Ethiopia to situations of stress and disaster caused by drought, crop failure, famine, epizootics and diseases over the last 100 years. Through field work and historical reconstruction the authors were able to establish that the key to survival is found in flexible networks of a social and economic nature spanning across different ecological and production zones. Individual peoples developed their survival strategies on the basis of the specific ecological niche inhabited and exploited by them. But the success of the system depended not so much on the strength of one partner only but 'on the interrelationships, interlocking and interdependence of all the strategies existing in the wider region' (Johnson and Anderson, (eds.) 1988:152). The wider regions were, however, internally self-sufficient and complete resource systems. Survival strategies, accordingly, were highly effective and capable of saving lives in most situations.

The authors insist that any rigid classification of 'traditional' societies by economic role as pastoralists, agriculturalists or hunter-gatherers or as belonging to equally rigid ethnicities is unhistorical. These rigid concepts misrepresent and distort the reality of the traditional situation, which was socially dynamic and ecologically adaptive and allowed for entry and exit from economic roles and ethnicities in answer to survival challenges. The success of survival depended on the ease with which individuals and groups could move between ethnicities and economic roles.

Reviewing the history of Maasai survival Waller (1988) indicates the following range of options among pastoralists: skillful management of resources, control of human reproduction, construction of networks of exchange and reciprocity with other communities across ecological boundaries, dispersal of herds and pawning or loaning out of livestock for certain time periods, dispersal of the human group itself as refugees, pawns or slaves in neighbouring communities for indefinite periods.

Freedom of movement was an important element in traditional survival strategies. Their successful operation was therefore negatively affected by colonial borders and land reserves of different kinds, restrictions on movement and transhumant herding or other practices built on traditionally free access.

The case studies show that colonial impositions of a restraining and border-setting nature destroyed many of the dynamic traditional arrangements of complementary interconnections. They left different traditional groups in isolation or in a competitive relationship to each other. The odds of survival accordingly fell in the early years of colonial administration and made the recurrence of famine appear as yet another aspect of African incompetence and backwardness.[10]

Health and Disease

In explaining the collapse of the man-controlled ecological system in the 1890s, I offered some preliminary ideas about the colonial government's understanding of the diseases encountered and the medical solutions chosen to alleviate the catastrophe of sleeping sickness. As historians have realized the enormous complexities of the African disease environment and its importance for understanding events and developments in the past, they have turned their priorities to explore these tangled relationships. The path-breaking study by William McNeill (1977) may have signalled the change.

Hartwig and Patterson (1978) laid the groundwork for such enquiries with a collection of case studies tracing the history of a series of infectious

[10] John Iliffe's study (1990) of famine in Zimbabwe also documents falling odds for local survival in the early colonial years. Iliffe shows that indigenous survival strategies were undermined by state intervention and boundary setting, commercialization and labour recruitment. Unwittingly, the colonial state disrupted the old pattern of famine-alleviating techniques, without replacing it with initiatives of its own. A new colonial relief system was only gradually put in place through the growth of settler farming, the building of transport networks and a humanitarian orientation in government. But it lasted the better part of three decades before the new disaster-preventing system was in place and operational. Only then was the colonial government able to alleviate recurrent famines and cause significant decline in famine mortality.

diseases in several regions of Africa. The authors also raised questions about the impact of diseases on overall population developments. Continent-wide surveys have been provided by Ransford (1983), Arnold (1988), and MacLeod and Lewis (1988). Field research has been facilitated by the appearance of a useful bibliographical work by Patterson (1979), followed a decade later by a much expanded volume by Muller *et al.* (1988).

Research into health and disease in Tanzania has been vigorously pursued in the last few years. The medical services have been studied by Clyde (1962) with emphasis on the administrative build-up. Ferguson (1980) underlined the selective concern of early medical services with the white population and with labour recruits. Two very useful studies (Beck, 1977, and Turshen, 1984) move away from a narrow medical focus to attempt more broadly oriented socio-economic approaches. They also discuss the history of important diseases in the Tanzanian setting.

Specific diseases are analysed by Clyde (1967) with respect to malaria and Dawson (1979) on smallpox with Kenya as background. I will also draw attention to Musere's historical study (1990) of sleeping sickness in Uganda and Maryinez Lyons' study (1992) of sleeping sickness in Northern Zaire. Both studies document the profound social and economic impact of the remedies that the colonial governments made use of to stop the disease which erupted almost simultaneously in the wider East African and Zaire regions. This disease and its antidotes together put a virtual end to important regional contacts of the pre-colonial period expressed most strongly in the many trading networks centred around water-borne transportation.

A common theme that seems to be emerging from much of the recent research on disease and health is the inability that western medicine for a long time demonstrated in understanding and coming to grips with the disease patterns of the colonial world. There were faltering responses to African wilderness diseases and some of the vector-borne diseases. Colonial medicine could on the whole do little to protect European settlers and soldiers in the unfamiliar environments or save indigenous populations from new and old diseases. Only the invention of advanced and potent drugs later in the current century (sulpha, antibiotics and DDT) gave colonial medicine a firmer command of health and disease problems. The invention of these drugs had less to do with African needs than with Euro-American developments. However, when these drugs were introduced into the African environment they had important effects on disease and mortality. Most certainly they impacted on the population development which showed rapid increases towards the end of the colonial era.

Gender Issues

Ecology Control does not single out women as a specific analytical category when presenting the various indigenous initiatives. In hindsight it appears clear to me that this dimension should have been given more careful consideration. At least two of my principal sources, Fülleborn (1906) and Weule (1908,1909) reported extensively on the role of women in the local societies, particularly in the matrilineal tribes of the southern regions of the *Schutzgebiet*. Information on women participating in trading, handicraft production and agriculture is found throughout *Ecology Control*, but the material is not given the specific gender recognition it deserves in the historical context.

Women's studies have flourished in Tanzania during the last two decades.[11] The move has been spearheaded by women and it has responded to national political goals as well as to the spread of a world culture of gender awareness and consciousness. In 1983 a thorough bibliographical work, *Women in Tanzania*, was published by Ophelia Mascarenhas and Marjorie Mbilinyi, indicating the wide appeal of this new field of research.

Most of the women's studies appearing so far – Shields (1980), Sender and Smith (1990), Swantz (1985), Ngaiza and Koda (eds.) (1991) and Mbilinyi (1991) – are contemporary studies of women's activities and daily duties in a changing socio-political context. The studies focus on women's struggle for recognition and visibility in today's society. They are making important sociological and political statements and are seeking to enlarge the space for women's recognition and participation in the current situation. The studies have opened up a number of questions that should be followed up by historians.

As far as I can ascertain there are at the moment no satisfactory historical studies of women in Tanzania bridging the rich contemporary insights with the equally abundant but widely scattered information about women's position in the past. Such integrative work seems to be needed. The recent study by Elias Mandala (1990) from neighbouring Malawi may be of relevance here. He demonstrates that women's subordination in that part of Africa was not embedded in tribal organizational traditions but was linked to specific historic situations, notably the slave trading era. At other periods, the role of women has been active, participatory and competitive in economic and social life.

Khasiani's insightful study from Kenya (1992) should also be mentioned

[11] For a short survey of the growth of women's studies in Tanzania see Bujra, Janet (1990) 'Taxing Development in Tanzania: Why Must People Pay?' *Review of African Political Economy*, 47:44–63.

since it approaches questions about the more specific roles of women in environmental management. The study, which relies partly on oral history, demonstrates women's central position in maintaining balanced ecologies in traditional Kenyan societies where women's daily tasks involved them fully in the utilization of available natural resources (see contribution by Kanogo, 1992). The local environmental balances were disrupted by the European colonization and the multiple changes that accompanied this process. The study demonstrates that Kenyan women are now re-emerging from marginalization to play an active part in creating environmental security.

In *Ecology Control* I retain the German term *Frauendorf/Frauendörfer* as typifying the most desperate and precarious rural situations following the ecological collapse that took place in the early years of the German occupation. These villages were widely identified in the German literature. The men had either been killed or drawn into the new economic order as forced labourers far away from home. In this period the *Frauendörfer* represented the last remains of human initiative in several Tanzanian communities. I believe studies of these village situations could yield valuable material on survival strategies under women's leadership and mark an appropriate bridge between historical and contemporary knowledge about women's agency in Tanzanian history.

Settlement Patterns and Ecological Control

The final subject I would like to deal with has to do with the traditional settlement pattern which in *Ecology Control* is seen as closely intertwined with the ecological control and economic exploitation of land through agricultural production and herding. I demonstrated that the traditional patterns of dispersed settlements related in a dynamic way to the man-controlled ecological system. I also outlined the historical origin of the policy of population concentration or villagization and traced it back to erroneous colonial ideas about the East Africans as useless agriculturalists. Finally, I documented the ideological continuity of the villagization idea and its successive introduction under different labels: as sleeping sickness concentrations from the 1920s onward and as development villages in the final years before Independence. The idea re-emerged in the *ujamaa* villages of President Nyerere in the 1960s. In different ways the manipulation of the traditional settlement pattern has been part of efforts by central authorities to gain control over the population for various worthy causes ranging from the prevention of diseases to planned development more generally.

The publication of *Ecology Control* in 1977 coincided with the implementation of the *ujamaa* policy which may be seen as the most massive confrontation of man with the Tanzanian ecosystem since the beginning of historic time. In the course of a little more than a decade the execution of this policy fundamentally altered the settlement pattern of millions of people in the rural areas to fit a model of nucleated settlements prescribed for them by the country's ruling party.

These changes gave an unexpected currency to the arguments about settlement patterns that I put forward in *Ecology Control*. This resulted in a paper about the Tanzanian development where I identified ecological viability as the weakest part of the *ujamaa* policy (Kjekshus, 1977a). Based on evidence available in 1977 (including an extended tour of central and southern Tanzania) I suggested the need to follow closely the ecological impact of the transformation to nucleated villages and raised questions of whether the uniform *ujamaa* model was at all sustainable in the country's diverse ecological situations.

The *ujamaa* experiment was from the beginning followed with intense interest and has been widely documented in a growing literature. A number of scholars have traced the ideology of *ujamaa* in Nyerere's philosophy and political writings (Ghai *et al.* eds., 1979; Mohiddin, 1981) and discussed the establishment of the villages and their first uncertain results (Mwansasu and Pratt eds., 1979; McHenry, 1979; Boesen *et al.*, 1978). Other observers have recorded the bureaucratic high-handedness surrounding the implementation of the policy and seen these negative features as the result of growing class differentiation (Coulson, 1979, 1982). Bernstein (1981) discussed the *ujamaa* movement as an extension of state control over the peasantry in government efforts to extract surpluses for ambitious development programmes in the industrial, health and education fields. Freyhold (1979) complained that villagization had not realized socialist ideals but furthered class formation and exploitation in the countryside instead.

Finally, Hyden (1980), resurrecting old colonial prejudices, identified the pre-modern mentality of the peasantry, or what he calls their 'economy of affection', as the major blockage to full *ujamaa* success. Although there is growing evidence that East African peasants historically have overcome local and temporary supply deficiencies through barter and trade arrangements, Hyden's study maintains that a narrow subsistence orientation prejudices the Tanzanian husbandmen to resist 'modern' markets and commodity production. As usual, the peasantry was to be blamed, and history was again misread in favour of political rulers and modernizing reforms. Full licence seems to be given to the Tanzanian Government to get on with its *ujamaa* revolution (see also Seavoy, 1989).

As far as I can see, only McCall (1985), Mung'ong'o (1991) and Giblin (1993) have so far attempted to address the ecological problematic raised by the Tanzanian villagization programme. McCall makes clear that the result of ten years of programme implementation has indeed caused major economic and ecological disasters. He describes important crop losses in the early years of implementation when the production systems were in disarray and important reductions took place in the arable land tilled by the households. McCall further documents deteriorating husbandry caused by physical fatigue and time-waste in movements between the new village homes and the old cultivation fields. He claims that household demand for firewood has caused concentrated pressure on the *miombo* woodland and scrub and that water problems are in evidence in a great number of villages. Resource requirements of livestock were largely neglected during the implementation phase and this led to overgrazing and land deterioration, as well as to violent clashes between pastoralists and farmers seeking to exploit the same land resources. Furthermore, the policy implementation alienated the peasantry from the political leadership and made it withdraw from a market system that functioned only as an instrument of forced surplus extraction (see also Ellis, 1983).

The tendencies cited by McCall seem to have intensified subsequently. They contributed to more widespread social unrest and political demands ending with the abolition of the one-party system through constitutional changes in 1992. In the new situation of competing ideas and intellectual diversity I believe one of the most important research tasks will be to understand fully the incompatibility of central features of the *ujamaa* policy with Tanzania's various ecological situations. Such studies will become necessary in order to chart viable options for the future which continue to be strongly tied to economic development in the rural areas. Such studies will, I believe, illuminate an important period of recent economic history while confirming central elements of the traditional knowledge system which formed the basis of people's earlier achievements.[12]

---

[12] Although the research agenda of 'Traditional Knowledge Systems' seems to have been set with a strong East African bias (Brokensha *et al.*, eds., 1980), its follow-up has been more clearly associated with West African research, notably with the outstanding contribution of Paul Richards (1983, 1985). His work, which takes the traditional agriculturalists seriously, has succeeded in bridging the gap between traditional practices and modern science and in gaining status and scientific recognition for past practices as the basis for future work to strengthen agriculture in West Africa's ecological diversity. Similar research based on Tanzanian and East African material is urgently needed. A major review of agricultural technology and field systems for East Africa (Sutton, ed., 1989) fails, with the exception of one or two contributions, to give serious consideration to the agricultural dynamics of the nineteenth century. According to McCann (1991), the entire subject of pre-colonial agriculture in East Africa still awaits historical reassessment on the basis of fresh field-based research (but see Anderson forthcoming; Berthelot, 1987; and Paul, 1993).

By Way of Clarification

The occasion of the second impression of *Ecology Control* gives me an opportunity to clear up misunderstandings that have arisen from the book. It was, on the whole, well received and has been an inspiration for further research rather than the cause of confusion or stale exchange. I have, of course, been surprised by some commentators' association of *Ecology Control* with a 'Merrie Africa' interpretation of African history.[13]

The portrait of East Africans that emerges from the book is that of hard workers, skillful planners, active learners and ultimate survivors. These are clearly not characteristics of the cast that made up A. G. Hopkins' myth of 'Merrie Africa'. Apart from this digression, I shall briefly comment on two issues that have given me cause for some concern.

The first difficulty arises from Koponen's opinion (1988:367) that the agencies and initiatives discussed in my book, including the ecological control situation, were presented by me as 'national' or 'countrywide' achievements of the pre-colonial period. They supposedly filled the entire geographical space negotiated in the Anglo-German Agreement of 1886 to become internationally defined as German East Africa.

This is rather misleading. *Ecology Control* has, throughout, a local focus on achievements and initiatives. The various activities are ascribed to peoples identified in my sources as tribes settled in relatively small areas of the total territorial space of German East Africa. Large parts of the total expanse were then as now uninhabited.

To guard against misunderstandings of this nature *Ecology Control* refers the reader to the population maps of Gillman (1936) and Porter (1966) both showing close correspondence between human settlement and ecological endowment of fertile soil, rainfall or permanent water.

While the total area of Tanzania is large, the population has until recently been small. However, population densities varied considerably. Kuczynski estimated the average population density to be 15 per square mile in Kenya and Tanganyika on the basis of census information at the time of his writing in the 1940s. This contrasted to real district situations of up to 180 inhabitants to the square mile in Kikuyu and Kavirondo districts in Kenya. Kuczynski gave no similar details for Tanzania, but indicated that 'two-thirds of the Territory are entirely uninhabited, and

---

[13] The term 'Merrie Africa' is first used by Hopkins (1973:10) as a contrast to 'Primitive Africa' of Alfred Marshall (1938) to set the stage for Hopkins' pioneering work on West African economic history. As the reader will recall 'Merrie Africa' denoted to Hopkins a mythical situation of populations living, without working, in abundance and plenty, but pursuing lives of ease and leisure of which major parts consisted of 'interminable dancing and drumming'.

the well watered parts of the country which cover one-tenth of the total area contain two-thirds of the population' (Kuczynski, 1948, II:102).

This is the approximate spatial setting within which the human agencies and initiatives of *Ecology Control* unfold. It was the local populations in their home areas that were the initiators and defenders of the ecological control situations. The populations acted on the basis of experience, observation and insight that was neither confined to the localities nor restricted by the new borders set by Europeans. Undoubtedly, the agro-pastoral prophylaxis of the past rested in the indigenous knowledge systems of East Africans that are only now being reconstructed on the basis of our cumulative historical insights.

A second misunderstanding of *Ecology Control* seems to arise from Giblin's excellent article on trypanosomiasis and history (1990). This is a thorough review of tsetse research, John Ford's contribution to it, and the relevance of tsetse research to history. In this process, Giblin seems to misread *Ecology Control* on important points. For those who are interested in pursuing the details of the matter, which deals with the interpretation of John Ford's work, let me say this: when writing *Ecology Control* I reflected repeatedly on how to present and describe the herders' role in relation to Ford's thesis that limited cattle contact with the vector is a key element in the control situation. I was concerned with conveying the traditional herding situation which was of course very different from the controlled field experiments of modern entomologists which had given Ford the scientific foundation for his thesis.

I concluded in line with Ford that cautious risk evasion was the safest herding policy in a fluid situation where the cattle could not escape the occasional infectious contacts in any case. The herders' role was to guard against overexposure that could put individual animals at risk and ultimately tilt the man-controlled balance from endemicity to epidemic.

Conclusions

Ecology Control was intended as an introduction to Tanzania's economic history. I wanted to restate and interpret the bold features of basic economic activities and material achievements and interrelate them within the time and space limits set by the study. The book portrays the East Africans as doers: as peoples living close to their environments, but as masters and shapers of them, not as their prisoners. The study aimed to be about and for ordinary people in a truly grassroots-oriented development. To advertise its populist inspiration the book was dedicated 'To the People of Tanzania'.

Reviewing recent literature in preparing this introduction, I find it encouraging that themes of economic history continue to generate vivid interest. In fact, such themes account for a large share of the impressive knowledge production that has come into print on Tanzanian and East African affairs over the last two decades. A number of recent books and articles have enriched our understanding of events and themes that were taken up for the first time in *Ecology Control*, sometimes only in their barest outlines. My study struck reviewers as an 'ideas book' (Larson, 1978), raising new questions while suggesting alternate solutions to old puzzles. In this sense it has remained in the mainstream of the ongoing historical discourse about Tanzania and East Africa. It may even have been 'enormously influential' as Maddox, Giblin and Kimambo (1996) have recently formulated their evaluation.

I conclude from this that the basic scholarship is rapidly being supplied to inform a more definitive economic history for Tanzania. I also realize that *Ecology Control* (which has been out of print for the last ten years) still remains the only comprehensive study of its kind in the field. The second impression of the book will therefore continue to fill a current gap in the literature and scholarship. Hopefully, the book will also continue to inspire reflection, provoke new questions and shake the sanctity of preconceived ideas.

Introduction
to 1977 Impression

HISTORIOGRAPHY

The move to political independence has altered East African historiography in a most fundamental way. Free peoples concerned with their future, their dignity and their nationhood will look to their own past for inspiration and instruction. Their particular concern will be the period antecedent to their involuntary tutelage and the achievements of the African peoples in this period.

Oliver and Mathew made the first important contribution to the new historiography, in which scholars would write the 'history of Africa and not only that of its invaders' (1963:xiii). Following this lead, historians writing about the newly independent nation-states have over the last few years brought out a number of books, pamphlets and articles aimed at restoring the African as an agent of his own past, and rejecting as biased and racist the neglect of African initiatives in the colonial historiography. Kimambo and Temu complained that 'most of the fragmentary material in print has either ignored or distorted the history of the Africans themselves' (1969:xi) and set out to rectify the perspective. A similar note was struck by Andrew Roberts (1968) in another effort to reinterpret the Tanzanian[1] past.

It is difficult to disagree with the urgency these and other scholars feel to explore the extent of 'African activity, African adaptation, African choice, African initiative': the words of Terence Ranger (1968a:xxi). Roberts' *Tanzania before 1900* thus opens with the broad announcement: 'In place of the old myth that the African past was more or less static, or at best repetitive, we have to acknowledge a continuous process of social and political innovation, economic improvement and technical change' (1968:ii). Kimambo and Temu's *A History of Tanzania* has a similarly wide commitment to the reconstruction of African agency in its widest manifestations.

---

[1] The United Republic of Tanzania came into existence in 1964 with the Union between Tanganyika and Zanzibar. Throughout this study, I shall use the name of Tanganyika when referring to the mainland before 1964.

The concrete achievements of the new historiography have, however, been far more narrowly focused than the sweeping promises that launched them. In fact, both works quoted on Tanzania are works of political history, preoccupied with changes of institutions and authority structures, the origin and growth of chiefship, tribal history and chiefly genealogy. In *Tanzania before 1900*, the African initiatives in statecraft are at the centre of attention with founder warriors like Nyungu-ya-Mawe and Mkwawa as the celebrated modernizers. The book deals largely with responses to that crisis of the peoples of the interior that Speke identified as a 'want of a strong protective government, without which nothing can prosper' (Speke 1864:344). According to Speke, in a situation where everybody warred against everybody, all scope for prosperity was undermined. To the contributors to *Tanzania before 1900*, this kind of constant warfare constituted a 'crisis of authority' to which the peoples responded with innovations in statecraft, the spread and consolidation of chiefships, and a shift in the basis of authority from ritual to military power. This development, identified as 'the enlargement of scale', is also a central theme in *A History of Tanzania* and *The Historical Study of African Religion*. In the latter book, Ranger and Kimambo have pursued the crisis of the interior and demonstrated important initiatives and responses in the spiritual domain. The tumult of tribal fission and war increased the contacts between peoples of different ethnicities and places. It exposed the members of a self-sufficient tribal cosmology (microcosmic society) to larger environments (macrocosmic society). The resulting confusion and spiritual crisis 'found its successful solution as Africans developed a newly effective system of prediction and control' (Ranger and Kimambo 1972:16). In *A History of Tanzania*, the 'enlargement of scale' theme has been expanded to cover incidents of polyethnic co-operation in warfare against the colonial intruder and the development of a common ideology to cement this African initiative.

Two objections have, as far as I am aware, been made to the latest historical works on Tanzania. Denoon and Kuper pointed to the *nationalist* character of *Tanzania before 1900* and *A History of Tanzania*. They felt that the works represented 'not simply an appeal to put the African back into African history. The demand is for a history of African national dignity and self-assertion—in current political terms, for an African nationalist history' (Denoon and Kuper 1970:333). Saul (1972) similarly pointed to pitfalls in the nationalist orientation of *A History of Tanzania*, but he found its major weakness in the negative—in not raising issues of class differentiation and related subjects that would be relevant to a *socialist* understanding of the past and the present options.

These are extremely valuable contributions to the discussion of the historian's responsibilities to his audience and to his sources. They point to the imperative for meaningful standards for selecting and giving historical significance to the uncountable facts at the historian's disposal.

My own objection, however, is not to the nationalist orientation of the works on Tanzania under discussion. Carr, concurring with Croce (1941) wrote about 'contemporary history', meaning that 'history consists essentially in seeing the past through the eyes of the present and in the light of its problems' (Carr 1961:21). In this sense all relevant history must take the present at its point of departure. Contemporary Tanzanian scholarship is reorienting itself along these lines. From this development there can be no going back.

My concerns arise from the historians' choice of specific themes (statecraft, ideology and religion) to demonstrate African agency, and from the weaknesses of the interpretative model pursued. This will be clear from my treatment of the warfare and slave-raiding themes later in this work.

My aim in this study is to move away from political history and the obvious Weberian model of societal development and change (from religious to military to legal/rational bases of power) which has been the framework for demonstrating East African agencies. In this study, attention is instead turned to issues relating to man and his environment and to the economic basis of indigenous initiatives. The study will show that far from being initiators only as a defensive reaction to a crisis situation, nineteenth-century East Africans were on the offensive against a hostile ecological system, and that until the end of the century, they were the victors in that struggle.

The study seeks to restore the *people* as agents of African initiatives. There will be no great men in the following pages, where focus is on man as a doer, husbandman, industrialist and trader. In these initiatives the individual takes on the anonymity of mere numbers, and purposeful action becomes that of great masses of people.

ECOLOGY CONTROL AND ECONOMIC DEVELOPMENT

The basis for economic development is an ecological system (ecosystem) controlled by man. Darby (1956) has described the creation of such a system in Northern Europe during the Middle Ages when the great continental forests were felled and the land put under the plough. Similar works had in earlier centuries laid the basis for the great Chinese, Egyptian and Indian civilizations (Heichelheim 1956).

In large parts of tropical Africa we are even now witnessing the struggle for mastery of nature by man. The very vitality and regenerative powers of nature—its flora, fauna, and microbial life—mean that mastery of it is a long and painful process. Nature will retaliate and take back what it has yielded to man as soon as man's will or ability to impose his control is weakened. The possibilities for permanent control are, however, more and more in the hands of man, and he is finally achieving ecological domination even in the tropics.

There has been a general assumption that this control of the ecosystem is now occurring for the first time in East Africa. Three major factors present themselves in support of the supposed failure of the pre-colonial African to master his environment. First, the state of constant warfare and destruction undermined any purposeful human impact on the physical surroundings. Second, the widespread presence of the tsetse fly confined man to limited settlement centres. Finally, the agricultural method—shifting cultivation—precluded the possibility of permanent control. Thus, until recently, the East African has been seen as a captive of his barbarism and his environment. Forced to live in overcrowded stockades where he could keep cattle, the East African soon exhausted the land with trampling and overgrazing. Soil erosion ensued and he frequently had to move his dwelling place to recommence his work of destruction somewhere else in the abundant waste of virgin land. Nature soon recovered to wipe out the traces of his spoliations.

Our study rejects this picture of pre-colonial Tanganyika. Its starting points are the puzzling testimonies of wholesome prosperity among the East African peasantry made by several explorers throughout the nineteenth century: 'The assertion may startle the reader's preconceived opinions concerning the savage state of Central Africa', wrote Richard Burton. 'But it is not less true that the African is in these regions superior in comforts, better dressed, fed, and lodged, and less worked than the unhappy Ryot of British India. His condition, where the slave trade is slack, may, indeed, be compared advantageously with that of the peasantry in some of the richest of European countries' (Burton 1860, II:278).

Casati traversed central Tanganyika twenty years after Burton and saw parts of the area that Burton never visited. Casati also left an impression of 'a rich and productive country; cattle, grain, rice, peas, and tobacco are found in abundance in every village' (Casati 1891, II:297). These villages were formed of scattered habitations that occupied almost the entire territory brought under cultivation. Lying in the shadow of the colossal baobab trees which gave dimension to the vastness of the cultivation plain, these villages showed 'in a pleasant and comforting manner the prosperity of the region and the well-being of its inhabitants' (Casati 1891, II:298).

Such observations (and those of other explorers and administrators that will be introduced later) call into question the idea that for hundreds of years intertribal warfare, the tsetse menace and wasteful cultivation practices dictated economic underdevelopment in East Africa, and restricted human activity to the cleared patches surrounding fortified villages. On the contrary, this study will show that East African man maintained an ecological control system throughout the nineteenth century in spite of intertribal warfare and slave-raiding. His economic activity was not restricted to diminutive clearings around isolated hamlets or villages. Fortified stockades existed and have been described by many of the early explorers, but rather as isolated frontier phenomena or periodic defence systems than as a form of settlement typifying the East African existence in the nineteenth century. The economic basis of this period, its production system, technological level and exchange activities will be analysed. The idea pursued in this study is that the reign of the tsetse fly in Tanganyika is a recent, twentieth-century phenomenon that followed the breakdown of the man-controlled ecological system that Burton and others witnessed.

THE APPROACH

The primary key to the control situation is people, and the idea will be maintained in Chapter 1 that the population of Tanganyika was relatively stable or even slowly expanding throughout the nineteenth century, and that there were no significant reversals to this overall trend. (This does not, of course, rule out localized and temporary tragedies.) This chapter seeks to resurrect a positive population initiative from the tales of 'darkness and doom' relating to internecine wars and slave-raiding. In writing this section I have relied extensively on Kuczynski's work (1949) on the demography of the British Empire, as well as on early German works on the population of their East African *Schutzgebiet* (protectorate).

Gillman (1936) recognized the reciprocal relationship between man and the tsetse fly and held that the tsetse problem would be solved naturally through population growth. While this is in principle correct, in practice it has proven fallacious as the vast population growth registered in the last few decades has failed to solve automatically the tsetse crisis. This lesson points to the fact that the distribution of the population and the settlement pattern are of greater importance in this context than a simple population increase. In the nineteenth century all expansion was channelled into rural endeavours and entered more directly into the ecological control effort. A smaller, but rurally oriented, population in the nineteenth century could therefore maintain command of land areas that the undoubtedly larger population of the mid-twentieth century still regarded as a problem.

Boserup's work (1965) has called attention to population expansion as an important agent for agricultural changes under conditions of sub-sistence production. Pursuing similar ideas, in Chapter 2 I shall attempt to show the fallacy of accepting 'shifting cultivation' as the overall system of pre-colonial agriculture in East Africa. I shall maintain that the majority of the Tanganyikan agriculturists operated systems of relative permanency, labour intensity and various degress of soil improvement in this period. I shall interpret the variety of pre-colonial agricultural systems as a confir-mation of the positive population thesis developed in Chapter 1. A second concern in this chapter is to integrate the information of agricultural systems in a dynamic model of settlement patterns for the area. This is another way of expressing the man-land relationship which found a successful solution in the ecological control system of the nineteenth century.

A second key to the ecological control situation is found in domestic animals, first and foremost cattle. Chapter 3 will point out that an im-portant cattle economy existed in East Africa throughout the nineteenth century. Contrary to Gourou (1961) who held that the introduction of cattle in the tropics was ecologically disastrous and economically in-significant, the view will be defended here that cattle constituted a signifi-cant aid in the maintenance of the ecological control system by the East African husbandman and that the presence of cattle in the nineteenth cen-tury is an important proof of the absence of tsetse fly. This chapter owes many of its insights to Austen (1903) and his discussion of the appearance of tsetse flies in East Africa.

Chapter 4 will challenge the common notion of East Africa as a wildlife paradise where man and beast lived in perfect harmony. It will demonstrate that competition existed between people and animals for control of the land and maintain that wildlife was already becoming managed by the end of the last century.

The basic economic activities of agriculture and animal husbandry gave rise to a number of industrial innovations. In Chapter 5 we shall sur-vey the most important of these initiatives, iron smelting and the forging of implements, salt production and cotton manufacturing. Chapter 6 focuses on trading relations which connected the supply and demand of agricultural produce and livestock, as well as a series of manufactured commodities and acted as dynamic stimuli to exploit comparative advan-tages within the indigenous economies. The chapter suggests that well-developed trading patterns existed by the time foreign interests became aware of the interior as a source of commercial riches. The chapter thus questions the idea (Hill 1963) that East Africa is uniquely set apart from the general African economic experience through a lack of traditional markets and trading activities.

The man-controlled ecological system came to a temporary (in some places lasting) end in the 1890s due to causes discussed in Chapters 7 and 8. These chapters give prominence to the writings of John Ford (1971) who saw the events of the 1890s as leading to an 'ecological catastrophe' for East Africa. After a period of depopulation of man and domestic animals, bush and wildlife reoccupied the cultivated areas where only isolated survivors of the former communities remained to eke out a meagre existence. Thus it was a people and an economy in rapid decline that the European colonialists encountered as they scrambled to take possession of the East African heartland. In Chapter 8, I pursue this ecological disaster into the colonial period in a review of two administrative measures, population concentrations and wildlife protection, which further weakened control of the environment. It is the periphery of the economy which retains the interest of this study during the colonial period, not the many initiatives of development that were launched to reorient the economy and subject it to the economic rationale of the colonial metropole. The achievements of this development, the building of an infrastructure of transport, harbours, towns, etc., fall outside this study. So does the development of the export economy. I am concerned with that section of the territory which, in the views of many observers, remained the untouched part of a dual economy. Alien policies aggravated the ecological control situation at this periphery where economic development in due time became identified with the surrender of human activity altogether. The background to these policies was based in deep-seated biases about a Tanganyikan past without initiative and agency, and I shall have occasion to stress the continued importance of these misconceptions until recent times.

The study has a vague time demarcation necessitated by an approach which neglects genealogies in favour of broad economic/ecological changes. The work spans roughly the period between 1850 and 1950, and seeks to judge events from the point of view of ecology control as a first principle of economic and other activities.

As distinct from most on-going investigations into East Africa's past—which have large components of oral research among their sources— this study is based entirely on written material. The reason for this is simply that I found the sources of untapped material of a recorded nature—particularly the German sources—too overwhelming to venture into any further original work in the field. The point should be made, of course, that most of the authors quoted in this study did, in fact, base most of their own observations on oral evidence. Important improvements have taken place in methodology and data-collecting techniques of oral research. But we are also many more years distant from events than Arning (1896, 1897) or Fromm (1912) who both utilized oral research and warned about its pitfalls. An entry in the *Geita District Book* should also spell caution. Frustrated by the difficulties of undertaking research on tribal lore and legend for the newly instituted District Book, the District officer wrote that except for those who have been to school at Kome, where the White Fathers endeavoured to teach local history, very few people were able to give any account of their tribal past.

The reliance on written evidence has, however, its own weaknesses that should be noted at the outset. One is the geographical limitations of many statements quoted in the text and the difficulties in generalizing from them. Many observations made along the trade routes, for instance, may not have been representative of the hinterlands. Also, situational descriptions may remain valid for short time-periods only. A second difficulty lies in the personal biases of the different observers. This problem will be directly confronted in Chapter 1, but remains an important interpretative consideration throughout the study.

The richness of the existing economic material, drawn from a variety of disciplines, is documented by numerous quotations in the text and in an extensive bibliography. I have chosen to present much of the evidence directly and, when necessary, at length. Many of the sources used in the work, for example, have not previously appeared in English. I have sought to substantiate my ideas by confronting the reader squarely with the original material—when necessary in translation. What emerges is a novel synthesis of the past which opens the mind to a fresh appreciation of African agencies. This study can be only an introduction to the economic history of Tanzania. Further research of greater intensity and more limited geographical scope will ultimately help us to correct our perspective and regain the full vision of the East African *homo economicus*.

CHAPTER 1

A Demographic Review

Little concrete information is available about the size, distribution and growth of the population of Tanganyika in the nineteenth century. On the one hand, the continental assessments of Africa's population by Wilcox (1940), Spengler and Duncan (1956) or Cox (1959) are of limited use. Wilcox suggested that the continental population had remained static at approximately 100 million people over the previous three centuries. He cited a number of factors like periodic famines caused by climatic conditions, poverty of food-producing plants, critical health conditions, warfare and slave-raiding as the main reasons for this long stagnation. Yet it is evident that these factors were applicable with different intensity in the various parts of the continent and that the total population aggregate was capable of containing important and contradictory developments in the various geographical regions. On the other hand, reliable data on local populations do not go back beyond 1900. Before that time, numerous explorers visited East Africa at various points and reported what they saw of the peoples and their economies. Save for Baumann (1891, 1894), who was interested in population densities based on the count of huts and villages, few of these explorers took a scientific interest in populations. Their reports were highly impressionistic. Lord Hailey rejected their assessment as 'little more than guesses based on insufficient or unreliable data' (Hailey 1938:104), devoid of demographic validity.

Ecological control is at the centre of attention in this study. Such control is predicated on the presence of people. It can be maintained only by people who either expand or hold their own numerically; depopulation spells crisis in the control system and may initiate its total collapse. It is therefore important to this study to gain at least a general picture of population patterns in pre-colonial Tanganyika. I am interested in extracting from the existing historical material crude indications of contrasts between depopulation and a positive population initiative. The discussion in this chapter will result in the hypothesis that the population of Tanganyika was either stable or showed slight tendencies to expansion throughout the nineteenth century until its last decade.

On the face of it, this seems an absurd position to take, given the numerous reports testifying to population disruption and even depopulation in this period. These reports deal firstly with occasional local tragedies caused by disease or famine. Secondly, they deal with two specific phenomena of destructive impact on the population, namely internecine wars and slave-raiding. These two latter events are of particular interest to this study not only because they are the twin pillars of what can be called the 'maximum population disruption theory', but also because acceptance of the primacy of these man-made events has had significant implications for historians' understanding of the economy and life in general in pre-colonial East Africa.

In undertaking a re-evaluation of the impact on the population from these events and putting forward a 'minimum population disruption theory', I have been struck by important biases in much of the source material on which East African historians have to rely. Already Cooley (1845) was aware of this danger and wrote about the general tendency to exaggeration among early reporters from Africa. They elevated 'petty wars and tumultuary movements' into 'grand conquests and revolutions', wrote Cooley, who felt that their evidence represented 'nothing remarkable or certain' except an 'extravagant bad taste with which they relate incredible barbarities perpetrated by natives' (Cooley 1845:194). Cooley thus pointed to the general assumption that a state of barbarism reigned in Africa, that the writers had not so much to prove this as to confirm it, and that the more solidly this impression could be imbedded the greater would be the glory of bringing Christian light and civilization, trade and administration to peoples suffering as much from self as from slavery. On what then, do the proponents of a 'maximum population disruption theory' found their ideas?

MAXIMUM POPULATION DISRUPTION

Internecine Wars

The early accounts of visitors to East Africa abound in vivid descriptions of constant warfare among the Africans. Almost every traveller seems to have come across one or more peoples that were said to have terrorized their neighbours and made life in East Africa 'nasty, brutish and short'.

Krapf singled out the Masai as the terror of the peaceful agriculturalists surrounding them:

> They (the Masai) are dreaded as warriors, laying all waste with fire and sword, so that the weaker tribes do not venture to resist them in the open field, but

leave them in possession of their herds, and seek only to save themselves by the quickest possible flight (Krapf 1860:359).

Krapf reported that the spear-throwing skills of the Masai were quite extraordinary: 'hurling (the spear) with the greatest precision, at a distance of from fifty to seventy paces they can dash out the brains of an enemy; and it is this weapon above all, which strikes terror into the East Africans' (Krapf 1860:359). The vanquished could expect little mercy from the Masai warrior, according to Krapf. The Masai, he wrote, 'do not make slaves of their prisoners, but kill men and women alike in cold blood, sparing only the very young girls' (Krapf 1860:364). In a similar way, Reichard wrote about the Masai *moran* that 'his only thought concerns killing and murder; he wants his weapon baptised in blood. The Masai are dreaded beyond belief; fear and panic ensues wherever they appear' (Reichard 1892:289–290).

Map 1.1. Tanganyikan Ethnicities. (Based on *Survey Division* 1948.)

Almost similar terms were used to identify the Turu people of Singida. They were 'warlike, cruel and wild' wrote Stadlbaur (1897:170), and had a reputation far outside their land for barbarous living.

The relationship between Masai, Wahehe and Wagogo was described by Lieutenant Herrmann. The Masai and the Wahehe were seen as 'deadly enemies who are at constant war with each other'. The weakness of the Wagogo was exploited in this relationship and Ugogo became the battleground for the 'plundering hordes' of the two warring tribes (Herrmann 1892:200). The *Deutsches Kolonialblatt* portrayed the Wahehe as 'enemies of every ordered way of life'. They were seen as 'nomads, robbers and highwaymen' who annually raided the weaker tribes in the interior. Easily overwhelmed by the Wahehe warfare, the vanquished tribesmen were either 'murdered in the most brutal way' or taken away as slaves (*DKB* 1891:409).

According to early reports, however, the most widespread destruction in pre-colonial Tanganyika resulted from the migration (*mfecane*) of the Wangoni. In response to population pressure and unrest in southern Africa, the Wangoni trekked northward and entered Tanganyika through Ufipa in the 1840s. To Elmslie, this was a wildfire from the south, leaving in its wake the 'fall of Kingdoms; rivers of blood shed; a million or more massacred, condemned to cannibalism, or to death by starvation; fathers slaying their children, and children their fathers; and God's fair earth made worse than Hell'. 'We see before us', wrote Elmslie, 'a horde of barbarians, their faces set to the north, who over hundreds and hundreds of miles, are to spread death and desolation' (Elmslie 1899:29).

A major portion of this tribe settled in Songea which soon became a veritable centre of plunder. Prince described the surroundings of Ungoni and the entire caravan route from the sources of the Ruvuma to close to Kilwa as a 'depopulated wasteland'. Several tribes had previously lived in these areas, but had been vanquished in wars with the Wangoni and were thought to have been partly exterminated (Prince 1894:215). Smith (1887:103) had made similar observations, but attributed the depopulation to the abandonment of the area by people fleeing not from the Wangoni, but from the Wangwangwara. This was one of several local tribes (*Ngoniaffen* in the German literature) said to have imitated the Ngoni warfare technique and to have carried the destructive vibrations of the *mfecane* further afield to areas and peoples never directly touched by the Zulu migration. A recent study (Redmond 1972) of the Wangoni of Songea is a remarkable review of existing reports about this tribe. The study underscores, above all, the tribesmen's barbaric mentality and innate desires, it would seem, to destroy, kill and lay waste.

The reverberations of the *mfecane* were felt also in the western parts of

Tanganyika where one section of the Ngoni people crossed the Fipa corridor to settle in smaller groups throughout Unyamwezi and eventually reached as far north as the shores of Victoria Nyanza. These people, variously called Vatuta, Mafitte or Wangoni, were reportedly responsible for destroying the southern expanses of the Waha cattle kingdom (Burton 1860) and of the Usinza chiefdom (Baumann 1894). Stanley saw in the Mafitte a true exponent of *homo diabolicus*: 'their hands are against every man, and every man's hand appears to be raised against them' (Stanley 1880:319).

From his study of the Zulu migrations, Omer-Cooper drew the conclusion that warfare came to eastern and central Africa with the Wangoni and wrote that the *mfecane* brought 'a long era of peaceful peasant exsistence to a violent end' (Omer-Cooper 1966:83). The early travellers insisted, however, on warfare as a general feature of the East African way of life much earlier than the coming of the Wangoni. Moreover, the warfare theme is generally encountered. It is not restricted to peoples and places falling within what we may call the sphere of *mfecane* influence. Warlike behaviour has been taken as part of the make-up of the East African psychology. Material destruction and depopulation have been seen by historians of the area as necessary results. To establish these points, a few cross-references to literature about the pre-colonial conditions in Kenya and Uganda are in order.

In Kenya, Lugard did much to propagate the impression that life in the colony had from time immemorial been an unending war of everybody against everybody. Due to tribal wars, the population was restricted to certain smaller areas. Constant wars went on between the Kamba, Kikuyu and Masai peoples, wrote Lugard (1893, I:283, 327). Ainsworth described Ukamba as 'inhabited by tribes whose everyday occupation had been for generations one of raiding and killing one another and enslaving and selling women and youths' (Ainsworth 1905). In Uganda the early reports replay the familiar warfare theme: 'the Waganda ... are constantly at war, making continual raids on the surrounding countries for cattle and slaves. Their fights are often very sanguinary, and they frequently lose 30 to 40 per cent of their men' (Felkin 1886:735). Portal wrote of outright depopulation in parts of the country due to 'the most incredible misgovernment, the barbarous enactment of its Kings, the cold-blooded massacres, the wars of extermination, the raids, the murders, and the internecine conflicts under which the country has groaned for the last thirty years' (Portal 1894:187). Sir Charles Eliot paraphrased Hobbes' description of the state of nature to characterize the general East African situation: 'Every tribe was at war with its neighbours' (Eliot 1905:239).

Slave-Raiding

The reports relating to slave-raiding and marketing in East Africa are too numerous to be summarized here even in quotation form. The standard historical works are Coupland's two books *East Africa and its Invaders* (1938) and *The Exploitation of East Africa* (1939) in which the different reports have been summarized. A typical example of Coupland's historiography is found in the following statement concerning the hinterlands of Kilwa which has already appeared in our discussion of inter-tribal warfare.

> Most of the explorers, indeed, described the areas scoured by the slave traders as not merely devastated, but depopulated. There is no reason to doubt the information given to Rigby (the British Consul in Zanzibar) by men who knew the Kilwa slave route. 'Natives of India who have resided many years at Kilwa . . . state that districts near Kilwa, extending to ten or twelve days' journey, which a few years ago were thickly populated, are now entirely uninhabited; and an Arab who has lately returned from Lake Nyasa informed me that he travelled for seventeen days through a country covered with ruined towns and villages which a few years ago were inhabited by the Mijana and Mijan tribes and where now no living soul is to be seen'. (Coupland, 1939:140.)

It is significant that depopulation in the area has been attributed on the one hand to plunder and warfare (see p. 12), and on the other to organized slave-raiding.

Coupland argued that slave-trading in Africa dated from the first contacts with peoples from Asia, and that for more than two thousand years it had been the central feature of East Africa's exploitation. He held that slave-trading had depopulated the country and directly accounted for the generally small number of people living in East Africa when compared to other parts of the continent.

Coupland's work has been attractive to subsequent historians. His presentation is repeated in two major works. Oliver and Mathew (1963) and Marsh and Kingsnorth (1957) acclaim Coupland's presentation and restate it with only minor modifications. Alpers (1967) confirmed Coupland's most gloomy views about slave-trading and depopulation and added substance to the earlier works by introducing estimates of the actual casualties of the trade (but see Alpers 1975).

Alpers indicates several figures for slaves sold via the Zanzibar market in the nineteenth century. These are useful for a reconstruction of the impact of the slave-raiding on the population. The following annual figures are given for the trade at its height:

1839, 40,000—45,000 'sold on the Zanzibar market'.
1860s, 50,000—70,000 'slaves reaching the coast'.
1873, n.a., 'the trade was actually at its highest' (Alpers 1967:11–12).

It seems to be implied in Alpers' material that the slave trade in the early 1870s reached proportions of from 65,000 to 80,000 people. Taking these figures to represent the average for the decades, we can now create Table 1.1, indicating the total population drain resulting from the trade:

TABLE 1.1.   *The East African Slave Trade*

1830s	$40,000 \times 10$	400,000
1840s	$45,000 \times 10$	450,000
1850s	$50,000 \times 10$	500,000
1860s	$60,000 \times 10$	600,000
1870s	$70,000 \times\ 3$	210,000
(until 1873)		
	Total	2,160,000

We must keep in mind that this staggering total represents only a fraction of the people actually removed from the East African economy. The authority for the 1860s figures is probably Sulivan (1873) who stated that only a third of the people captured by slavers reached the markets on the coast. Others held the rate of survival to be even smaller. Coupland states that it was Kirk's and Waller's view that 'four or five lives were lost for every slave delivered safe at Zanzibar' (Coupland 1939:140). He reported that Livingstone estimated that at least ten deaths occurred for every slave sold on the market. This was apparently also the opinion of Elton, who vividly described the horrors of Kilwa, the main slave port on the coast.

'Places of skulls' mark the various roads on which the slave traffic is carried on; skeletons are strewn on the beach. The country behind is a desert for a week's journey; and at every step some new experience of the desolation of the slave-trade is apparent (Elton 1879:102).

A very heavy death rate operated throughout the period of raiding, and we must accordingly adjust our figures to this fact. A minimum estimate (based on the calculation that one out of three slaves reached the market) reveals that some 6,480,000 people were removed from the East African economies in the 43 years between 1830 and 1873. A maximum estimate (one out of ten slaves reached the market) would give us a total removal of 21,160,000. Somewhere between these two figures is the mental image that has determined historians' choice of words when describing the nineteenth century in East Africa. Added to the ravages of the intertribal wars, all evidence seems to prove that the East African populations were in rapid decline in the nineteenth century.

We can now sum up the demographic trend implied by the writers we have presented so far: prior to the establishment of the European colonial governments, the East African population suffered the disrupting effects of two major events, intertribal warfare and slave-raiding. The first of these extended indefinitely backward in time, the second reached maximum impact after 1850. We cannot be sure where in the nineteenth century the demographic collapse occurred according to this thesis; most likely it took place between 1840 and 1860. From then onwards, East Africa took on all the characteristics of a human jungle where everybody made war on his neighbour, killed or enslaved him and took away his property. In demographic terms, such conditions must have spelt depopulation. Enter *Pax Britannica* and *Deutsches Schutzgebiet* and an immediate improvement can be registered. The critical turning points may have differed by some years in the various parts of East Africa, but can in the case of Tanganyika be portrayed as in Figure 1.1 with demographic 'breaks' in 1850 and 1890.

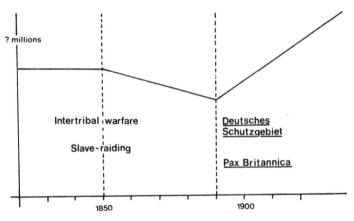

Figure 1.1.   The Demographic Trends of the Nineteenth Century in East Africa (Maximum Population Disruption).

MINIMUM POPULATION DISRUPTION

Twenty-five years ago, the eminent demographer Kuczynski, in his survey of the populations of the then British Empire, rejected the population trends suggested in Figure 1.1. He felt that the literature supporting depopulation from the middle of the nineteenth century onwards had been tailored to fit preconceived notions about African conditions. He pointed to a distinct ideology underpinning the observations and warned that the recorded views of many early explorers and administrators should not be taken as serious history. Kuczynski's position on these opinions is graphically supported in the following quotation by one of those administrators, Sir Charles Eliot, who wrote in an early dispatch about conditions in Kenya:

> Modern East Africa is the greatest philanthropic achievement of the later nineteenth century. . . . Perhaps political philanthropy is never quite disinterested; but when a Government can point to the triumphant accomplishment of the great work of humanity there is no reason why it should not receive due recognition. . . . It is only a few years ago since East Africa was nothing but a human hunting-ground where the hunters did not even take ordinary precautions for preserving the game. On the coast the Arab Chiefs required two children out of every three from the neighbouring tribes as slaves; Arab caravans ravaged the interior and carried off the population of whole villages, of whom a terribly small proportion reached the coast alive as slaves for exportation. The native tribes warred with one another in order to get slaves to sell to the Arabs, and this picture of slavery and bloodshed was chiefly diversified by interludes of terrible famine. . . . How great is the difference now! There can be no doubt of the immense progress made in rendering the civilization of the African at least possible, and it is a progress which need occasion no regrets, for we are not destroying any old or interesting system, but simply introducing order into blank, uninteresting, brutal barbarism (Eliot 1903:29).

This attitude towards their mission in Tanganyika was also shared by German administrators. They wrote confidently about population increases that had come about through their cultural and sanitary improvements, and first and foremost because they had put an end to warfare and slaving (*DDS* 1909–10:6).

Kuczynski thought that instead of creating conditions for an increase in population, the coming of the Europeans had led to a worsening of the situation. Disruption of tribal life, introduction of new diseases, recruitment of labourers and war-time carriers had greatly outweighed the beneficial sides of the early colonization. Moreover, Kuczynski felt that the early administrators had 'overestimated mortality caused by slave-raids and intertribal wars' (1949, II:118) and thus been able to create a false dichotomy between tribal and colonial conditions. 'An unbiased appraisal', he wrote, 'therefore, leads to the following conclusions. There is no evidence that population decreased essentially in the decades preceding the advent of the British. . . . There can, however, be no doubt that the population in 1895–1920 was decreasing' (Kuczynski 1949, II:122, 123).[1]

It will be of value to indicate some of the sources that support a 'minimum interpretation' of intertribal warfare and slave-raiding and thus force our attention to the many other activities that engaged the East

---

[1] Kuczynski is here writing generally about the colonial impact in East Africa. East Africa in this context means Kenya, Uganda and Tanganyika.

African peoples in the nineteenth century. I shall again present a number of excerpts from various sources that together cover the Tanganyikan situation.

Internecine Wars

As much evidence points to a minimum interpretation of internecine wars as to the maximum views already surveyed. Many of the writers we have seen so far made their observations on preconceived assumptions of a state of barbarism prevailing in the region. In their writings, the African was equipped with a savage mind, and acts of violence therefore needed no further explanation. Not all writers viewed the situation in these terms, however, and many injected an element of economic rationality in the explanation of warfare. Fischer's observations on the Masai, for instance, are in clear contrast to the description of them by Krapf and Reichard as irrational barbarians. The warfare theme is not absent, but violence is explained as serving the limited economic objectives of the young *moran*. Acquisition of cattle was seen by Fischer as the only motivation for warlike action against other peoples. Young men with modest material demands or those inheriting herds from their fathers would not join in the warfare (Fischer 1884:62). The recent work by Jacobs has also done much to scale down the old impression of the Masai as the perpetrators of wanton destruction. Jacobs states that apart from the serious encounters between the Masai and the Wakwaia (the War of Laikipia) of 1870–75, the Masai have not encroached on others, but have in fact been the object of a number of smaller aggressions that can hardly be spoken of as wars:

> Though they (the Masai) admit to cattle-raiding, both among their own tribes and against Bantu tribes, they are quick to point out that these were invariably small-scale ventures, rarely involving more than 20–30 warriors (Jacobs 1968:27).

Jacobs thus confirms what Kuczynski had said much earlier with respect to the Masai as the major military dominance in the nineteenth century:

> The total number of Masai now living in Kenya and Tanganyika seems to be approximately 80,000. Before the cattle plagues and famines of 1884 and 1890–1 which apparently reduced their numbers to something like 150,000 or 100,000 there may have been as many as 400,000 or 500,000 scattered over an enormous territory. Their warriors were the young bachelors; they lived with their girl-friends (in many cases at a month's walking distance from the nearest Wakamba or Kikuyu), and they ceased to be warriors when they married, which they were not allowed to do until they had been on several raids. There were probably never more than 50,000 warriors at the utmost, and the number who took part

in a raid probably seldom exceeded 500. The Masai ... had not the power to restrict the population in East Africa to certain areas (Kuczynski 1949, II:122, footnote).

Similarly, in contrast to the uncontrolled destruction that is seen as characteristic of the Wahehe earlier in this chapter, Schele gave to the Hehe raids a limited and economic interpretation. He wrote:

> The Wahehe are primarily peasants and cattle keepers, with the qualification that the ruling class does not work and that the tilling of the fields is done by women and slaves. This situation explains the frequent raids among the surrounding tribes. It is not need that drives the Wahehe to raiding, the object is to secure fresh labour forces (Schele 1896:72).

Fülleborn described the Ngoni people not as warriors, but as agriculturists of high standing. He praised their farming skill and stated that 'agriculture in Ungoni is of a very high quality' (Fülleborn 1906:163). Lieder (1897) told a similar story which I shall refer to in greater detail in the next chapter. Also Redmond (1972) writes at one stage about 'the cattle economy' of the Wangoni of Songea, but he nowhere pursues this idea or deviates from the general presentation of the Wangoni as a warrior people supported by a raiding economy. Yet, it is possible that the concept of a raiding economy misrepresents even the Ngoni existence in the closing decades of the nineteenth century. The majority of the East African peoples practised either an agricultural economy or a cattle economy, neither of which had any built-in necessities for extensive warfare. Where raiding took place, it is therefore possible to understand it in limited terms. Tanner (1966) has given statistics of cattle-raiding in Musoma in the 1950s when no more than 1·5 per cent of the cattle was affected. There is no reason to believe that the raiding incidence, under normal conditions in the nineteenth century, should have been very much higher.

It is quite possible that our impressions of a warlike past have come about partially through uncritical translation into accepted history of tribal lore and legend despite their well-known tendencies to exaggerate past achievements on the battlefield. John Ford quotes a West Lake tradition recorded in the *Bukoba District Book* that fully illustrates the exaggerating tendency. After one of the tribal battles in Karagwe, four piles of testicles, each four feet high, were reportedly exhibited as trophies of victory. Ford thought that at least 75,000 men would have been slaughtered to collect this unusual booty. He noted that the entire chiefdom in the 1948 census had less than 13,000 males over 16 years of age (Ford 1971:426).

Stressing tribal wars as very limited affairs, Richter reduced the succession struggles of Rumanyka's sons to 'the harmless nightly thieving of quarrelsome people' (Richter 1899:96). He had a generally poor opinion of warfare among the West Lake peoples. 'The battle opens with an exchange of prodigious insults', he wrote, 'for there is no proper war cry. Angry tongues maintain and the *pombe* (beer) flask stimulates battle among the Wahaya' (Richter 1899:96). Rehse said much the same thing. He thought that the local weaponry revealed that the people were no warriors (*kein Kriegesvolk*) and that their 'wars' were simply a matter of play-acting. There were few people wounded in skirmish, he reported, and it was extremely rare to find people killed in action (Rehse 1910:90–91). Most wars among the Wanyamwezi, wrote Bösch, 'are nothing more than clever nocturnal surprises' (Bösch 1930:520).

Richard Burton depicted limited warfare as the norm in East Africa. The settled tribes—who clearly were in the majority—were described by him as unwarlike and evading armed conflict rather than seeking it out for pleasure and plunder:

> Even the bravest East African, though, like all men, a combative entity, has a valour tempered by discretion and cooled by a high development of cautiousness. His tactics are of the Fabian order: he loves surprises and safe ambuscades; and in common frays and forays the loss of one per cent justifies a *sauve qui peut* (Burton 1860, II:331).

I have previously reviewed some of the literature on the *mfecane* in Tanganyika. One important weakness of that literature is the complete absence of any real appraisal of the numerical side of the Ngoni invasions. Stuhlmann (1894) identified one of the so-called *Rauberneste* (literally 'robbernest') of the Wangoni, the village of Idabura in the district of Bukoba. The village was said to have tyrannized the entire Usindja (now Geita) peninsula and was accordingly destroyed by German troops. The village was defended by only 600–700 men.

Redmond (1972) estimated that there were 200–400 people in the original band of South African Wangoni who crossed the Zambezi River in 1838 and advanced northwards. He thought that the number might have been doubled by the time the tribe entered Upangwa in 1858. It is not likely that small bands of people numbering a few hundred tribesmen could have anything more than a nuisance effect on the large settled populations of Tanganyika. The impact may have been different in the frontier regions of recent settlement, but even there it is likely to have caused population displacements and temporary chaos rather than permanent destruction. 'They (the Wangoni) shake their shields and the people fly like stricken deer', wrote Livingstone from one such marginal area on the Ruvuma (Livingstone 1874, I:39). Even there, the Ngoni bands seem to have had the power of disruption only. Redmond estimated that the total number of Wangoni in Southern Tanganyika was 16,000–18,000 in the early 1880s. It is evident that this growth had not taken place through natural increases, but was the result of the successful incorporation of people—the so-called *sutu*—as distinguished from the Wangoni proper, from other tribes. The principle of *incorporation* is clearly different from that of *extermination* which is the one with which historians have been uncritically eager to associate the *mfecane*.

The foregoing material has sought to assess the impact of intertribal wars on the population. It does not refute such wars as a social reality in the nineteenth century, but suggests that their impact may have been small. This was Kuczynski's position in 1949 when he warned that the impression given by much of the colonial literature that whole populations or tribes were constantly fighting each other was a gross exaggeration. Statements such as the one mentioned by Felkin, that the Waganda frequently lost 30 to 40 per cent of their men, can only fall into this category. Kuczynski thought that the wars in most instances were limited in scope and intent. 'The object of these "wars" was usually plunder', he wrote, 'the stealing of cattle and women; the numbers of warriors engaged in those raids were seldom large, and the casualties as a rule were not very heavy . . . if there was a depopulation of the country in the decades preceding British administration intertribal warfare cannot have been one of the main causes' (Kuczynski 1949, II:122).

Slave-Raiding

Kuczynski also raised doubts about the information circulated by the anti-slavery groups on the East African trade in his 1949 treatise. He wrote:

> The export of slaves from East Africa rightly attracted enormous attention because it began to flourish when the slave-trade from West Africa had been nearly exterminated, but this should not make us lose sight of the fact that the traffic from East Africa, except for a few decades, was numerically absolutely irrelevant, that even at its worst it was smaller than it had been from West Africa for fully two centuries, and that it is therefore a gross exaggeration to say that it caused depopulation in British East Africa (Kuczynski 1949, II:121).

From what has been said earlier, it is evident that Kuczynski's views have been lost on some later historians. The 'maximum' interpretation has often been maintained, it would seem, because some historians have generally failed to confront and explore the question of the slave market. Repeatedly we are told of rising demands, with little identification of where and why the demand existed. It is clear, however, that as a means of production, the commodity had to fit a production mode of concrete dimensions. It is the latter consideration which had been missing from historiography in the area and its absence has prolonged the realm of speculation in this important chapter of East African history.

It is only in a recent work by Sheriff (1971) that the tortuous problem of the slave *market* has been squarely faced and a start made to treating the East African slave trade with anything like historical method. For the first time, the slave trade was related to the economic demands and the mode of production that gave rise to the traffic. While the slave trade was an integral part of the Zanzibar economic enterprise, it ceased to be the island's most important trading factor with the end of the French markets in the Indian Ocean after 1810. After this date, and particularly after 1830, Zanzibar developed its clove economy, based on plantation production by slave labour on the islands of Zanzibar and Pemba, and gradually also in several coastal areas of Tanganyika and Kenya as far north as Lamu. The development of large-scale plantations on the coast may have commenced simultaneously with the Zanzibar plantation system in the 1830s and 1840s. Burton reported this build-up to be well advanced in the 1850s when he found 'large plantations of cereals and vegetables' operated by slaves, on the Nyika coast (Burton 1860; I:16). These plantations supplied the islands of Zanzibar and Pemba and even the cities of Arabia. Similar developments were reported by Elton (1879) and Baur and Le Roy (1886).

Zanzibar's economic power in the nineteenth century was founded on the export trade in ivory, copal and hides from the mainland and of slave-produced cloves from the islands. Export of slaves outside the island and coast-centred plantation economy was insignificant. The demand for slaves in nineteenth-century East Africa was, therefore, largely limited to the expanses of the local plantation economy.

On the basis of the known trading figures (slavery was legal in Zanzibar until 1873), Sheriff indicates a total figure of 19,600 as the annual demand for slaves in the terminal 15 years of the trade. Of these 8,800 were retained in Zanzibar, 1,800 were re-exported to Pemba, and 4,100 to Lamu. A total of 1,200 were re-exported to unknown destinations. The latter group probably made up the bulk of illicit trading north of Lamu and south of Cabo Delgado.

The export of slaves to destinations south of Cabo Delgado had been prohibited by the Moresby Treaty of 1822. Export to areas north of Lamu had similarly been prohibited by the Hamerton Treaty of 1845. After 1850, British warships were able to search and destroy slave vessels found in the waters south of Kilwa and from 1864 all trade in slaves was prohibited in Zanzibar between the months of January and May. The

1864 prohibition may seem an unimportant gesture, but those familiar with the East African monsoons will know that it effectively sealed off sale and export to areas north of Lamu. Sheriff argues that the Zanzibar rulers agreed to these restrictions to the slave trade, because its export aspect was in fact insignificant in comparison to the plantation demand of Zanzibar and Pemba. The slave market was indigenous rather than external. The legal arrangements of 1822, 1845, 1850 and 1864 reflected this economic fact.

> All concessions relating to the export of slaves outside of East Africa were granted with little resistance on the part of the Sultan. The implication is that the Zanzibar authorities were decreasingly interested in the foreign slave trade which was not considered worth defying the British about (Sheriff 1971:435).

British policy in the area (and following this nearly all East African history) was predicated on the assumption that the slave export out of Zanzibar was of formidable proportions. Sheriff quotes Kirk (the British Consul in Zanzibar) as the source of this assumption. Kirk's estimate was that slave transfers to Benadir, Arabia and Persia totalled 9,792 per year, and that it was more than double the 'normal local demand' (4,100) in Zanzibar/Pemba, Mombasa, Malindi and Lamu. The parliamentary committee which recommended the policing of the East African coast understood the economy of the slave trade through Kirk's impressions. The dhow-chasing in Zanzibar waters that followed until the final abolishment of slavery in 1873 was accordingly predicated on erroneous assumptions. The dhow-chasing of course, produced *some* evidence of slave transport. This evidence was, however, largely created through the prize-money incentive to the British captains who—behind presumed integrity—turned the occasion into one of wholesale looting of local shipping. The evidence is therefore highly suspect and calls for further investigation. Sheriff's work, which broke much new ground there, entirely confirms Devereux' old confession about the patrolling by the Royal Navy that 'the name of the British sailor is sadly compromised by acts which come under no other name than piracy' (Devereux 1869:41–42).

The market question is clearly the most important key to an assessment of the size of the slave trade. One other factor also merits further investigation, namely the reported wastage of human material during the transport to the coast. Little attention has been paid to Burton's observation regarding this that 'no man was foolish enough to spoil his own property' (Burton 1860, I:51), or to explore some of the evidence that destructions due to other causes than slave-raiding have been uncritically attributed to the brutalities of the trade. Thus Burton and Stanley, for instance, reported the dangers of communicable diseases breaking out in the trading caravans. Both identified smallpox as a real killer among the porters. Against this disease few remedies were known, although Burton states that the Arabs practised extensive inoculation (Burton 1860, II:318). When smallpox entered a caravan, those struck by the disease were left to die on the roadside. Burton reported the gruesome sights of smallpox in a trading caravan in the Usagara mountains. He wrote about 'the clean-picked skeletons, and here and there the swollen corpses, of porters who had perished' (Burton 1860, I:165). Stanley wrote: 'The bleached skulls of the victims to this fell disease which lie along every caravan road, indicate but too clearly the havoc it makes annually, not only among the ranks of the several trading expeditions, but also among the villages of the respective tribes' (Stanley 1872:533).

A New Demographic Hypothesis

I have dwelt at length with the slave trade because it is a most difficult subject to approach. After a long line of historians have uncritically magnified its dimensions, one cannot commence a more searching enquiry without running the risk of being branded an apologist of the slave trade. For a proper understanding of the African initiative in the nineteenth century, however, a more realistic evaluation of the size and impact of the trade would seem to be called for.

The important element emerging from the previous discussion is the demographic model of the century that it seems possible to draw from it, namely a zero-growth situation or a situation of slow population growth. According to this model, the period as a whole was a relatively stable and prosperous one in East African history that contained, absorbed and overcame internal difficulties with minimum disruption. The overall vitality of the century came to an end in the 1890s through the events that I shall discuss in Chapter 7. Contrary to the previous population hypothesis (Figure 1.1), this model shows no break in the population in the middle years of the century. It rejects the idea of immediate growth signs in the population after the establishment of foreign rule and so-called 'pacification', and instead sees 1890 as the beginning of the long downward dip which population counts, available from 1903 onwards, have reported.[1] Figure 1.2 is therefore partly an hypothesis; and partly it presents the earliest population counts made in Tanganyika by German and British authorities.

[1] The earliest population figures published for German East Africa exclusive of Ruanda-Urundi indicated totals of 4,622,000 in 1902–3, 4,009,500 in 1906–7, and 4,043,500 in 1913. Sources: *Jahresbericht über die Entwicklung der Deutschen Schutzgebiete* (different years) and Supan (1904).

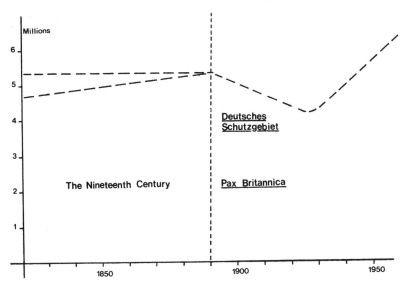

Figure 1.2.   The Demographic Trends of the Nineteenth Century in East Africa (Minimum Population Disruption).

In the final analysis, of course, all early population figures are only speculation. What we have done in this chapter is to question the picture of the pre-colonial East African as either a violent, war-crazed individual or his hapless victim. There is no serious evidence that the population of the nineteenth century was on the decline. Admittedly, there is also no *statistical* evidence to the contrary. The economic evidence which we shall take up in the next chapter will, however, support the population hypothesis that has been outlined here. I shall maintain that the existence of a variety of labour-intensive agricultural systems in Tanganyika during the nineteenth century is an indication of a positive population initiative. Along with the thriving cattle economy, the agricultural effort supported an 'agro-horticultural prophylaxis' (Ford 1971) which among other things held trypanosomiasis (sleeping sickness) in abeyance as an endemic disease throughout the century.

CHAPTER 2

Agricultural Systems and Settlement Patterns

The possibility of a population increase in nineteenth-century Tanganyika has not been seriously considered partly because of the widespread belief that the East African peasantry was incapable of providing food for a large number of people. The East African has been regarded as a useless farmer, too lazy or ignorant to conserve the soil through fertilization and the prevention of erosion. His interaction with the land has been held to be predatory, never actively improving it, but exhausting it through thoughtless tilling. After a few years, the peasant faced declining yields and eventual starvation. He then was forced to move on to new land where the cycle of clearing and settlement recommenced. Differences in the indigenous systems have been seen as automatic adaptations to soil differences and amounted to little more than minor variations in the length of the fallow. We can take Wrigley's account as a typical statement of historians' views of pre-colonial agriculture in East Africa:

> Indigenous (agricultural) practices, varying in detail, conformed to the general pattern known as 'shifting cultivation'. Land was tilled until its yield began to diminish. It was then abandoned to the slow regenerative agencies of nature and new fields were taken out of the surrounding waste. No attempt was made, by systematic rotation of crops or the application of manure, to maintain the soil at a high level of fertility under continuous cultivation. To do so would not only have been exceedingly difficult under African conditions but would also have been entirely pointless. For the system was based on the hitherto valid premise that land was not a scarce factor (Wrigley 1965:254).

Agriculture becomes a matter of concern to historians only with the colonial period. Colonial initiatives and the diffusion of new knowledge, crops and techniques are seen as having brought about profound changes in a static economic situation which only the abundance of virgin land could salvage from deterioration and ruin.

A few authorities have noted some advanced cultivation methods encountered in parts of Tanganyika, but attribute them to a 'special emergency situation' (Ruthenberg 1971:119). These are instances where historians' views of the past have, in turn, influenced agricultural researchers and framed their understanding of past cultivation systems: threatened by surrounding barbarism, slave-raiding and internecine wars, a tribe might have been prevented from shifting cultivation and forced to invent techniques of soil conservation and manuring for permanent settlements. Thus, Gourou (1961) identifies advanced agricultural systems as 'siege methods' developed under duress.

More sympathetic studies of African agriculture were made by Trapnell (1937) and Allan (1965). Both are in agreement on the vast ecological knowledge of the African husbandman. The native could define the forests where he could not define the soil, Trapnell claimed. He suggests that indicator trees and grasses were traditionally used to identify the quality of soil and its suitability for crops. Allan pursues these ideas when paying tribute to the soundness of a number of 'traditional' agricultural practices and to the measure of ecological expertise possessed by the pre-colonial husbandman. He describes the pastoralists as authorities on grasses, capable of assessing the feed value of different grazing lands and their stock-carrying capacity at different seasons of the year. This 'fund of ecological knowledge', which Allan rates as 'precise and remarkably complete', was the basis for pre-colonial agriculture and animal husbandry in Africa (Allan 1965:5).

This chapter will demonstrate that shifting cultivation—rather than being the system pursued by most East Africans—was probably operated by only a small minority of peasants in pre-colonial Tanganyika. Gourou's 'seige method' thesis presupposes a state of warfare in Tanganyika which we called into question in the previous chapter. Even Trapnell and Allan tend to pass off the so-called 'surprisingly advanced' systems as environmentally blessed by excellent conditions of soil and water. Allan never escapes the passive quality of man's always adapting to the environment, despite the fact that many of the systems he analyses bear clear evidence that man has altered the environment to fit the prescriptions of his changing needs.

In the following description of Tanganyika's pre-colonial agriculture we shall see a rich variety of traditional systems. Having rejected the warfare theme in the previous chapter, we must seek new explanations for this variety. It seems natural to turn to Boserup's thesis (1965) that population growth is an independent variable determining agricultural innovation under subsistence conditions. According to Boserup, an increasing population causes food shortages and forces man to intensify his efforts through technological inventions and longer hours of work. The agricultural development that ensues is an adoption of new methods that make possible a more intensive land-use through soil conservation, irrigation systems, and fertilization. These innovations are usually accompanied by falling productivity of labour, in other words, by more work per unit of output.

Boserup develops the idea of 'frequency of cropping' to create a continuum of change from the simplest and unintensive swidden (slash-and-burn) type of agriculture to the more labour-intensive forms of permanent cultivation. The following gradation of land-use is found in her thesis:

1 Forest fallow cultivation (long fallow periods)
2 Bush fallow cultivation (medium fallow periods)
3 Short fallow cultivation (short fallow periods)
4 Annual cropping (perhaps with seasonal fallow)
5 Multiple cropping (two or more successive crops each year).

It will be recalled that Wrigley's statement quoted above places traditional East African agriculture within the first three of these categories. I shall maintain that the majority of Tanganyika's population engaged in agriculture in the nineteenth century operated under some variations of the latter three categories. The correlation of advanced agricultural systems with population pressure will be a powerful argument in support of the population thesis developed in the previous chapter. The labour-intensive techniques we shall observe presuppose a population large enough to practise them.

From Allan's work in Northern and Southern Rhodesia and parts of Tanganyika, we shall use another relationship between agriculture and population. Allan proposes the concept of 'critical density of population', defined as 'the maximum population density the system is capable of supporting permanently in that environment *without damage to the land*' (Allan 1965:9). He establishes this 'critical density' in some of the parts of Tanganyika we shall study, and his figures will be useful in showing that the specific techniques used were in fact capable of maintaining a sizable population.

The object of this chapter therefore is to review a representative number of agricultural systems and to point to those features of the systems that clearly are unrelated to happenstance. As far as possible information on population relationships will be provided. Throughout I am interested in seeing both continuity and change, so that where possible, recent analysis will be contrasted to early historical descriptions from the same areas. Finally, I shall show the relationship between settlement patterns and ecological control.

AGRICULTURAL SYSTEMS

It will be seen that my critical disagreement with Wrigley pertains to the degree to which permanent settlement or migratory practices characterized pre-colonial agriculture. Whereas Wrigley tends to stress the latter, I find that contemporary descriptions by early explorers indicate that the vast majority of Tanganyika's husbandmen were settled permanently or semi-permanently. Many of them had introduced perennial crops and practised a number of devices that helped them to maintain the fertility of the soil. Such features were in many areas reinforced by soil conservation practices and with occasional irrigation schemes.

Coastal Agriculture

The shifting cultivation described by Wrigley and most East African historians was practised by a minority of the peoples of Tanganyika. The Makonde/Makua thicket cultivation and the 'Mashokora' cultivation of some of the central coastal peoples seem to correspond most readily to Wrigley's generalization.

The coastal cultivation system was described by Hartnoll and Fuggles-Couchman (1937) as a long-fallow practice of three to four years of successive harvests of maize, rice, sorghum and cassava, intergrown with different legumes. The land was then abandoned to fallow and the regrowth of grass and secondary bush. In a few years' time the land would gain the character of 'Mashokora' thicket—a succession forest of generally low type that replaced the big trees that covered the land before man's first onslaught. In this area (inland from Dar es Salaam) soil regeneration is slow and a fallow of at least twenty years has been regarded as a minimum. A change of settlement is not necessarily demanded by each cultivation shift. Allan (1965:218) judges the critical population density to be in the region of fifteen per square mile for people fully dependent on this form of cultivation.

Gillman described the Makonde Plateau in 1945 as 'scattered clearings in this overall blanket of thicket' (Gillman 1945:43). The thicket resulted from regrowth of bush during the period of soil-resting indicated to be at least twenty years. A few remnants of the original vegetation revealed that tall trees had once covered the plateau. Allan points to similar cultivation among the neighbouring Makua people, but indicates important local variations where fertile pockets are cultivated more or less permanently with occasional fallow for control of weeds (Allan 1965:213).

There is an almost total similarity between these descriptions of the Makonde/Makua cultivation and those given by early visitors to the area before the turn of the century. Livingstone (1874) experienced much bush-cutting in the area and the terms 'bush' and 'thicket' repeat themselves in the early literature from the northern side of Ruvuma River, indicating that the travellers encountered the regrowth of the long-fallow cultivations. Behr (1893:77) stated that a maximum of three years' cultivation would be tried on one plot before the regrowth of thicket was allowed. These rapid shifts were held to cause serious destruction of the forest potential, and Bornhardt (1900:270), who thought that at least ten hectares of forest (thicket) land would be destroyed for every one under cultivation, recommended that the government force the people to settle permanently.

Permanent settlement apparently occurred in this region only near the fertile river floodplains. Livingstone was surprised to find rice grown along the Ruvuma and its confluents and offered for sale in abundance (1874, I:29). Agriculture in such areas, which were described as densely populated, was seen as an ideal contrast to the long-fallow practices in the neighbouring hills and plateaus (Adams 1902).

The Impact of Urbanism and Trade

Behr contended that the agricultural efforts of the Makonde peoples had regressed considerably since they had learnt to collect wild rubber and copal and discovered their easy market on the coast. These sales gave quick returns, and the Wamakonde soon preferred to buy their needed grain from coastal traders rather than to grow it themselves (Behr 1893:78). This development is part of the loss of self-sufficiency which took place throughout the nineteenth century as the result of economic specialization.

We should remember that the city formation of the East African coast dates back several centuries (Nicholls 1972, Strandes 1899), and that the string of townships in varying stages of prosperity included Bagamoyo with 25,000 inhabitants in 1889, which besides Kilwa Kivinje with 15,000, Tanga, Pangani, Sadani, Lindi and Zanzibar must have added up to a considerable demand for foodstuffs. This demand caused reverberations in a number of agricultural areas near the coast and stimulated their specialization as grain and vegetable suppliers for the urban centres. It seems likely that part of the flat and enormously fertile river valleys in the south were particularly affected by these developments. The greater urban concentration on the northern half of the coast also caused a deep penetration of agricultural demands. It seems likely that the village complexes surrounding Bwana Heri's *boma* at Palamakaa were part of the Sadani grainchamber and possibly that of Bagamoyo. Leue described the country of the Wadoe around the village of Mandera as well populated; its extensive maize fields exhibited proof of the extraordinary fertility of the soil (*DKB* 1893:247). The supply line may at that time have stretched as far inland as Mhonda in the Nguru mountains, also described as heavily populated and cultivated (*DKB* 1893:248). Further north many of the Usambara peoples were similarly drawn in as food suppliers to the urban centres along the coast, like Pangani, Tanga and Moa (Farler 1882). It is likely that food demands from the trading caravans criss-crossing the country had an impact deep into inland communities like Ugogo and Unyamwezi. We must therefore reckon with trade and urbanism as factors stimulating, to some extent, changes in the agricultural production. Such changes are not, however, restricted to contact points with trading caravans and urban centres and demand a wider explanation of general applicability.

The River Floodplains

In addition to the normal rain-fed agriculture, the Warufiji are given a bonus harvest in the form of the *mlau* cultivation which exploits the sinking water table in the river plains following the annual floods. This cultivation is fully independent of the rainfall during the growth season, if the fall of the water table is slow and does not outpace the downward growth of the crop roots. No clearing for cultivation is necessary in the *mlau* areas, but the fields are hoed after the seeds germinate in order to reduce the evaporation of moisture. 'In this process', wrote Marsland, 'we have an unconscious application by the native of the theory of papillarity and the movement of soil moisture' (1938:58). More work is needed where the land has been only partly inundated and it is necessary to clear weeds before and after planting. In these instances green manuring, utilizing the weeds, is practised. Intercropping is extensive and makes possible harvest seasons at different intervals throughout the year. The total system is extremely labour intensive and work goes on without any seasonal breaks. Summing up his impressions of the Rufiji valley, Marsland (1938:59) wrote of it as a 'veritable agricultural Eldorado'. Its cultivation system seems, however, to have changed little over the last one hundred years.

The rich alluvial deposits of the lower Rufiji valley stretch approximately one hundred miles upstream from the delta. Elton crossed the lower parts of the area in the 1870s and left this impression:

> The fertility of the lands lying between the Mahoro and Rufiji is extraordinary. Maize, rice, millet, ground-nuts and peas are largely cultivated, and heavy crops are garnered every year, the periodical inundations bringing fresh life to the soil. Sheep, cattle, and goats are in sufficient numbers to be bought for export and shipped at either Murengu or Samanga. In fact, from the Mahoro to the Rufiji was a three hours' march through a land of plenty (Elton 1879:97).

The export of large quantities of foodstuffs (beans, maize, rice and sesame seeds) from the Rufiji villages to Zanzibar was recorded by Ziegenhorn (1896). His review indicated relatively heavy population concentrations near the fertile flood plains where the main villages were located. Indigenous food demands must have been considerable. The agricultural production in most villages aimed, however, beyond self-sufficiency to create a considerable surplus for export outside the tribal boundaries. Because of the important rice exports, the area was referred to as 'Calcutta *Mdogo*'—'Little Calcutta' (*DKB* 1893:495).

Further inland along the Rufiji tributary system Joseph Thomson passed through the land of the Wamahenge in 1879. Part of this tribe was then living along the Great Ruaha River where rich alluvial soil made their area 'one of the most fertile spots in Africa'. Thomson observed:

> All the cereals of the coast, such as rice (the favourite food), millet, and maize, are grown extensively. So also are such vegetables as sweet potatoes, yams, ground-nuts, melons, pumpkins, and cucumbers, and many other excellent articles of food. Tobacco is grown very abundantly. The sugar-cane, the castor-oil plant, and cotton, are also cultivated. Curiously enough in what appears to be an extremely favourable country for bananas none appear (Thomson 1881, I:189).

The Mahenge cultivations tied in with another important rice-growing area higher up along the Ulanga/Kilombero River and its numerous tributaries (Stolowsky 1903). These areas together produced important surpluses estimated to have amounted to annual deliveries around 1900 of nearly 4 million kilos (Braun 1906:206). Braun singled out the Wambunga for their devices of artificial irrigation and for their particularly large production. It is likely that the grain surpluses from these areas eventually were included in the regional trading network and made places like Mgunda, Kondoa/Kilosa and Morore important provisioning stations along the central trade routes.

The Ruaha/Ulanga area was in the early 1890s a hotbed for Mafitte (Ngoni) raids. The Governor, Schele, inspected the district and expressed astonishment at the heavy population and agricultural skills of the area. Production was extremely work-intensive (ridges and irrigation works), and much effort went into the cultivation. A large labour force was accordingly needed, and Schele judged that the Mafitte raids expressed the labour needs of an expanding agricultural economy (*DKB* 1894:228, see also Lieder 1894).

Many of the Mahenge settlements of the nineteenth century have since then been abandoned, and new sites taken up, oriented to the recent road network in the highlands away from the main river valleys. This is not because present day farmers *prefer* other soils than those of their forefathers as claimed by Braun (1968:24). The people had little choice in the matter when the dangers of sleeping sickness and the decision to create the Selous Game Reserve made their move away from the main river plains necessary. In terms of agricultural techniques, this move has entailed a step backwards from the permanent irrigation systems of the nineteenth century to the shifting cultivation (long fallow) described by Braun as the prevailing pattern among the Wamahenge of today. A second feature has been the replacement of cassava as the main staple crop for the variety of crops mentioned by Thomson.

The Usambaras

In Feierman's analysis (1970), the Sambaa culture can be summed up as a people's total adaptation to an ecological niche where language and economic practices as well as political institutions bear the marks of the formative environment. Feierman describes the traditional Sambaa cultivation and crop patterns as enormously complex and explains this complexity as caused by the constraints of the subsistence economy and the need for survival in the absence of adequate methods of storage. Complexity of crops, growing seasons and field practices developed 'to defeat famine, to cheat death'. Feierman nevertheless thinks that the economy sustained a 'relatively high density of population' (Feierman 1970:21, 126).

One striking difference between this 1970 analysis and German observations approximately 80 years earlier is that the Sambaa people then produced large food surpluses which were carried by local caravans to Wanga, Pangani and Tanga (Baumann 1891; Holst 1893, 1893a; and Warburg 1894). Another indication of important surpluses was the production of sugar-cane which was used for alcoholic beverages. Cows and small stock were part of every household. The people must have been permanently settled for some time. The town of Vuga was surrounded by banana groves and counted some 500 dwellings already in 1857 (Burton 1872, II:229). The cultivation circuit had clearly become overextended by the 1890s. In most of the 'outer' plantations temporary huts were then erected so that people could stay for longer periods away from their permanent dwellings in Vuga (Warburg 1894).

Irrigation systems of great complexity had to a large extent removed the risk of drought. The Wasambaa were described as 'excellent water technicians', and irrigation channels of several miles' length were not uncommon (Warburg 1894:134). The fields were cleared of stones which were piled in walls and ridges giving support to the steep fields. The ridges were often reinforced by planted hedges. The latter practice was still in use in the 1930s (Swynnerton 1939).

The Wasegua also traded food surpluses to Sadani and Pangani, according to Baumann (1891:273). They seem to have specialized in grain production which was undertaken in near permanent cropping. Baumann contended that cultivation took place for three years followed by one year of fallow. The permanence of the settlements was evident in the presence of bananas. A certain seasonality must have operated in the agricultural time-table, because the Seguas found occasion to organize trading caravans, going mostly to Irangi (Baumann 1891:274).

Large quantities of maize, sorghum and rice originating in Bondei country were also delivered to the coast (Baumann 1891:126–27). Fish was usually brought back to form part of the standard diet. Tobacco, tomatoes and sugar-cane were also grown.

Of all the Usambara peoples, only the Wadigo seem not to have been part of this pattern. Baumann described them as recent converts from cattle-keeping to agriculture due to Masai raids. They adopted as their staple food-crop the easily grown cassava which at that time was cultivated to a very limited extent in Tanganyika. Whereas other tribes traded only surpluses of food crops like maize, beans and sorghum, the Wadigo apparently adopted these as cash crops which entered the export market without becoming part of the local diet.

Kilimanjaro and Upare

It is difficult to know whether trade routes from the coast also acted as stimuli to agricultural growth in the more northerly parts of Tanganyika, in Upare and Kilimanjaro. In the 1840s, Rebmann described Kilimanjaro as an extremely isolated place (Krapf 1860:245); but important routes skirted the mountain on its populated sides in the later parts of the century, when Taveta became an important provisioning station. It seems, however, that the main characteristics of the Kilimanjaro agricultural system had been developed already by the 1840s. Rebmann, for instance, reported the existence of extensive irrigation systems at the time, and a recent review (Masao 1974) has dated a number of important furrows to the period before 1850. Besides being trained to serve their chief in the defence of the land, all male Chagga youths were educated as 'engineers, in the construction of water-courses' (Krapf 1860:243). People were permanently settled in individual family homesteads, and Rebmann commented on the absence of nucleated (fortified) villages. The settlements were generally planted with bananas which were seen as the most important food crop among the Chagga. The banana plant also served as building material for houses, fodder for the cows and pipes for irrigation.

Later travellers like Decken (1869) and Johnston (1886) stressed the abundant riches of the Chagga country and in particular detailed the irrigation systems. These were cut out from the mountain streams often several miles above the settled areas and the water conducted in skilfully constructed troughs and tunnels along the mountainside to reach the individual settlements by way of innumerable branches and rivulets. Elaborate rights and privileges attached to the irrigation system and were seen as the origin of the strong political systems among the mountain clans (Gutmann 1926).

The irrigation system assured virtually a third cropping season beyond the normal two connected with the long and the short rainy seasons. Volkens (1897:240) claimed that dry-season irrigation had fully insured the Chagga peoples against drought dangers and practically eliminated food shortages from the area.

Shortage of land in this period is indicated by the information on stall-fed cattle. Contrary to the popular belief that the Chagga cattle were hidden in huts due to the dangers of Masai raids, stall-feeding has a simple and general economic explanation in pressure on the land. This will, under mixed agriculture, result in the early transformation of grazing ground to cultivated fields. By the end of the nineteenth century, very little land was left for cattle-grazing. Only Rombo still had extensive fields where the chiefs of Marangu and Moshi reportedly tended their herds during some parts of the year (Brehme 1894:125). Most Chagga cattle were, however, stall-fed in this period.

This picture corresponds to information about the Chagga population. Although such reports vary considerably, the consensus seems to be that the mountain was densely populated (Widenmann 1899). At least two German administrators (Brehme 1894, and Widenmann 1895) warned against optimistic schemes for European settlement on Kilimanjaro on the ground that the land was heavily populated and that most fertile land had already been occupied. Settlement by foreigners would therefore only result in conflict. According to Allan's calculations, the critical population density for pre-colonial Chaggaland was up to 400 people per square mile (Allan 1965:166). There is no reason to believe that the actual population was much below this. One advantage of the stall-feeding technique was probably that the peasants could utilize manure on their plots. Although Johnston (1886:124,440) claimed that only ashes, usually from the burning of refuse and weeds, served as fertilizers among the Chagga, Volkens (1897:232–33) found evidence from Kibosho Chiefdom that the cow dung and stall-bedding were spread on the banana fields. Allan (1965:164) claims that manuring of the permanent banana groves was a common practice all over Chaggaland. A second half of the peasant-holding was traditionally kept under short fallow (2 years) after 3 years' cropping. These fields were probably manured with ashes. Maize, sweet potatoes, yams, beans, peas and millet are mentioned as the pre-colonial crops in addition to the all-important bananas.

Much of what has been said above apparently also fitted Pare agriculture in the pre-colonial period. The steep mountain terrain caused added difficulties for cultivation, but these had successfully been overcome through terracing. Baumann found the Pare stone ridges surprisingly similar to the terracings in the European wine regions (1891:228). Equally remarkable was the Pare irrigation system which Baumann held to be a 'truly outstanding feat of construction' of a preindustrial people (1891:229). As in Kilimanjaro, bananas were the main crop.

The Usagaras

Important dry-season irrigation systems also existed in the Southern Usagaras in the heavily populated valleys of Mwega, Rumuma and Munaga (Tiller 1913). German travellers were struck by the very advanced irrigation techniques and by the scale of the operations, where water from the main rivers was for several miles directed towards the cultivated fields in the valley bottoms. Dams of stone and timber were built high in the valleys from which the irrigation furrows branched out. In Marore district, numerous troughs running parallel to the Mwega River irrigated all cultivated land. The peasants in this region were also quite familiar with animal dung as a fertilizer (Tiller 1913:57), and their system was extremely productive. The crops grown were sorghum, maize, sweet potatoes, beans, groundnuts, sesame seeds, sugar-cane and—less frequently—rice, bananas, cassava and cucumbers. In the fertilized irrigation fields up to three crops were planted simultaneously. Grain was always planted with legumes. The crop production was primarily for local consumption, but part of it was sold to the caravan carriers between Kilosa and Iringa who probably provisioned in Marore. Nevertheless, it was tobacco production which characterized the area. Tobacco was produced in large quantities, particularly in the Widunda mountains, and was mostly exported towards Ugogo.

Ukonde/Unyakyusa

Of the different agricultural systems of the southern Tanganyika highlands, those of the Matengo and Nyakyusa peoples have been singled out as exceptional developments. Thwaites' appraisal (1943) brings out the important environmental differences within short distances in Unyakyusa due to sharp altitude changes and corresponding rainfall variations. He was able to demonstrate man's careful adaptation of different crop systems and methods of land-use to these environmental zones. Variations in crop selection and rotation, ridging methods and conservation works resulted from profound insights into environmental nuances. Thwaites also demonstrated the general use of leguminous plants with their nitrogen-fixing qualities as an important rotation crop. He described the Nyakyusa agriculture as mixed, with cattle manure playing an important part in the upkeep of soil fertility. Cattle were stalled 'owing to the prevalence of thieving' (Thwaites 1943:236).

With one exception, the essential features described by Thwaites were present in pre-colonial times when people like Harry Johnston (1897) and Merensky (1894) agreed that the banana cultures of the Konde peoples represented 'the arcadia of Africa'. Merensky mentions the use of green manure, ashes, mulchings and animal dung to fertilize the banana fields and garden plots where three successive crops of maize, beans and sweet potatoes were harvested in one year. All vegetation was controlled, and tree-planting for bark cloth production, shielding and firewood was widespread (Merensky 1894:148). The exception pertains to cattle-keeping, where it seems judicious to reject Thwaites' slander in favour of Fülleborn's explanation that cattle were stall-fed due to grazing shortages. As in Kilimanjaro, population pressures transformed the available land from grassland to fields cultivated for staples and fodder. Already in the 1870s, Elton had been amazed at the extent of the Konde cultivations. Hamlets dotted the countryside and were surrounded by farmland, 'the appearance of some of the valleys showing a greater extention of cultivation than has been reached in our South African colonies' (Elton 1879:331).

Stall-feeding of the cattle also gave additional advantages to the farmer in gathering the manure for his household plots. Allan's calculation is that the traditional agricultural system of this area could have supported up to 200 people per square mile (critical population density) (Allan 1965:194).

Umatengo

The agricultural system of the Matengo people has been extensively analysed by Pike (1938) and Stenhouse (1944). The terrain is steep and the main achievement of the Matengo system is the ingenious combination of anti-erosion techniques and green manuring through field methods of pits and ridges. Cultivation is permanent and must have been so for a considerable period of time. Thus, Stenhouse claimed that 'shifting cultivation is unknown to the older generation of Wamatengo' (1944:23). Fertility has been built up through the box-pit method which exposes the subsoil while green manure is building up the humus and gradually deepening the layer of fertile soil. Both Pike and Stenhouse deplored the fact that the system was disintegrating due to the loss of labour. Matengo agriculture is extremely labour intensive, and young people were attracted to easier ways of making a living elsewhere in the country. Moreover, the Matengo system was seen as having developed in response to threats by marauding Wangoni. When *Pax Germanica* fell over the land, the mainspring of development was broken and the system went into rapid decline.

It was still working well when Busse visited the Matengo highlands around the turn of the century. He was struck by the extreme isolation of the Wamatengo whom he encountered after crossing what he described as an endless stone desert (Busse 1902). His general impression was very favourable, and he rated the agricultural achievement as one of the finest in the colony. Irrigation systems abounded (*DKB* 1898:349), and all cultivation was man-controlled. Tree-planting was frequent in the vicinity of settlements, for bark-cloth production, building material, firewood and shade. There is no doubt that the agricultural system developed under heavy population pressures. The number of people was found to be considerable, and Busse mentioned the chief's village as a dwelling cluster of more than 5000 people. Maize, peas, beans, tobacco and cotton were grown by the highlanders.

Uhehe

We know a lot less about the agricultural systems of other peoples in southern Tanganyika, notably the Wahehe, Wabena, Wasangu and the Wangoni, all of whom have been assumed to have been raiding peoples with a very limited economic base, consuming more than they produced. Their agricultural systems are seen as recent developments that commenced after the imposition of colonial pacification. Winans (1965), for instance, has great praise for the Hehe adaptations to the variety of environmental conditions of the area they occupy today. To each environment, defined by altitude and rainfall, corresponds a particular form of adjustment. Cattle-herding is practised in the lowlands, where nucleated settlements organized around permanent water are the general rule. In the middle highlands and uplands, where settlement takes the form of dispersed homesteads, various forms of mixed agriculture prevail. The Hehe agriculture developed from what is described as the raiding economy of the nineteenth century which could accommodate only cattle as an economic asset. Winans observes: 'Under such a (raiding) regime herding, with its great mobility, was the optimum adaptation and the greater the agricultural involvement the greater the risk of domination by more mobile neighbours. In other words, herding versus farming activity was a straight-forward index of military success and political dominance' (Winans 1965:437). In due course the military prowess went from the Wasangu to the Wabena and finally to the Wahehe, whose zenith of power may have been reached in the 1880s. Their raiding mentality provoked the imposition of the *Pax Germanica* in a series of particularly fierce battles throughout the 1890s.

In the previous chapter, however, I have described the Wahehe and the Wangoni as excellent agriculturists. This view is fully substantiated by German reports from Hehe country in the early 1890s. Schele's observations (1896), for instance, leave little doubt that the ecological adaptations praised by Winans have a pre-colonial origin, and that agriculture played a far greater role in the Wahehe economy than is normally allowed for. Schele recorded that crops, field methods and settlement patterns changed with the clearly defined altitude/rain zones. Differences were found between the valleys of the lower Hehe highlands (*Randgebirge*), where sweet potatoes, millet, maize, cucumbers, rice and beans, peas and tobacco were cultivated, and the real highlands (*Hochplateau*) where grain, peas and maize were the main crops. Field methods also changed with the ecological zones. Thus high ridges were used for cultivation on level ground, whereas terraces were built for anti-erosion purposes on the steeper hillsides. The terraces were skillfully constructed and resembled those of the German vineyards, wrote Schele (1896:72). The upkeep of these terraces required very intensive work which was not carried out by the Wahehe proper, but by the dispossessed peoples who had been forced into the hills through the arrival of the basically cattle-keeping Wahehe. Field work was carried out with large iron hoes of Kinga make.

Surplus produce from the highland zones undoubtedly went to feed the large *tembe*-villages[1] that developed among the cattle keepers in this period. Old Iringa was a relatively modest township when Giraud (1890) saw it in the early 1880s. By 1890, it had grown to a considerable size with 5000–6000 people (Engelhardt 1895). We should note that such *tembe*-villages were not restricted to Hehe country only. Gawiro in Ubena was also a large *tembe*-village (Fülleborn 1906:254), Mhenge and Idinda sprawled for more than a kilometre across the plains (Adams 1899:36), and Utengule in Usangu was estimated to have had more than 2000 inhabitants before its move after the destruction of Hehe power in 1896–97 (Bornhardt 1900:167).

Schele could not report about the cattle component of the traditional Hehe economy, because it had been recently destroyed through the Rinderpest. It was this component that amazed earlier travellers like

---

[1] *Tembe* refers to the traditional house type of the Sangu, Hehe, Gogo and Nyamwezi peoples.

Thomson (1881) who must have visited the lower parts of the Hehe ecological zones only. In these parts, cattle abounded everywhere, and Thomson rightly wondered that he could travel for miles upon miles through settled country without encountering cultivated fields (1881, I:215, 225). Adams (1898) travelled through the same ecological zone following the Hehe wars and the defeat of Mkwawa. Both cattle and people were gone, and the vast plains were destroyed and deserted. The terrain was becoming overgrown with young bush not yet high enough to cover the ruins of the old *tembe*-villages that were strewn throughout the countryside.

Ungoni

As in the case of the Wahehe, it is possible that the strength of the Ngoni agricultural system was based on involuntary labour. The Wangoni seem to have practised a medium-fallow system. An early report from Shambruna's country around Songea stated that the ground was everywhere well cultivated, and that groundnuts were the main crop (*DKB* 1894:229). The Songea Wangoni were compared favourably to their tribesmen (the Mafitte) of Ulanga as expert agriculturists. Their system was seen as far more advanced than that practised among the coastal tribes (probably Makonde/Makua of the long-fallow system). The fields were well hoed and the ridges straight. Everywhere the German observer found 'signs of man's industrious hands' (*DKB* 1894:229). Need was not judged to be the mainspring of the Ngoni raids. The country was thickly populated and Shambruna was thought to rule over from 50,000 to 60,000 people. An equal number of people were ruled by Mharulli, another Ngoni chief. Approximately one-third of the countryside was under cultivation.

Lieder had similar praise for Ngoni agriculture:

> Nowhere in East Africa have I seen such well tended fields as in Ngoniland. During the hoeing season, people come out in long lines and dig with their huge hoes—their long handles are swung with both hands—to prepare approximately 2-metre broad seedbeds which are planted. In the execution of these ridges the fields gain a completely European appearance (Lieder 1897:103).

Busse found features of controlled vegetation in Ungoni, where tree-planting was as much a part of the agricultural system as it was among the Wamatengo (Busse 1902).

It is possible that cattle and small stock were integrated into the agricultural economy, and Fülleborn observed cattle stalls in the upper Ruvuma region and reported that the cattle were brought into the villages at night (Fülleborn 1906:97). It was such features of the Ngoni territory which made Fülleborn recommend Songea as more attractive for European settlers than the land of the Wahehe (1906:131).

Ufipa

An important technique for retaining soil fertility for long cultivation periods had been developed by the Wafipa. Lunan (1950) correctly pointed to the importance of the so-called mound cultivation in maintaining fertility and lengthening the cropping period before exhaustion. Grass and other plant remains are placed in mounds built of up-turned sods. While the green manure is allowed to rot nearly a year before the mounds are broken down and spread over the fields, beans are grown in the mounds during the first year. Later cropping alternates between flat cultivation and mounds or ridges, with different crops alternating on the plots. First-year planting of legumes in the mounds has been judged to be an important sign of microbiological insights: 'This tribe has discovered for themselves the importance of nitrogen in the crop cycle,' stated the *East African Agricultural Journal* in an editorial (*EAAJ* 1950:63).

Fromm's work on the Wafipa, which was undertaken in 1908–09, described in detail the same green manuring in mounds and ridges. He contrasted this practice, which was carried out on grass fallow, with the use of ashes (*Chitemere*) in the longer fallows in the miombo forests. Only in the tobacco plantings, which were always found next to the villages, would the Wafipa of 1908 utilize animal manure in the form of urine from goats and sheep. Fromm implied that a deterioration had taken place in agriculture from the time before the great Rinderpest of the 1890s when the integration of the cattle economy and agriculture may have been far greater than it became later. Fromm made his remarks in connection with the shifting of village sites undertaken because the land could not be adequately fertilized by the reduced herds. The shifting of plots—and villagers—was held to take place more frequently than before the Rinderpest. Because of these changes, abandoned villages (*tongo*) were frequently encountered and, on the other hand, settlements and fields under cultivation were found where earlier maps indicated wilderness (Fromm 1912:81).

The loss of cattle undoubtedly created a heavier pressure on the land as the main supplier of foodstuff. This also must have acted to increase the exhaustion of the land and sharpen the need to shift more frequently. The drawing-off of seasonal labour from the land had commenced at this time and may have been particularly critical in this agricultural system which knew no slack season. Where Fromm (1912:90) indicated a period of cultivation of 6 successive years on the average, Allan (1965:140) gave 4–5 years as the maximum cultivation period of today's Wafipa.

Unyamwezi

In his portrait of Ingereza Ng'wana Sweya, Rounce (1939) has given us an insight into what the colonial agricultural officer would regard as a progressive Unyamwezi farmer in the 1930s. Born around 1870, Ingereza Sweya had lived a varied career, including several trips to the coast as a porter and a session on a plantation in Muheza before returning to settle at Ilalanguru village on the Tabora-Kigoma road in 1908. Rounce saw Ingereza Sweya as a rather unique peasant in that he had learnt to restore some degree of fertility to the ground. He knew the importance of cow dung, but as manure he generally used a compost of ant-hill soil and the leaves of the mango tree in addition to household waste and ashes. These practices enabled him to settle permanently and to cultivate almost continuously with occasional fallows of unstated duration. Rounce regarded him as a lone innovator: 'In spite of his success not a single individual has followed his royal road to soil rehabilitation' (Rounce 1939:215).

The story can be put into perspective only by anticipating a later chapter (see pp. 62–4). In Ilalanguru village, Ingereza Sweya's house was located near an *itongo*—a disused cattle kraal—on which ground he planted his first garden. Although he understood the importance of cattle manure for the soil, he had apparently never made use of it in his farming. In the next chapter, I shall quote German evidence that the entire western and southern Tabora district was strewn with empty cattle kraals in the period around 1910, as the cattle had died out following the Rinderpest and the spreading tsetse flies. The cattle component has since then been lacking in the agricultural system of this part of the cultivation steppe. Allan included the general area under his description of 'the Miombo Woodlands' where shifting cultivation, low or moderate population densities and widespread distribution of tsetse fly (*Glossina Morsitans*) were typical features (1965:210–11).

The term 'Unyamwezi' as used by nineteenth-century explorers is extremely imprecise. It seems possible, however, that Ilalanguru village formed part of the 'land of the Moon' which deeply impressed Richard Burton. He held the Nyamwezi population to be 'comparatively numerous' and described the 'well-hoed plains' surrounding the villages. Numerous herds of cattle, as well as flocks of goats and sheep suggested to him conditions of 'barbarous comfort and plenty' (Burton 1860, II:7).

This prosperity was maintained twenty years later when Casati saw the cultivation steppe of the Wanyamwezi and confirmed 'the prosperity of the region and the well-being of its inhabitants' (Casati 1891, II:299).

Such impressions of Nyamwezi agriculture would in the twentieth century ring true only of Sukumaland. A number of studies have detailed the

Sukuma agricultural system and its merits (Allnutt 1942, Rounce 1949, Rounce and Thornton 1939, Smith 1938) and made possible a number of comparisons.

Rounce pointed to the high population density in Sukumaland where the average exceeded 100 people per square mile with isolated centres ranging between 400 and 700. The cultivation systems was of a short-fallow type with three years of cultivation followed by three years of fallow. By the time Rounce undertook his study, the Sukuma agriculture was beset with a number of problems, of which soil erosion was seen as the major one. This was linked directly to overstocking, i.e. the presence of cattle, but it is evident that pressure on the land had equally been caused by the extensive growing of the new cash crop, cotton, which was destined for direct export.

To the 'well-hoed plains' corresponds the use of high ridges in Sukumaland, developed in response to problems of fertility depletion and soil erosion. For the latter purpose the ridges follow the contours of the hill slopes. The ridging practice is also connected with the weeding problem and the incorporation of field refuse and weeds (green manure) into the soil. The aeration of the soil caused by hoeing into high ridges has also been proven beneficial, as Rounce and Thornton (1939) have demonstrated a constant pattern of higher yields on ridges than on flat cultivation.

Finally, Allnutt (1942) discussed rice-growing in Sukumaland. He expressed surprise over the practical possibility of growing rice in the dry areas of the cultivation steppe, but saw the effort as yet another example of Sukuma industry and quick adoption of new crops and farming techniques. Allnutt did not refer back to the long tradition of rice-growing in Unyamwezi where the crop probably entered with traders returning from the coast in the early years of the nineteenth century. This led to an important expansion of cultivated land as the *mbuga* of Unyanyembe for the first time become attractive farmland (Unomah 1972:4). The rice-growing initiative still rested in western Unyamwezi around the turn of the century. Braun's review (1906:204) of rice-growing in Tanganyika then singled out the areas of Urambo, Ubagwe, Umakarundi and Ugunda as the particular rice-growing areas of the cultivation steppe.

Returning to Rounce's progressive farmer, it now appears correct to see him less as an innovator than as a last struggling survivor of an earlier agricultural tradition in Unyamwezi. It also seems possible to conclude that Sukumaland alone of the many areas making up the Unyamwezi of the nineteenth-century explorers retained this tradition and carried its positive achievements into the twentieth century.

Ukara

Some of the most convincing examples of Africa agency in the agricultural field come from communities around Victoria Nyanza, notably from Bukoba district and Ukara Island. The latter has attracted considerable attention and the impression is easily gathered that Ukara agricultural ingenuity is a unique exception to a general situation of unfortunate malpractices.

There is no need to describe in detail the intensive farming system of the Wakara, their integration of livestock (which is stall-fed) and crop husbandry, soil conservation and improvement methods, different forms of manuring, intercropping, crop rotation, etc. Such descriptions are readily available in the works of Ludwig (1968), Lunan and Brewin (1956), Patterson (1956) and Rounce and Thornton (1936). Their findings add up to a system where man has not stopped at adapting himself to the limits of the environment, but where these limits have been considerably stretched through human activities. Even the trees on the island form part of the agricultural system. They are man-controlled and planted for lopping purposes to provide fodder and bedding for livestock (French 1938). Allan praised the system enthusiastically as 'the ideal of agricultural perfection, the highest attainment of the indigenous systems' (Allan 1965:199–200). The Wakara achievement is particularly significant because the soil is generally weak and of no exceptional fertility.

The Wakara system is labour intensive in the extreme, and the return per hour of work is far below that of neighbouring peoples (Ludwig 1968:133). This fact has led to a great deal of migration which Allan (1965:206) sees as the reason for falling standards of excellence in the system and increasing signs of its disintegration. His estimate that the critical population density for the island exceeds 500 per square mile is conditioned on a human agency: that fertility can be maintained indefinitely through man-made devices under continuous cropping.

The essential features of the Wakara agriculture as outlined here were reported by Baumann (1894) and Kollmann (1899). It seems likely that the agricultural development on the island reached a peak in the last decades of the nineteenth century, and that the system has gradually disintegrated since then.

Bukoba

Stanley saw the Bukoba coastline from Musira Island in Bukoba Bay in 1875. He thought it 'one of the strangest yet fairest portions of Africa', and wrote of 'hundreds of square miles of pastoral upland dotted thickly with villages and groves of banana' (Stanley 1880:142–143). He reported herds upon herds of cattle and huge flocks of goats and sheep spread over the grazing fields.

As on Ukara Island, agriculture on the western shores of Victoria Nyanza depended in Stanley's time on mixed animal husbandry and crop farming. This system was given a lasting jolt through the Rinderpest, after which the upkeep of soil fertility must have become a severe problem due to the loss of animal manure. The problem could partly be solved through other long-standing devices for retaining soil fertility, like green manure and mulch—the return of all possible grass and household refuse to the soil. Kollmann (1899) and Rehse (1910) observed the system in this period and described its settled character with individual plots of land (*vibanja*) lying adjacent to each other throughout the village areas. These were sharply demarcated and separated by the communal grasslands, the *raya*. The villages were densely populated and all vegetation was under human control.

Milne (1938) has given the soil-scientist's description of the Bukoba soils as impoverished through geological and climatic factors and with a ruling tendency towards laterization. He explained the existence of small enclaves (up to one-fifth of the terrain) of relatively fertile land in the midst of the characteristic sandstone ridges as the result of geological formations. These enclaves were found to coincide with the settled areas. Milne stressed, however, that the soil was cultivated by 'enlightened and intensive agricultural methods that are well worth study' (Milne 1938:14). Taking this point still further, Schmidt (1974) claims that the relatively good soil quality of the Bukoba village sites is due largely to human enterprise. Schmidt thinks that an intense and rapid up-grading of the soil took place when the grassland was first opened for cultivation, and that the area did not undergo a prolonged transition of shifting cultivation with a gradual shortening of the fallow. Such gradualism is ruled out by the nature of the soil. When the Bukoba grassland is opened to cultivation, one commences a laterization process which in a few years' time transforms the soil mantle into oxides of iron and aluminum. Various forms of soil upgrading, including the use of mulch and cattle manure, were therefore part of the original opening of the Bukoba coastal strip for agriculture. The first cultivators carried grasses from the swamps and marshes to deposit over the plots to be cultivated. This added nutrients, protected the soil and prevented leaching by retaining moisture. Humus in enormous quantities was in effect artificially created by the early Bukoba husbandmen. Schmidt refers to oral traditions in the area that the chiefs in several instances had large volumes of grass and compost carried to the laterite mantles so that successful agriculture could be commenced in the vicinity of the royal headquarters (Schmidt 1974:36–37).

The German and British experience in bringing European agriculture to Bukoba confirms the soundness of the oral tradition reported by Schmidt. The German administrators in Bukoba made several brisk efforts to cultivate in the open grassland adjacent to the military station. They all failed, and the Germans took the local advice and planted their new crops in old banana groves (Stuhlmann 1894:138). The mistake was apparently repeated again in the 1930s when British agricultural officers demanded that coffee (coffee is a pre-colonial crop in Bukoba) should be planted on the open grassland as a countermeasure against the coffee berry disease. This disease was thought to have originated from the 'silly' local practice of intercropping bananas, coffee and legumes (Schmidt 1974).[1] The effort had been met with local scepticism and resistance and was a total failure. Reining claims that all European agriculture in Bukoba was eventually carried out in old village sites. A final European effort to make the *raya* blossom—with a coffee plantation east of Mushondi—ground to a halt in the 1950s after years of failure (Reining 1967:77–78).

Summary

A number of points emerge from this discussion. First of all, the data tend to show a correlation between a dense population and agricultural innovations and to add further material to the ongoing discussion of Boserup's thesis. A number of the agricultural systems reviewed were labour intensive in the extreme and based their success on the ability to keep labour on the land. Clearly there was some reason peasants resorted to farming methods which gave them a lower return per hour of work, but ultimately gave a larger harvest. The pressure to increase yields could have come from several sources. I have rejected Gourou's 'siege' thesis: permanent settlement was far more widespread in Tanganyika than this thesis implies. I have mentioned the provisioning of the caravans and coastal centres as an external stimulus, and surely this force had some effect. Yet at the same time we have seen that in most cases the abundance and variety of crops were part of the local consumption. The evidence seems to indicate that there was an important indigenous pressure: Tanganyikans at least in part grew more food to feed a growing population.

Allan analysed the problem of population and agricultural methods from a different perspective. Historians have implied that a rising population in Tanganyika could not have been fed under 'primitive'

---

[1] Intercropping of this kind provides a 'triple canopy protection for the soil' (Schmidt 1974:54). The deep-growing banana roots keep up the circulation of mineral nutrients to the surface and the legumes fix nitrogen to the soil.

agricultural methods; Allan's figures for some of the areas discussed show that in fact the systems were capable of supporting sizable populations. In many cases some of the food produced by these systems entered a wider market as surplus. This precludes us from using Allan's 'maximum density' figures as actual population statistics for the areas. However, in many cases, the reports of early explorers suggest that the populations may in fact have been in the vicinity of Allan's figures.

Secondly, the data indicate a great variety of cultural innovations: new crops, irrigation, manuring systems, crop rotation, intercropping, nitrogen-fixing through legumes, anti-erosion methods and field techniques which had taken most of the Tanganyikan husbandmen far beyond the adaptive stage of shifting cultivation. Some of these techniques have been the object of detailed studies: manuring systems by Sommerfeld (1912a), nitrogen-fixing by Rounce (1936) and Sturdy (1939), intercropping by Robertson (1941), field practice by Hartley (1938) and Rounce and Thornton (1939) to mention only a few. All of these authorities came to realize the essential soundness of a number of traditional methods and thought that useful agricultural science for the area would have to incorporate the wisdom of experience acquired by the local peoples.

Thirdly, the term 'subsistence production' emerges from the discussion as a misnomer in describing the pre-colonial agricultural situation. Allan (1965:36) recognized the presence of a 'normal surplus' in the economy and saw the traditional beer party as an indication of this. Among the early travellers to Tanganyika, the term 'sitting on *pombe*' (indicating the after-effects of a beer party) was as frequent as the descriptions of material plenty. It demonstrated that important surpluses were present and that the people generally produced in excess of their normal diet. Moreover, as we shall see in a later chapter, several of the systems we have discussed delivered specialized produce, for instance tobacco, coffee and rice, that went beyond the normal tribal exchange to a larger trading network. One agricultural system not discussed in this chapter is that of the Wagogo, which Stanley (1872:181) had already judged to be superior to any systems encountered further east. It was capable of yielding important surpluses to the caravan carriers passing through the country. Kanneberg (1900) quantified the annual grain demand of the caravans to 1,200,000 pounds, of which a large part was grown in Ugogo.

Such evidence casts doubt on the contention that famine was a regular phenomenon in pre-colonial Tanganyika. Miracle (1961) has doubted that hunger was a frequent and widespread occurrence in savannah agriculture in Africa. The evidence discussed here would support his views. It is possible, for instance, that famine problems were far less

prevalent in the pre-colonial period than they became later. It is significant that the only major study of food shortages in Tanganyika (Brooke
1967) was based on twentieth-century evidence; Brooke's claim that
periodic famines were a historic phenomenon is only a backward projection of this evidence. Later on in this study, we shall see the famines in the
1890s as the result of important disruptions in the traditional systems.
Periodic catastrophes due to structural imbalances and maladaptations to
the new economic system of colonialism then replaced the *random* disasters that characterized the nineteenth century. A complete review of
storage constructions in the pre-colonial period would probably support
these contentions. It would demonstrate that the traditional economy was
carefully planned and that important volumes of food were grown and
stored for future use. Yet, we should notice that the need for storage
facilities is environmentally conditioned and that their absence would not
necessarily indicate any lack of planning. Storage is necessitated by long
lean seasons when no cropping is possible. In other areas crop storage is
not an issue because agricultural adaptations have made regular year-
round cropping possible.

SETTLEMENT PATTERNS

We have earlier been interested in general population patterns for
Tanganyika in the nineteenth century and ended the discussion of
Chapter 1 with an hypothesis that the population was either stable or in
slight expansion throughout the century. In this chapter we have seen
vastly uneven patterns of population distribution for the country and
related these as possible causative agents for agricultural developments.
Despite the vastness of the country's total terrain, land for agricultural
uses may in fact have been experienced as a scarcity at a relatively early
date. We should immediately recognize that large parts of the country
have never been vied for as areas of human exploitation. Ecological
expertise was undoubtedly responsible for the original land selection
where indicator trees and grasses helped to identify the more promising
areas for human settlement. The resulting variations in population distribution can be seen from the population maps of Gillman (1936) and
Porter (1966) which indicate an important continuity in the pattern over
the last 30–40 years. Several major settlement shifts may however have
taken place since the pre-colonial period along the lines discussed for the
West Lake region by McMaster (1962). We have seen similar shifts in this
chapter in connection with the Ulanga Valley and Unyamwezi, and shall
point to numerous other areas throughout this study.

There are also wide differences in the actual land occupied by the tribes. This question is clearly related to population and agricultural patterns. Among the long-fallow agriculturists, the picture of agricultural islands in a sea of wilderness (Jäger 1910) may seem appropriate. This does not mean a contrast between man-controlled terrain and its absence, however. It is likely that the settlement pattern in the swidden areas was organized around permanent water. As Matzke (1972) has shown, even widely dispersed human settlements around the permanent water occurrences have an extraordinary effect on the surrounding fauna, and force its decline in a way which approaches direct wildlife control. This is an essential point to keep in mind for our later discussion of the break-down of man's ecological control system in East Africa and the increase in the incidence of wildlife, tsetse flies and trypanosomiasis.

Among the more advanced agricultural peoples, the wilderness had been forced into the background to become narrow border strips—a *Grenzpori* or *Grenzwildniss* in the German literature—between the tribal heartlands. Where cattle-keeping was added to the economic activities, considerable areas were kept under permanent control, usually through periodic fires. 'Once forest, but now clear and cultivated', wrote Hore (1892:59) about the undulating plains of Unyamwezi. Busse (1908) made the claim that the high grasslands and savannahs of East Africa had a man-made origin, largely through the use of fire. Early Europeans tended to regard this practice as stupid and wasteful, and the German authorities prohibited grass-burning in 1893 (*Verordnung* 12 Dec. 1893), basing themselves on British practice in southern Africa.

A clear man-land relationship is expressed in the settlement pattern. Apart from Moore's study (1971) little attention has been paid to this question in East African research, and I shall restrict the discussion to two recent models proposed for West Africa (Udo 1963, and Prothero 1972) and to a few observations on their relevance to Tanganyika and to the problem under consideration.

In one of the few theoretical statements on this problem, Udo (1963) claimed that compact settlements characterize the periphery of human land occupation, whereas the dispersed dwellings represent the more developed centre. Udo found the compact settlement to be historically tied to collective agricultural practices, and to a system of defence. Both features are identified as frontier (periphery) phenomena that break down with peace, population expansion and consolidation of man's control over the land. Changes then take place in the agricultural system where block farming by the entire compound gives way to individual farming on separate plots. Land scarcity arises through population expansion, and places a premium on the occupation of plots: the best proof of one's claim to land is to settle on it. Along with such changes there is a shift from rotation of bush and forest fallow as the entire compound moves to annual cropping in permanent settlements.

Prothero (1972:332) operates with similar ideas and tends—with some qualifications—to support Boserup's population thesis. He suggests a model of population-land relationships which involves a continuum of changing phases:

1 from extensive and unsettled to fixed and intensive modes of land exploitation
2 from virgin land to total use of all cultivable land
3 from low population density to high density
4 from shifting cultivation to rotation cultivation, semi-permanent and finally permanent cultivation, with the gradual introduction of manuring techniques
5 from communal land rights to individual land rights
6 from non-permanent (migratory) settlement to permanent settlement and from nucleated villages to dispersed settlement.

A large part of the material presented in this chapter falls readily into these models. The exceptions would seem to be explainable through local warfare which caused a retrenchment to the original pioneer traditions of fortification and nucleization. Hore's comments confirm the model in two distinct scenes which summed up his 12 years' experience in western Tanganyika. In the uncertain frontier areas of recent settlement 'native villages, with houses in close array within stockades, are seen perched upon peninsulas and other easily defended positions', wrote Hore. He contrasted this situation to a settlement pattern developed under more normal conditions. In such areas 'mile after mile of scattered houses, peeping out from amongst groves of bananas, indicate peace and plenty; and widestretching fields of corn and cassava are spread over the country' (Hore 1892:152). These contrasting scenes represent different stages of technology and environmental adaptations, with the former struggling to transform bush to cultivation and pasture. From the point of view of ecological control the two interacted and reinforced each other. The prosperity of the centre depended in a remarkable way on the control of the periphery. The key to this relationship is again Matzke's thesis referred to above. Even a relatively small population at the periphery of the human settlement could neutralize the fauna and keep under control the dangerous combination of trypanosomes, their hosts (wildlife) and their vectors (tsetse flies) which in later decades became the major obstacle to development in large parts of the country.

CHAPTER 3

The Nineteenth-Century Cattle Complex

Man alone did not maintain the ecological control situation of the nineteenth century. We have already mentioned the importance of cattle in the agricultural systems of different peoples and shall now discuss in fuller detail the cattle complex of Tanganyika and its part in man's control of the environment.

The overwhelming feature in the study of cattle-keeping in East Africa is the presence of the tsetse fly. This has become a less important problem with the development of effective drugs combating trypanosomiasis. Historically, however, the presence of flies has meant the absence of cattle, and even today, cattle is normally not found in the so-called fly belts. *The Atlas of the Tanganyika Territory* assessed the problem in these terms:

> Tsetse flies (*Genus Glossina*), which infect man and his domestic animals with the parasitic trypanosomes causing fatal diseases in both, occupy over two-thirds of the Territory. Seven species occur. . . . The most important are the *Common Tsetse (Glossina Morsitans)*, *Bruce's Tsetse (G. Pallidipes)*, *Swynnerton's Tsetse (G. Swynnertoni)* and the *Waterside Tsetse (G. Papalis)*. All these species have been responsible for epidemics of sleeping sickness either in this Territory or elsewhere in Eastern Africa, and are potential carriers. They all cause trypanosomiasis in domestic animals, so that wherever they are established, man cannot keep cattle or other stock (Survey Division 1948).

A later edition of the Atlas went further to state that the tsetse flies 'confine man and his animals to specific settlement centres' (Survey Division 1956). This had already become official dogma in 1925 when the Ormsby-Gore Commission identified the tsetse fly as 'the greatest menace to the development of tropical Africa' (Ormsby-Gore 1925).

In a curious way, colonial administrators saw their own efforts as unwittingly responsible for these developments. Tsetse fly was held to have been a general menace in the tropics from time immemorial. Intertribal warfare and slave-raiding had for centuries depopulated the interior and opened the terrain for the spread of *Glossina*. The social organization of pre-colonial times arising from these double dangers was, however, held to have afforded protection to man and beast from the fly dangers. East African man, so the thinking went, had before the European arrival been living in large fortified villages for protection against marauding tribes and slave-raiders. The nucleated villages were localities of dense population around which effective barriers of cleared ground could be maintained against the surrounding fly. Within these sanctuaries agriculture could be practised and livestock kept. With the arrival of Europeans, however, and the suppression of intertribal warfare, Tanganyikans began to spread into the bush to escape from the demands of civilization. Exposed to the ravages of the tsetse, these people were unable to keep cattle. Fairbairn (1943) has recorded this historical explanation of the tsetse crisis of his time. We shall meet it again in the thinking of later administrators.

We have already seen that the colonial explanation cannot be valid because it presupposes a pre-colonial settlement pattern which existed in only a few areas of Tanganyika. In the following discussion we shall see that in fact the colonial administrators overestimated the presence of tsetse fly in the nineteenth century and underestimated the African's ability to deal with this complex problem. I shall first document the East African's general understanding of the tsetse dangers to his livestock. Second, I shall review the flourishing cattle economy in the nineteenth century in areas where bush and wildlife have later dominated.

Pre-Colonial Entomology

The reports of the early explorers of East and Central Africa document that the local people knew and understood the relationship between tsetse flies, wild animals and bush and the survival of their own cattle. It is probable that the shared knowledge of the tsetse dangers—as well as the methods evolved for keeping cattle despite the natural obstacles—would truly justify the term 'cattle complex of Eastern Africa' and make it meaningful beyond Herskovits' psychological/anthropological speculations on man-cattle relationships in the region (Herskovits 1926).

The African cattle initiative resulted from successful imposition of a man-controlled ecological system. Cattle herders benefitted from the prior advance of agricultural pioneers who, largely by the help of fire, cleared the land and isolated the wild animals and their accompanying tsetse flies to the unattractive 'jungles' or 'badlands' that formed the boundary zones between the settlements of the larger peoples or tribes. The cattle-keeping peoples seem to have explored and known these localities and evaded them when herding. Burton testified to such awareness among the Nyamwezi peoples. He wrote of 'a fly which infests the forest-patches of Unyamwezi: it is about the size of a small wasp, and is so fatal that cattle attacked by it are at once killed and eaten before they become carrion from its venomous effects' (Burton 1860, II:18–19). John Kirk had observed a similar understanding among the peoples of the Zambezi valley and wrote about it in a paper on the tsetse fly published in 1865. Kirk conceded that 'much of what we know on these points rests on native information', and he told about isolated and identified fly habitats that the people avoided during movements with their herds:

> The Makalolo are a people from infancy accustomed to tend cattle, possessing a thorough knowledge of the most fattening pastures to be sought, and noxious herbs to be avoided. Their only wealth consists in cattle, which they number by thousands. All affirm that on entering certain localities by day the oxen die shortly afterwards; this they have proven. . . . They have further learned that these deadly places may be crossed with safety by night if sufficiently narrow to allow of the cattle being driven through before sunrise (Kirk 1865:153–54).

Similar knowledge was undoubtedly present among the cattle keepers óf Tanganyika. Evidence of this comes from the most unlikely of places, namely the Ulanga Valley, where Bishop Spreiter recorded the following information in 1908:

> The Sultan told me the very interesting fact that the cattle on the plateau die if they eat a plant called *mitukutu* which tastes bitter. Everywhere where this plant is, there are also *dudu*, which go *suusuu* and also *ng'ombe waharibu*. Is that not the tsetse??? He further told me that only one camp, Igimba, on the way from Iringa has this plant and *dudu*. They do not exist in Ifakara. He says the cattle must be grazed in the fields in these places, and not in the bush. The last fact agrees with the findings of the latest tsetse investigations. Tsetse loves underbrush and disappears completely when it is cleared away. In the interest of development of cattle breeding, I would ask you to carefully check this business out with various people. The *Wachenzi* often know more about these things than we highly educated Europeans . . . (Spreiter 1908).[1]

Long experience and keen observation thus seem to have equipped the African husbandmen, who knew no medical prophylaxis against the tsetse dangers, to make curative measures largely superfluous through what John Ford calls 'an agro-horticultural prophylaxis' (Ford 1971:474) where the flies were naturally isolated to limited and well-known foci that could be evaded when herding and annually controlled through fire.

It seems that such fly-infested areas were opened up for emergency grazing during times of drought. The cattle owners would then deliberately drive their herds into the ungrassed tsetse bush gambling that the *possible* death through fly-infection was a better risk than the *certain*

---

[1] I am grateful to Dr. Loren Larsen for this quotation.

death from famine. This extreme measure, which has recently been reported to have been put to use by Gogo herders (Brooke 1967) and by the Sukuma peoples in Shinyanga (Ford 1971:234), is probably a traditional survival technique utilized by the East African herdsmen. It underlines the point made earlier, that the tsetse infested areas were known to the herders and were avoided under normal circumstances.

Beyond the discovery that nocturnal movements of the cattle were a relatively safe undertaking in tsetse territory, it appears that several experiments had been made with repellents of an unsavoury—but reportedly efficient—nature. John Kirk wrote about such measures in his paper on the tsetse:

> The fly avoids human excrement, so the natives told us, and we have found it true, and they say that cattle have been passed by day through fly country when smeared with a composition containing this. Native doctors have an herb to which they attribute a similar effect, but they never assert that it will save all (Kirk 1865:154).

David Livingstone, writing from Manyuema country to the east of the Lualaba River in the Congo (Zaire) in 1871, reported further advances in the repellent technique:

> Lion's fat is regarded as a sure preventive of tsetse or bungo . . . It is smeared on the ox's tail, and preserves hundreds of the Banyamwezi cattle in safety while going to the coast (Livingstone 1874, II:87).

Stuhlmann also mentions the practice of smoking the cattle as a temporary repellent against tsetse fly. Among the Wanyamwezi such fires were made from sun-dried cattle dung. Fires burnt in the cattle kraals during the nights generated a very strong smell from which the cattle received a certain degree of protection (Stuhlmann 1894:78). The smoke treatment was apparently a widely used practice among many tribes both against tsetse flies and ordinary house flies (Fülleborn 1906). It was also adopted by the caravan captains when bringing cattle for sale or as provisioning for the porters in the trading caravans. Thus Gregory (1896) reported this practice in caravans going inland from Pangani.

Writing about the meat market in Zanzibar in the 1860s, Burton observed that cattle were seldom brought from the interior 'on account of the length and risk of the journey' (Burton 1860, II:413). He thought, however, that the trade was capable of extensive development and improvement. When cattle taken to the coast were traversing tsetse-infested areas, the herders apparently made use of the standard technique of smoke and nightly transports practised all over Eastern, Central and Southern Africa. These techniques may have been well developed in

Tanganyika territory later in the century (Wölfel 1911a) when large herds were driven to the coastal towns from the interior. Some indication of the size of this trade has been provided by two German officers, Behr and Herrmann. Behr reported the arrival of a caravan, consisting of about 2,500 men bringing 350 ivory tusks and 2,000 head of cattle, in Bagamoyo in September 1889 (Behr 1891). Lieutenant Herrmann observed a cattle caravan passing the military station of Mpwapwa in 1891. The caravan brought with it 2,000 head of cattle and 2,000 goats and sheep in addition to 600 elephant tusks (Herrmann 1893:82). It was on the way to Bagamoyo, Sadani and Pangani, and may have been one of the last of the great cattle transports to go to the coast before the wholesale destruction of livestock which took place during the next few years.

Advancing beyond the simple use of smoke for fly protection, some people apparently ventured into herbal devices for medicinal cures against the illness caused by tsetse flies in cattle. David and Charles Livingstone mention evidence of such experiments:

> Moyara showed us a plant ... and likewise told us how the medicine was prepared; the bark of the root, and what might please our homoeopathic friends, a dozen of the tsetse are dried, and ground together into a fine powder. This mixture is administered internally; and the cattle are fumigated by burning under them the rest of the plant collected. The treatment must be continued for weeks, whenever the symptoms of poison appear (David and Charles Livingstone 1865:233).

The 1888 edition of *Encyclopedia Britannica* summed up the 'civilized' world's knowledge of the tsetse flies at that time. One can easily recognize the African contribution to the knowledge:

> At present no cure is known for the bite, nor does innoculation seem to afford any protection. The fly is said to avoid animal excreta, and in some parts a paste composed of milk and manure is smeared on cattle which are about to pass through the 'fly-belts'. This affords a certain amount of protection. Lion fat is used in the same way, and is said to be efficacious. The fly is found as a rule in the neighbourhood of water, and its habitat is usually sharply defined. Often it occurs on one side of a stream, but not on the other. The limits of the 'fly-belts' are well known to the natives, and travellers can ensure comparative safety to their cattle by passing through these districts after sundown (*Encyclopedia Britannica* 1888, XXIII:601, quoted in Austen 1903).

John Ford (1971) mentions the massive bush-clearing and wildlife eradication scheme utilized by Mzilla, one of the Ngoni chiefs of Northern Mozambique, in the resettlement of cattle and people in the Mzilizwe Valley in 1861. Swynnerton (1921) apparently learned from Mzilla and repeated the approach sixty years later in Shinyanga in Tanganyika.

Finally, in frank recognition of the African tsetse-control initiative, Franz Stuhlmann, in a lengthy paper on the tsetse problem, listed as one of the top research priorities in the *Schutzgebiet*: 'To find out the places where, according to the experience of the local peoples, cattle can never be kept' (Stuhlmann 1902:152). By this time (1902) most of the cattle were dead, and bush and tsetse flies were on the offensive.

The argument that is implicit in this discussion is that there were cattle in Tanganyika and elsewhere in East Africa in the nineteenth century where there have been none during most of the twentieth. The fly-areas were isolated and known and were therefore no absolute hindrance to economic development. It was the systematic mapping of these fly-foci that Stuhlmann seems to have had in mind in his outline of needed research in 1902. With one exception, that of John Ford (1971), nobody has since taken up the challenge. This is largely due to the acceptance of the proposition that where there are tsetse flies there can be no cattle and that the tsetse belt has been a long-term and largely static obstacle to cattle-keeping and other economic activity. The result has been that no historian has addressed himself seriously to the real achievements of the nineteenth century in this important field of economic development. The historians' fascination has been captured by the wars of chiefs and the intrusion of foreign elements into the area at the exclusion of the peaceful and constructive endeavours of the East African peoples themselves. To reconstruct the dimensions of the nineteenth-century cattle complex is a formidable undertaking, to which only a preliminary contribution can be made here. It is nevertheless a necessary and challenging task for anyone interested in readjusting the historical perspective and adding economic variables to the inquiry into the past.

In the rest of this chapter, I shall briefly outline some of the areas where a large-scale cattle initiative existed in the nineteenth century but where serious obstacles to cattle-keeping have been present in more recent years. I am initially relying for information on the written records of some of the first European travellers in East Africa. I have raised a number of questions about their reporting in Chapter 1 and shall continue to do so here. Their habit of systematically recording what they saw, however, and their keen interest in matters of an economic nature make it possible to gain an initial purchase on the problem from their accounts.

The Coast and Inland Caravan Routes

According to Richard Burton, cattle were not very numerous along the east coast. They were not entirely absent, however, and places like Kunduchi north of Dar es Salaam and the areas along the Pangani River were mentioned as cattle country (Burton 1859).[1] For the Dar es Salaam area, this general impression was later confirmed by Franz Stuhlmann who wrote that 'domestic animals are seldom seen, only some of the chiefs like those of Mboe Madji, Vikindo and Kisarawe possess a few oxen of the small Zebu type' (Stuhlmann, 1894a:231). Cattle were thriving at Kitmangao in Kwale south of Dar es Salaam, wrote Elton (1879:89). The township was identified as the centre of copal trading in the district. Elton's map of the coast indicates numerous plantations in the area extending all the way to the slopes of the Mtoni hills.

When Emin Pasha and Stuhlmann departed for the interior from Bagamoyo in 1890, they brought with them horses, donkeys and cattle. There is no later report of any of these suffering from the tsetse. It was quite common for the caravans to bring cattle along as part of the provisioning, apparently with no difficulty. The areas around Bagamoyo may not have been cattle-breeding districts in this period, but the town—reported to have had 25,000 inhabitants before the Arab uprising (Behr 1891)— must certainly have offered an attractive cattle market. Jerome Becker (1887, II:472) even wrote about wagon transport by cattle on the Mrina coast and in Bagamoyo. It was probably the normal occurrence of such transport sights that encouraged the London Missionary Society to undertake a major experiment with ox-drawn transport to the interior in 1876. In that year a group of missionaries set out from Sadani to found a mission station at Ujiji and managed to bring some 70 oxen (all bought on the coast) and carts successfully to Mpwapwa, a distance of around 200 miles through what is today miombo bush carrying tsetse. The experiment was initially successful (Mullens 1877, Hore 1892). It broke down probably because of overwork of the animals on poor or nonexistent roads rather than for reasons of trypanosomiasis.

Donkeys were a normal means of transportation in the long-distance caravans, although they were probably more utilized in those bound for Pangani than in those ending up in Bagamoyo (Fischer 1884). Burton wrote that the Wanyamwezi 'rear asses and load them lightly when travelling to the coast' (Burton 1860, II:30). His own expedition with Speke made use of numerous donkeys for transport, and so did Stanley on his way to find Livingstone in 1871 (Stanley 1872, see also Baumann 1894:8).

Emin Pasha's caravan took a northern route towards the Uluguru mountains. When the caravan settled outside the present town of

[1] Cattle-keeping in the coastal areas is—besides the tsetse menace—complicated by the presence of ticks which cause a dangerous cattle fever.

Morogoro, the Zigua ruler, Kingo, sent oxen, sheep and flour as gifts to the travellers (Stuhlmann 1894:26). Later, in his very detailed description of the Ulugurus, Stuhlmann wrote:

> Stock breeding has not been well developed; some sheep and a few more goats make up the lot. . . . It is only at the upper Mbakana brook that one finds half a dozen cattle. Later settlers will have to make use of the areas around Kissaki in order to satisfy their demands for meat and manure. In those areas cattle and pigs are thriving well (Stuhlmann 1895:225–26).

Entries in the *Morogoro District Book* confirm this. Uluguru is described as a relatively recent settlement (dating back 150–200 years), the southern and eastern slopes being peopled with immigrants of Bena stock, the northern side by the Ziguas. About the southern settlements, the local chief stated that the original founder, Kingalu, 'came from Ubena in Iringa Province with his people and their women and cattle. . . . The whole country was partitioned among the clans, each under its own Mndewa, a hereditary headman. The forests in those days descended the slopes much further than they do today and the people, then cattle owners, lived below them' (Bagshawe, 1930). The settlements of Kingalu were said to have been in the Kolero and Mgeta areas.

Another entry in the *District Book* states:

> According to German records, the Waluguru before the War had 4,500 head of cattle but they have all gone though I am not sure what happened to them . . . Increasing cultivation above forced the cattle to graze always lower down the slopes until they were killed off by tsetse fly. The people own a few goats and sheep (Bagshawe 1930).

Young and Fosbrooke (1960) claimed that cattle had never been part of the Uluguru economy and denied any trace of cattle in the history of the area. The presence of tsetse flies had, in their opinion, always prevented the Waluguru peoples from becoming stock-breeders.

Stuhlmann described the Wasegua (Zigua), through whose territory he travelled on the way to the Ulugurus, as keen businessmen, who traded cotton from the coast for tobacco, goats, cattle or skins to take back to the coast for further trade (Stuhlmann 1894:25). The Segua area may have been more hospitable for cattle in this period and more thickly populated and therefore probably more open and cultivated. A British administrator, who proposed to bring the Zigua-Nguru tribe together in a new district at Turiani, wrote:

> There is little doubt that the Turiani area in those (pre-colonial) days was very much more thickly populated than it is at present; severe epidemics and migra-

tion during the war (1914–18) would probably account for this depreciation (Hutchins n.d.).

Baumann stated that cattle—both of the longhorned (Sanga) and shorthorned (Zebu) types—could be seen in the Usegua villages in 1890. He thought, however, that stock-keeping was on the decline (Baumann, 1891:273). About the district of Kwambugu by Handei (Handeni), he wrote that 'stock breeding is the main economic enterprise. The only riches of the people are the magnificent herds which in recent times have been threatened through Masai raids' (Baumann 1891:185).

Along with Fischer, Baumann is one of the best informants on the cattle situation among the northern coastal peoples before the turn of the century. Fischer reported important cattle holdings along the Pangani River among the Waruvu, whom he described as close relatives of the Wasegua. The Waruvu possessed rich herds and were exposed to Masai raids (Fischer 1884:40). The territory of the Waruvu, who were also excellent agriculturists, was said to extend northwards along the Pangani up to a populous place called Maurui where numerous villages were located. Baumann confirmed the fame of the Waruvu cattle in 1890 (Baumann 1891:273).

Fischer also reported numerous cattle in the Pare mountains where they were kept and fed in barns. He thought that this was done for security reasons as a preventive measure against Masai raids. Baumann found stall-feeding in North Pare only. In the south, which he held to be the richest cattle area, Baumann thought that stock-breeding enjoyed natural defences in the steep mountain slopes from where the Wapare were able to control all outside intrusion (Baumann 1891:226). He made a distinction between the shorthorned Zebu cattle of the Pare people and the longhorned cattle of the Usambaras and Usegua.

Fischer found that the Wasambaa excelled as agriculturists as well as stock-breeders. Their chief, Samboja, had friendly ties with the Masai to whom he had granted grazing rights in the mountains during the dry season. A brisk trade in cattle and grain was carried on from the Usambaras to Pangani in this period (Fischer 1884:97).

Fischer's travels took him from the coast to Arusha and northwards through Masailand to Lake Naivasha. He returned via Lake Natron and took a westerly road to return to Pangani via Handeni. Fischer was clearly alerted to the dangers of the tsetse fly, but found few signs of its active presence. 'The Dondorobo or tsetse fly does not occur in the areas that have been traversed', he wrote. 'This fly is, however, reported to be very frequent at Taweta during the rainy season when many donkeys die from the fly bites' (Fischer 1884:41).

The Kilombero Valley

Another area of great interest is the Kilombero valley. Stolowsky, who travelled through the valley in the early 1890s, stressed the excellent opportunities for cattle-farming in some of the smaller side-valleys. He singled out the valley of Kihansi and the undulating plains along the Njera and Mpanga rivers as good areas for cattle. These valleys, he reported, 'offer such good conditions for stock-breeding that they could hardly be imagined to be more favourable'. He wrote that the Bena ruler in the Mpanga valley, Sultan Kiwanga, 'possesses a splendid looking herd of cattle which thrives marvellously (in the area)' (Stolowsky 1903:263). The district was apparently free of tsetse fly. Hauptmann Fonck, in a 1908 report, claimed that cattle had been kept in Fakarra (Ifakara) before the Maji Maji war. He also referred to Kiwanga's cattle. These were said to have suffered from an unidentified illness and had been sizably reduced in numbers. Fonck thought, however, that the real reason for the decline in the herds was the 'childish unreason' of Kiwanga's successor who was said to have sold off the cattle in order to buy all kinds of European junk (*Kramm*) that had become available on the local markets (Fonck 1908).[1] Einseidel reported that Ulanga District, by 1913, had practically no cattle at all. Forty-nine head were said to be in the hands of the local chiefs. The spread of tsetse fly was identified as the reason for this almost total demise of the cattle (Einseidel 193).

Jätzold, in his book about the Kilombero valley, reports the coming of the Wangoni as settlers in the valley around Kilosa kwa Mpepo after a tribal dispute in 1885. They brought cattle with them. Jätzold describes the area as 'miombo forest hill country, similar to their earlier domain near Songea . . . In spite of the tsetse flies the Ngoni kept cattle in the valley plains up to 1945, and goats in the hill country as late as 1955' (Jätzold 1968:40).

Cattle-keeping in the Kilombero valley today is apparently restricted to the main river basin, 'up river from Ngombo and Biro as far as Lupunga . . . (where) only about one in ten farmers owns cattle'. Jätzold explains:

Today the stock of cattle in the Kilombero plain is approaching 2,000 head, of which the vast majority is concentrated on Ngombo and Biro . . . This area is the most suitable for cattle rearing, as it consists almost wholly of treeless, open flood savanna, where tsetse flies do not occur as there is no shade. Consequently there is no danger of trypanosomiasis in contrast with all the marginal areas of the Kilombero valley (Jätzold 1968:67).

[1] I am grateful to Dr. Loren Larsen for this reference.

Sleeping sickness concentrations were carried out in the Kilombero valley in the interwar period. Five settlements were created, among them Ngombo. These concentrations 'fit in excellently with the scheme to protect the Bena-Ndamba cattle area and expand it' wrote the Provincial Commissioner (Letter to Chief Secretary, 19.3.45, *TNA* 28446).

The South East and Ruvuma Valley

There is little historical evidence that points to important cattle areas in the southeastern part of Tanganyika in the nineteenth century. Yet, it is important to stress that cattle here, as on the northern coastal strip, were not entirely absent. Stuhlmann's map of cattle in the territory (1909) indicated cattle-keeping at Kilwa and inland from Lindi, probably in Masasi. Further south, Livingstone had lost his oxen along the Ruvuma River when travelling towards Lake Nyassa in 1866. He reflected in his diaries on the reason for these losses, sometimes blaming the tsetse flies that he encountered and sometimes the cattle drivers who constantly mistreated the animals. Livingstone reported no cattle—only goats and sheep—in the villages along the lower Ruvuma. Referring to the Mazitu (Ngoni) raiders in the area, he wrote that they trekked with their women, children, oxen and goats (Livingstone 1874, I:41). It is clear that any extensive movements of cattle in this area could be successful only if the incidence of tsetse fly was considerably less than it is today.

Weule found cattle in the lower Ruvuma valley at the settlement of Chief Matola at Chingulungulu. The settlement was basically concerned with rubber production, but had also a number of pigs and cattle (Weule 1909:138). Fülleborn is somewhat ambiguous on the question of cattle along the Ruvuma. He wrote about the existence of separate barns (*Viehställe*), but testified to having seen only goats, not cattle. Yet he reported that 'the goats and cattle are in many places accommodated in the villages', and cattle were apparently housed jointly with the people during the nights (Fülleborn 1906:97). In a report on the border areas along the Ruvuma, Stuhlmann indicated oral information that there had been numerous cattle both close to the sea and along the river in earlier times. No date indicated when this golden age might have been lost (Stuhlmann 1897). The *Newala District Book* has an interesting entry under 'Laws, Manners and Customs' about one of the peoples in the area, the Wandendeule. They are described as 'originally cattle-folk on a limited scale, each freeman owning 5–10 head and sometimes more'.

Behr reported no cattle along the upper Ruvuma in an 1892 article. He mentioned, however, shields made of cowhide, and wooden carvings of cows among the Ngoni people. He attributed this to their traditions of cattle-keeping in southern Africa some 50 years previously (Behr, 1892). An entry in *Songea District Book*, however, recording the 'Laws of the Wangoni' at the time of Hawaya (ca. 1860–75), indicates cattle as the basic marriage dowry among the Wangoni. Whereas first wives were said to have been captured in warfare, additional wives were paid for in cattle (three head) and called *bibi ya ng'ombe*. The riches in cattle can be deduced from the information that the more important chiefs had more than 30 wives.

Fülleborn described the Ngoni people as both cattle-keepers and agriculturists. He put the cattle population around Songea at 3,000 head in addition to even more numerous goats and sheep. He added: 'At the moment, cattle breeding plays no major role in Ungoni after the Rinderpest swept away most of the animals in the (eighteen) nineties' (Fülleborn 1906:162). The Ngoni countryside was extremely fertile, and well watered. The terrain was held to be even better suited for European settlement than the lands of the Wahehe. Very little wildlife was reported in the surroundings of Ungoni, but the presence of lions was felt to be a very disturbing factor (Leue 1903).

Greater Unyamwezi

Richard Burton's description of central Tanganyika in the 1850s was one of a peasant economy sustaining relative comfort and prosperity:

> The land of the Moon, which is the garden of Central Intertropical Africa, presents an aspect of peaceful rural beauty which soothes the eye like a medicine after the red glare of barren Ugogo, and the dark monotonous verdure of the western provinces. The inhabitants are comparatively numerous in the villages, which rise at short intervals above their impervious walls of the lustrous green milk-bush, with its coral-shaped arms, variegating the well-hoed plains; whilst in the pasture-lands frequent herds of many-coloured cattle, plump, round-barrelled, and high-humped, like the Indian breeds, and mingled flocks of goats and sheep dispersed over the landscape, suggest ideas of barbarous comfort and plenty (Burton 1860, II:7).

Burton reported that Chief Fundikira of Unyamwezi possessed 300 houses for his wives and slaves and owned 2,000 head of cattle (Burton 1860, II:32). Speke, who travelled northwards from Tabora to discover Victoria Nyanza, thought that Msalala district exhibited signs of the most impressive wealth he had encountered in Africa. The area was densely populated and the villages 'followed one on the other, with few intervals of jungle'. The district, wrote Speke, 'abounds in flesh, milk, eggs, and vegetables of every variety' (Speke 1864:280). He continued:

The quantity of cattle in Msalala surpasses anything I have seen in Africa. Large droves, tended by a few men each, are to be seen in every direction over the extensive plains, and every village is filled with them at night. The cultivation also is abundant and the cattle are numerous, and the climate is delightful (Speke 1864:286).

The cattle that Burton and Speke saw in the 1850s had been starkly reduced by the time the German veterinarian Wölfel wrote from Tabora in 1911. Wölfel observed the spreading of the tsetse flies and the peasants' retreat before them. He reported wide areas in the northwest and south of Tabora town that until a few years previously had been inhabitable for man and cattle:

> Over half of the Tabora District is overgrown with bush and forest (*Trockenwald*). *Glossina morsitans* are found throughout and cattle-keeping is possible only in limited areas of the district. At present, the entire western part is unsuited for cattle. With few exceptions, the situation is similar in the south.
>
> According to several sources, there were previously numerous cattle herds in the north-western parts of the district. There were also many more cattle in the south, as the half-empty cattle kraals that can still be seen provide evidence of. This is caused by the spreading depopulation (*zunehmende Entvölkerung*) **and the resulting reduction in the size of the cultivated land. Already, some cattle are grazing in the tsetse infested bush. This practice causes losses through nagana** and prevents the herds from reaching their previous size. Today, there are only around 2,500 cattle left in the north-western part of Tabora....
>
> The same reasons that apply in the west and south, have made it impossible to keep cattle in Kigwa, Rubugwa, kwa Mtoni and along the Tabora-Kilimatinde road where the Government cattle was previously kept ... The situation is similar in places like Uyuwi, Jsikaza and all along the eastern road to Mwanza (Wölfel 1911:77–78).

Wölfel went on to outline in detail the boundaries of the tsetse belt at that time. He estimated that the entire Tabora District hardly contained more than 110,000 head of cattle. Both Zebu and Sanga cattle were represented.

A report written a few years later (Schaele 1913) indicating overstocking in Tabora and Mwanza and discussing the need for a cattle market can only be understood in light of the extensive reduction that had taken place in the area of grazable land. The surviving cattle were crowded into the safe districts initiating problems of dustbowls and soil erosion. The real issue was, therefore, not a problem of too many cattle, but of too little land available for safe economic exploitation.

There are further illustrations from western Unyamwezi and southern Kigoma of similar developments. In 1883, Jerome Becker bought a number of cattle in Tabora for delivery to the Belgian mission station of Karema on the east coast of Lake Tanganyika. The 200 mile delivery took place without incidents and prompted Becker to believe that the dangers of the tsetse had been greatly exaggerated. The fly had been misrepresented, he wrote, as maintaining everywhere a war of extermination against domestic animals (Becker 1887, II:340).

Livingstone had travelled to Karema in 1872 and continued to the south end of Lake Tanganyika, also with a number of cattle in his caravan (Livingstone 1874). These probably routine cattle movements took place through an area that the tsetse maps of the twentieth century (see p. 165) indicate is an uninterrupted tsetse belt. Contained within this area are the Ugalla River and Katavi Plains game reserves. A later commentator wrote about Livingstone's passage as 'a noteworthy event from the veterinary standpoint', having taken place through an area where tsetse flies 'have ensured that it is unlikely to happen again' (Young 1957). The Provincial Commissioner (P.C.) of Kigoma in 1948 included Karema and its hinterland in what he called 'the Southern Wilderness of Kigoma' where extensive sleeping sickness concentrations were recommended to combat the dangers of the spreading tsetse fly (*TNA* 23892 II). Between Becker's and Livingstone's cattle transport and the P.C.'s field assessment some 70 years later lies the fall of the nineteenth-century cattle initiative in Eastern Africa.

Ukimbu

Wölfel (1911) identified the Wakimbu, along with the Wasangu, as the important cattle people to the south of Unyamwezi. He described a deteriorating ecological situation in the areas of Ngulu, Ugunda and Unyamwira. These fall within the Kimbu tribal land, the history of which has recently been reviewed by Shorter (1972). Shorter tells us that Ukimbu today is dense miombo woodland, only occasionally broken by grassland steppes bordering the rivers. Large parts of the woodland are made up of forest and game reserves: Nyahua, Iswangala and Itulu Hill forest reserves in the north, Mwipa and Lukwati forest reserves in the southwest, and Rungwa River game reserve in the southeast. Virtually the entire area is infected with tsetse fly so that 'animal husbandry and large-scale agriculture are impossible in Ukimbu' (Shorter 1972:39). Besides natural obstacles to agriculture and stock-breeding, the mind of the Mkimbu is said to favour a hunter/gatherer existence: 'The call of the forest is stronger than that of the fields . . . Honey-collecting, perhaps even more than hunting, interests the Kimbu' (Shorter 1972:46). Responding to the ecological conditions, the people live in small and highly impermanent settlements. One factor that is said to explain the smallness of the villages is the need to build palisades around the cultivated land to defend against vermin destroying the crops. Dislike for hard work dissuades the Wakimbu from building palisades beyond a certain extension, and an optimum village size therefore seems to have established itself (Shorter 1972:42). The small and impermanent settlement pattern is seen by Shorter as giving the clue to Kimbu social and political organization which is the main subject of his book. The current ecological situation is said to have commenced in the 1840s with a devastating famine, the *ilogo*, which 'came near to wiping out the entire population' (Shorter 1972:249). Shortly afterwards, the Sangu people conquered the country and added to the chaos and disruption.

Cattle do not play any important part in Shorter's account of the Wakimbu. Yet it is clear that stock-breeding was for a long time part of the local economy. 'The founders of Igulwibi chiefdoms brought cattle to Ukimbu, as the Mya had also done', writes Shorter, 'and so enabled the Kimbu to keep cattle for nearly a century, before the spread of the tsetse fly belt made this once more impossible' (Shorter 1967:105). Burton recorded that the Wakimbu held numerous cattle in the Rungwa River area in the 1850s. In the chiefdoms of Kiwele and Nkokolo, cattle were traded for beads to the passing caravans (Burton 1859:300, 305). Rungwa River has since then given its name to a vast game reserve created in 1937.

Meyer reported stock-raising in Kipembabwe at the turn of the century when he also described an important iron industry in the area. The Chief of Kipembabwe, Chandang'ombe (meaning 'receiver or collector of cattle'), who ruled from 1878 to 1907, was reported to possess a splendid cattle herd (Meyer 1901). Büttner mentioned cattle in his discussion of Ukimbu property rights and held that goats and sheep had replaced cattle as the normal bridewealth only very recently (Büttner 1909), probably after the Rinderpest of the 1890s.

I would suggest, therefore that the Ukimbu situation differs little from the development of central Tanganyika we have traced so far. It seems likely that the Kimbu economy continued to progress throughout the nineteenth century, and that a relative prosperity—not poverty—was the basis of Njungu ya Mawe's political unification of the area. This prosperity came to an end in the last decade of the nineteenth century. The demise coincided with the disruption of Njungu's political achievement. Wölfel's article pointed to the first inroads in the cattle economy. By the 1920s, the miombo had overgrown the entire area, and sleeping sickness was rife, particularly in the Rungwa valley. Village concentration started north of Lake Rukwa in 1926–27, and the *Sumbawanga (Ufipa) District Book* recorded the movement of 13,000 people in 1926 alone: 3,750 in Myonga, 4,500 in Rungwa, 2,500 in Ilungwa and 2,880 in Uruwira. It would seem that the ecological situation that forced the hunter-gatherer existence on the Wakimbu of today is a twentieth-century phenomenon. It was not part of the formative reality of the nineteenth century when the Wakimbu, like their neighbours to the north and west, exercized a far greater control over the environment than they do today.

Uha and Ujiji

The great cattle kingdom of the Waha extended in the 1850s apparently all the way south and east to the Malagarasi River. Burton (1860) was impressed by reports of vast herds of longhorned Sanga cattle grazing on the river banks. He reported, however, that Watuta raids a few years prior to his visit and reduced cattle-keeping to the highland regions.

The immediate surroundings of Ujiji were also reported to harbour important herds of cattle. Milk and butter could be obtained every day in the town market from cattle belonging to Chief Kannina. Speke wrote about the breed in enthusiastic terms:

> The cattle this milk was taken from are of a uniform red colour, like our Devonshire breed; but they attain a very great height and size, and have horns of the most stupendous dimensions (Speke 1864:253).

Prior to the closing-up of the country with miombo bush and tsetse flies, there apparently was a brisk exchange of cattle between the Watussi herders in Unyamwezi country and the cattle-keepers further west. Wölfel saw this exchange as part of stock-improving efforts of the Watussi:

> Prior to the Rinderpest, they (the Watussi) used to import halfbreed cattle (crossings of Uha and Ussukuma stock) from the western parts of the district, from the sultanates of Shirambo, Sunsewe etc., with the aim of improving the milk yield of their own cattle. At that time, cattle raising was still possible in the western domains. The supply of pure bred bulls from Uha proper was difficult—not to say impossible—because of the evil of cattle raiding taking place there. Immediately after the Rinderpest the then District Officer succeeded in negotiating for procurations of cattle from Uha. The Watussi then brought some stock, largely bulls, but also some cows from Uha. This trade is said to have continued for 8–9 years. It then became impossible to carry on because the areas were invaded by vast numbers of tsetse flies. These had practically disappeared after the Rinderpest (Wölfel 1911:83).

Wölfel here recognized the concern with *quality* in the cattle and the conscious effort to improve the stock through selective breeding. Most literature will deny any such initiative among the African herders. It is therefore interesting to note what Lichtenheld had to say in an article which discussed the bad practices, particularly the keeping of too many and inferior bulls in the herds:

It is this practice (keeping of many inferior bulls) which primarily accounts for the uneven nature of the herds. But this practice is not the result of lack of understanding (of breeding) but stems from the present economic situation. As long as the local people have wide open fields at their disposal and no extra cost is incurred in the operation, the rearing of even inferior stock is advantageous and rational (Lichtenheld 1913:271).

Concern with numbers rather than quality probably prevailed in the situation where men were looking back to a period of more cattle. To recreate the large herds was the primary objective. In 1913 concern with quality was something of the past.

Karagwe, Geita and Sukumaland

John Ford's remarkable book, *The Role of the Trypanosomiases in African Ecology* (1971), has in many ways given the clue to this study. His work makes it possible to understand more fully Kuczynski's population thesis, elaborated earlier, and to undertake fresh research on ecology-control as the crucial variable in the history of the nineteenth century.

Ford's case studies of the development of the fly-belts of northwestern Tanganyika, the areas of Karagwe, Geita and Sukumaland, are of direct relevance to this discussion. Rather than repeat the rich evidence for important cattle initiatives in these areas we shall anticipate the arguments of Chapters 7 and 8 by pursuing the highlights of Ford's analysis of these districts.

Considering the historical evidence, Ford was forced to reject one of the standard colonial explanations of the 'advancing' fly belts: that agricultural malpractices leading to soil exhaustion and abandonment of land resulted in the regeneration of bush which allowed wildlife and flies to reoccupy the terrain. In this explanation, soil-exhaustion and shifting settlement were seen as a never-ending process of give and take between man and nature. Only European-type land use, destocking and soil conservation could free the Africans from this vicious circle of poverty.

Challenging this view, Ford undertook a detailed reconstruction of the situation in the nineteenth century based on the existing reports from the areas. He revealed evidence for long-standing cattle traditions, huge herds and general prosperity. A series of historical events led to the demise of the cattle kingdoms. Intertribal warfare and slave-raiding did not figure among the most important of his explanations. Instead he concentrated attention on events occurring very late in the nineteenth century, the Rinderpest and later tragedies, like smallpox and famine which, within a few decades, transformed prosperity into degradation and ruin. The loss of ecological control was the central result of these changes.

Of the three areas discussed by Ford, only Sukumaland was able to recover and its people regained the basic mastery over the environment. The old cattle kingdom of Karagwe suffered an almost total demise:

> Karagwe, where in 1861, Speke and Grant had gone 'tripping down the greensward' of 'this charming land'; where in 1891, Emin had remarked that Karagwe 'is only suitable for cattle-breeding' and 'noted, 'for the future' that the presence of a few 'flat topped acacias' was 'a sign that the hills of Karagwe would be capable of producing trees,' is now a waste of tsetse bush, with its small population crowded into concentrations as a prophylactic measures against the spread of sleeping sickness (Ford and Hall 1947:23).

In the case of Geita, its people never regained the initiative and the Zinza and Rongo peoples lost their 'confrontation with the woodland ecosystem' (Ford 1971:226). The ecological factor is well presented by Wyatt in his discussion of the Geita situation, where the loss of cattle triggered the large-scale ecological transformation. After analysing reports of local warfare, Wyatt wrote:

> In spite of these petty tribal wars, the period (pre-1890) is looked back upon by the old men as a time of great prosperity. There is every sign that the country carried a very much greater population than it does now, whilst vast herds of cattle roamed on Nyamirembe and in Lusahunga. Indeed, Kaihura (a local chief) . . . spoke of the cattle 'as grass', a statement which has been supported by several other sources. Every man had his herd and 'it was a poor man who could number but a hundred head.' Tsetse fly was unknown in the country except in the extreme South, nor were the pig the menace they are to-day. The Wazinza still hunted but the game was confined to the areas West of Burigi. Towards the end of Mankorongo's rule, rinderpest swept through the country and decimated the herds followed later by a second outbreak together with an epidemic of 'Kondera' (plureopneumonia?) which wiped out practically all the cattle; this latter about 1890, during Kasusura's rule. Emigration to Mwanza and to the South began and has continued since, resulting in decreased cultivation and the increasing area abandoned to the wild pig, the baboon and the tsetse fly (*Geita District Book*).

By the 1940s the old tribal land of the Wazinza and Warongo was gradually taken over by the expanding Wasukuma who today make up the dominant population group on the Geita peninsula.

CHAPTER 4

Wildlife and Ecological Control

In the previous chapter we have pointed out that the East African herdsmen understood the dangers of the tsetse fly to his domestic animals, notably to cattle. In this chapter I shall maintain that the man-fly and cattle-fly interactions were kept at a tolerable minimum throughout the nineteenth century and that this may have resulted from a certain wildlife control exercised through the settlement pattern and man's economic activities. This situation was altered during the ecological collapse of the 1890s. It further deteriorated as alien decision-makers later commenced a wildlife conservation policy predicated on the idea that man and wildlife had for centuries lived in harmonious co-existence in the East African plains and fields. After developing this general argument, I shall discuss the historical evidence of a human agency in some of the more famous game concentrations in Tanzania today. Of the examples discussed, only the Ngorongoro Crater lies outside of the present tsetse belts where people and cattle are at risk of trypanosomiasis.

MAN—WILDLIFE CONFRONTATION

Early British administration in Tanganyika coincided with a number of serious sleeping-sickness epidemics in Maswa, Kigoma, Liwale, and Rukwa, and I shall later review the measures taken to combat these. *Glossina Morsitans*, the game tsetse, was the principal vector involved in these epidemics. The *Annual Medical Report* of 1924 mentioned the closeness of the epidemic foci to major game concentrations and suggested a possible connection (*AMR* 1924:44). No conclusion was drawn from this observation which seems to have remained the isolated opinion of Dr. Davey (1924), the Principal Medical Officer. It was the views of the Chief Game Warden, Mr. Swynnerton, who later became the Director of Tsetse Research, which carried the day. He thought it possible that direct transmission of trypanosomes from man to man via the vector was very common, that man was the sole reservoir of the trypanosomes, and that the presence of game could indeed be seen as a protection against sleeping sickness (Swynnerton 1923). By 1927 these views were also accepted among the medical people. The medical report for that year stated that 'all the available evidence points to a man-fly-man spread (of sleeping sickness) . . . it is not necessary to assume the existence of a vertebrate host other than man' (*AMR* 1926:129). This remained the official doctrine for the next decade and a half. Only in the medical report of 1943 were doubts again raised about wild animals acting as reservoirs of human trypanosomiasis (*AMR* 1943:8). This change was undoubtedly stimulated by the valuable research findings of Corson (1935) that strains of trypanosomes remained infectious to man after several generations' existence in different animal hosts. It was probably a more direct reflection of the war situation which forced British decision-makers to become more interested in food production in the colonies—and incidentally in food producers—than in creating conditions for game safaris for Europe's idle rich.

The research undertaken by Weitz and Glasgow (1956) and Weitz (1963) has fully established the feeding dependence of the tsetse fly on certain well-defined species of wildlife such as antelopes, buffaloes, warthogs and bushpigs. Ashcroft (1959a) has reviewed the incidence of trypanosomes in the animal hosts and further sharpened the understanding of specific species of wildlife as permanent reservoirs of trypanosomiasis. If such game species disappear, so does the tsetse. Wölfel (1911a) made this observation in connection with the Rinderpest and the disappearance of tsetse fly in Uha and western Unyamwezi. Potts and Jackson (1952) reported the complete disappearance of *Glossina* following an experiment of controlled game-destruction in Shinyanga. Ford has made similar observations from Southern Rhodesia (Ford 1960). Thus, along with the climatic and vegetational conditions favourable to the fly, the presence of wild-life is essential to the existence and spread of tsetse and trypanosomes in the Tanganyikan situation where flies of the *Morsitans* group have been the primary vector in diseases involving man and domestic animals. The discussion of the cattle complex in the nineteenth century suggests that tsetse fly was less of an obstacle to cattle-keeping a hundred years ago than it is now. This further suggests that wildlife—the vital host of *Glossina*—may have been less prevalent, and that a gradual wildlife eradication was a necessary part of the economic expansion of the East African husbandman.

There is strong evidence that East Africa in the nineteenth century was not the wildlife paradise which it is today with approximately one-fourth of its land area set aside as national parks and game sanctuaries in Tanzania alone. Until recently such sanctuaries enclosed major towns like Dar es Salaam and Dodoma. The nineteenth-century situation was quite different. Whenever man and animals came into conflict over the occupation of land, the animals were inevitably driven out. In East Africa, as everywhere else in the world where people have expanded as farmers and cattle keepers, wildlife was gradually becoming extinct. A particularly critical situation existed for the elephant, as the commercial demand for ivory increased throughout the century. The introduction of firearms for hunting purposes greatly accelerated the process, although it is evident that the locally invented traps and game pits could effectively meet the needs of an expanding population for the removal of wildlife. Grant wrote from Biharamulo that 'the lads of several villages would assemble with dogs, horns and spears, to have a battue of the different forests—partridges, hares, coneys, and sometimes antelopes, being the result' (Grant 1864 :89). Larger animals had long since been driven out of the area. From the Nyassa–Tanganyika plateau, Boileau gave detailed descriptions of the system of game pits utilized by the villagers:

> They (the local people) build a high fence of brushwood and felled trees, sometimes 3 or 4 miles long, with various sorts of traps at intervals of about 30 yards. The whole village turns out, and drives the game towards these, and at times they make very big 'bags' (Boileau 1899 :582).

From the western edges of the Serengeti plains in Ushashi, Kollmann wrote about pre-colonial agriculturists subduing the wildlife:

> In the extensive woods in the Ruwana Plain, as well as in Nata, the traveller often comes across small hunting boxes and pitfalls for game. These are deep, narrow pits covered with thin brushwood, dug in scattered places in the wood, or in great numbers to the right and to the left of the footpaths. On one occasion I counted over 200 in a half hour's walk. In Nata I saw several such small pitfalls, arranged like a chess-board. Near the Ruwana River I saw a peculiar contrivance for catching game on a large scale. Two high walls of palisades, pretty far asunder at first, gradually converge like a wedge, leaving an exit at the narrow end. Just outside the exit numerous pitfalls covered with foliage were dug, and lay round in concentric semi-circles, so that the game driven through the double hedge had to pass them, and naturally fell in. In addition, the Washashi catch their game with large nets (Kollmann 1899 :199–201).

Similar systems of hunting and trapping were probably used widely in areas where man-wildlife confrontation was on the agenda.

Yet, wildlife was found in rich abundance in the 'jungles' or 'badlands' that were not contested for human habitats but existed between the larger tribal settlements. These were undoubtedly sanctuaries for wild animals, although it is possible that the settlement pattern was such that vast areas of land could be controlled by relatively small populations occupying critical locations, notably those associated with permanent water. The number of wild animals could thus be kept down to levels co-existent with human expansion and economic exploitation. Matzke (1972) has shown this to be true with regard to the Selous Game Reserve and advocated the complete segregation of wildlife and man to shield the animals from the large-scale effects of small human populations.

Burton claimed that grass-burning in conjunction with organized hunting greatly checked the animals and accounted, he thought, 'for the scarcity of animal life so remarkable in this animals' paradise' (Burton 1860, I:119). He observed:

> In the more populous parts game has melted away before the woodman's axe and the hunters' arrows: even where large tracks of jungle abound with water and forage, the note of a bird rarely strikes the air, and during a long day's march not a single large animal will be seen from the beaten track (Burton 1860, I:268).

He singled out 'the park lands' of Dut'humi south of the Uluguru mountains, 'the jungles and forests' of Ugogo and Mgunda Mk'hali, 'the barrens' of Usukuma and 'the tangled thickets of Ujiji' as the game areas along the central caravan route. These were also the isolated places where Burton reported having seen what he thought to be the tsetse fly. Writing from Bagamoyo, Behr described the coastal areas as practically empty of wildlife. He added:

> The still widespread opinion in Germany that you need only step outside of your door to shoot an antelope or a pheasant anywhere in Africa is founded on a complete misunderstanding. The entire coast is as poor in game as can possibly be imagined, and I believe that the chances are equally good to shoot a stag on the Lüneburger Heide as they are to lay down an antelope anywhere on the east coast of our territory (Behr 1891:127).

More significantly, similar reports abound from areas that are today the country's major game sanctuaries. We shall in the following pages review some of this evidence.

The Selous Game Reserve

Decken had been struck by the absence of wildlife along the main Kilwa-Lake Nyassa road in 1860. In search of news of his countryman, Rocher, who had disappeared somewhere along the lake, Decken set out with a small caravan and reached approximately 150 miles inland before he decided to turn around at the village of Mesule on the upper reaches of the Mbwemkuru River. Decken skirted the southern borders of what later became the Selous Game Reserve. In these surroundings he hunted pigeons only. He complained repeatedly about the absence of big game, and reflected that the generally dense population along the caravan road had driven wildlife out. He thought that the rich cultivation among the Ngindo belied the information received on the coast that their country had been heavily raided and that most of the slaves delivered on the coast were Ngindo (Decken 1869, I:185). 'Forests alternate with heavily populated cultivation land', he wrote about the areas west of the rivers Kiperele (Kipererere) and Mibuhu (Mihumo) (Decken 1869, I:169):

> With the exception of a few places, the land was extremely well settled and cultivated in an excellent manner. Provisions were offered for sale almost everywhere along the road. Their abundance and variety reminded us of the conditions in the blessed coastal regions. People offered us goats, chicken, peas, beans, millet, sweet potatoes, flour, sugar cane, mangoes, and pistachio nuts for sale. (Decken 1869, I:170).

In a later passage (I:184), Decken added cows to the list of animals kept by the villagers. He found the settlements to be located close to the hillsides and wondered whether the reason for this was security concerns or the greater abundance of water found there. Some of the settlements were evidently of considerable size:

> In the middle of the forest there were often large clearings with extensive settlements (*Ortschaften*); not real villages (*Dörfer*) in our sense, but widely extended cultivations and huts. On the well watered (west) side of the Ruhuhu (Tuhuu) River, the roads would now and then lead through fields and huts over distances that it took as much as two hours to pass through (Decken 1869, I:184–85).

The areas described were populated by the Ngindo people and lie immediately south of Liwale district, the heartland of the Ngindo-speaking peoples in the early parts of this century (Crosse-Upcott 1956). It seems reasonable to guess that the economic conditions of the Liwale Ngindo in the nineteenth century were not unlike those described by Decken, although the caravan traffic may have stimulated further developments in the south. The *Old Liwale District Book* stresses the absence of wildlife in the areas populated by Ndonde and Ngindo tribesmen at the time of European colonization. Crosse-Upcott, who interviewed people in the area wrote that 'elders speak of a time when people made special trips to the west in order to verify that an elephant was indeed as big as a hut' (Crosse-Upcott 1956:32).

Crosse-Upcott discussed the Ngindo people in the 1950s as essentially a tribe of hunters and gatherers who were less interested in the settled life than in roaming the forest:

Children with their toy bows and arrows delight to wander alone on its fringes. In time of want the population simply takes to the forest *en masse*. For the forest is more friendly than hostile, supplying almost every physical need of the Ngindo, who are essentially forest-minded (Crosse-Upcott 1956:50).

Quoting a Ngindo proverb that 'we do not stay long enough to eat our own mangoes', Crosse-Upcott concluded: 'Clearly, Ngindo do not anchor themselves firmly to one site, or even area. They have such short roots that they can readily be transplanted' (Crosse-Upcott 1956:106). The author failed to ask the question why this vagrant attitude prevailed, and to draw comparisons between the economic conditions as reported by Decken and his own observations in the 1950s. If he had done so he would probably have been struck by the enormous 'de-development' that must have taken place in the intervening years. This resulted in an almost total loss of control over the environment and led to a mental accommodation to that situation. Crosse-Upcott's work therefore never challenged the myth of the Ngindo woodsman prevailing among the British administrators at the time. Their conviction underpinned the decision to move 40,000 people out of the area to create the world's largest concentration of game in the Selous Reserve.

The Ngorongoro Crater and the Serengeti Plains

Poor game conditions do not seem to have been characteristic of the coast and immediate inland areas only. 'It is hardly a country one would recommend the sportsman to visit for shooting purposes', wrote Boileau from the Nyassa–Tanganyika Plateau (Boileau 1899:582). Many of the now famous game concentrations were—like the Selous Reserve—thriving human communities. A report by Farler about the inland caravans from Pangani described the Ngorongoro Crater as 'a thickly populated Masai district with many villages. The country is full of big game, harboured in the neighbouring forest. A strong boma is made here, and the caravan remains about twenty days to trade and hunt' (Farler 1882:735).

The Rinderpest removed the Masai and their cattle from the crater in the 1890s. Its rich pasture was then discovered by Siedentopf, a German settler who laid claim to approximately one-third of the crater floor to build a cattle and ostrich ranch. By 1905 he held more than 2,000 head of cattle and had plans to expand up to 5,000 (Fuchs 1907:252). The Siedentopf farm was sold as enemy property after the First World War to the American millionaire, Sir Charles Ross, who kept it up as a hunting lodge for his friends. The crater was gradually turned over to the animals from 1928 onwards when the first complete reserve was created. The Masai have since then fought a losing battle to reclaim old tribal lands.

Farler reported numerous Masai settlements west of Ngorongoro Crater into the present-day Serengeti National Park. The name is derived from a Masai village that prospered under chief Aramantuka. 'There are several wells here', wrote Farler, 'with good water and much cattle. The country is very open, with a good pasturage of short sweet grass, and no trees. This appears to be the limit of the Masai country in the west, for they are not met with again between this and the lake' (Farler 1882:735–36). Fuchs confirmed the existence of water wells throughout the eastern part of the plains during his research for the projected Northern Railroad which would have run through the Serengeti Plains to Mwanza. The water holes were thought to have been originally dug by the Wataturu or Tatoga peoples before the area was taken over by the Masai who utilized them un-til the Rinderpest put an end to the cattle domain in the eastern Serengeti in the 1890s (Fuchs 1907:253). The water wells fell into complete disuse after the forceful evacuation of all people in the area took place early in this century. The move into the Masai Reserve took place to prevent cattle thefts and clamp down on the unruly behaviour of the Masai. Their reserve was restricted southwards by the fourth parallel and westwards by the Rift Valley escarpment. From an old grazing area of more than 40,000 square kilometres the tribe was restricted to a mere 6,000 (Jäger 1913, Prittwitz and Gaffron 1910).

The Masai territory of the 1890s seems to have run westwards close to present day Seronera. Immediately to the west and northwest, another people, the Wandorobo, had settled. They are alternately described by Farler as elephant hunters 'who neither cultivate nor keep cattle', and as settled peasants. The Ndorobo village of Nata, was reported to be pop-ulated by 'agriculturists, and have large plantations. Food and grain are very plentiful and cheap' (Farler 1882:736). Baumann described several Waschaschi settlements along the Grumeti and Urtuti rivers. One such settlement was Ikoma or Elmarau surrounded by 'fields where sorghum, maize, millet and other food plants were carefully cultivated' (Baumann 1894:38). Another village was Niasiro, composed of over 100 huts. Foodstuffs were generously offered to the travellers in both settlements.

Lake Manyara

Oscar Baumann reported no trace of animals in the area presently covered by Lake Manyara National Park when he went through it in 1892. He brought with him a herd of 250 cattle looted from the Mangati (Umbugwe) people at the southern end of the lake. Baumann's caravan spent three nights within the boundaries of the present park. He described in detail what he saw and referred to the well-known hot springs (Maji Moto), to the flamingoes and the white soda crusts forming on the flat lake shore. Emerging on the north side of the lake into open grassland, Baumann again wrote about wildlife, ostriches, antelopes and numerous rhinoceroses. From the Rift Valley escarpment westwards to Ngorongoro Crater and the Serengeti plains he travelled on '*tief eingetretenen Viehwegen*'—deeply worn cattle paths (Baumann 1894:34). There is little reason to agree with later commentators that Baumann failed to report a supposedly rich wildlife in the area because he was 'distracted by an encounter with Masai raiders' (Watermeyer and Elliott 1943:58). It seems more likely that the entire area was part of the Mbugwe expansion from the south (Gray 1955), and that this people effectively controlled the strip of land up to the north end of the Lake for grazing purposes.

A suggestion to create a national park in the area in 1935 was rejected by the governor who wrote about the western lakeshore as 'one of the richest agricultural areas in the Territory' (*TNA* 11234, II). Although there were no local interests involved in claiming the land, he felt that 'it cannot be sound to close a rich agricultural area in the interest of game, when there are unlimited areas which are useless for cultivation and equally suitable for game on the Serengeti and in its vicinity' (*TNA* 11234, II). The park was nevertheless created a few years later. The official guidebook to the park now claims that the area 'carries a remarkably high biomass, or weight of live animals per acre or square mile' (*TNP* 1970:7). The entire park is infested with tsetse flies, which undoubtedly would make a repetition of Baumann's cattle-crossing impossible.

Lake Rukwa

One of the first Europeans to see Lake Rukwa was Joseph Thomson in 1880. He advanced northwards across the Fipa plateau and saw the lake from the edge of the escarpment above the present town of Zimba. The lake was then at maximum water level and Thomson wrote that 'from the place we halted we could almost throw stones into the lake; only we lost sight of them before they reached the ground' (Thomson 1881, II:225). He observed a dark green strip of land surrounding the lake between the mountains and the shore. Many villages were located in this belt which was highly cultivated. At the north end of the lake, the strip broadened into a 'marshy expanse formed doubtless by the detritus of the river Mkafu (Kayuu)' (Thomson 1881, II:226). Wallace toured the lake with a large caravan in 1897, when he visited most of the settlements observed by

Thomson. He wrote about numerous well-populated villages where a certain material abundance could be detected:

> Food was very plentiful the whole way around, and in presents alone I got almost enough to feed my caravan of over one hundred men. It consisted principally of flour, beans, pumpkins, and maize, and mostly a few fowls and a goat were given to me at each village. Cattle I only saw twice . . . (Wallace 1899:613).

It was probably the dense population which first attracted the White Fathers to the area and encouraged the early construction of three mission stations, at Zimba (St. Peter Claver), at Mkurue or Mkulwe (St. Boniface) and at Igalula (St. Moritz). At the time of Wallace's visit, the ecology of the area had changed radically as the lake had dried up to approximately one-third of its size in 1880. Langheld, who also saw Lake Rukwa in 1897, stated that the lake was almost dry and that the water had given place to a very game-rich steppe. He attributed the stockades of the Fipa and Mpimbwe villages to the need for protection against destructive vermin and thought that the extremely weak fortifications (*ausserst mangelhafte Befestigung*) would be useless against human attacks (Langheld 1897:511). The local opinion quoted by Langheld that the lake would not go back to its former level suggests that there was no historical memory among people in the area of earlier periods of extended drought (Langheld 1897:512).

Gunn's review (1956) of outbreaks of red locust in the Rukwa Valley is of interest for its periodization of high and low water levels in the lake. The important dates—which seem to have marked turning points in the water level of Lake Rukwa—are as follows:

1882	very high water level	reported by Kaiser
1897	very low	reported by Langheld
1905	very high	reported by Meyer
1929	low	reported by White Fathers
1937–38	very high	reported by D. C. Ufipa
1950	dry—low	reported by International Red Locust Control Society

From about 1905 to 1929 a prolonged period of drought apparently existed. When hundreds of acres of grassland opened up as the water receded, wild animals penetrated the cordon of settlements described by Thomson and established a habitat in the plains. This was the beginning of the rich wildlife for which the area has since become famous (Vesey-FitzGerald 1964). By the time the British administration entered Tanganyika animals were firmly entrenched. Their vast numbers became most noticeable as the gradual filling up of the lake recommenced from

1930 onwards. This caused game congestion and forced the animal population into contact with the human settlements around the lake. As large-scale hunting by settlers and prospectors commenced, an effort was made to save the game from extinction. A game reserve was created in 1932 and greatly extended westwards five years later when the lake had risen to its old high level. By this time the people in the cultivation areas seen by Wallace had been concentrated into two big sleeping-sickness settlements at Rungwa and Udinde, leaving only Manda and Sala undisturbed on the northern side of the lake (Gunn 1956). The 1937 extension of the Lake Rukwa Game Reserve enclosed approximately 10,000 people within its border (TNA 21210). Since then, a continuous struggle has been going on as to who, man or animals, should have the right of occupancy to the lake shore.

END TO TERRITORIAL CONFRONTATION

This review has been neither complete nor balanced. It is intended as a follow-up to previous chapters to further document the nineteenth-century economic initiative of the East African and to show its presence even in areas that we have come to regard as the last remains of untouched nature. I have also sought to correct the old misconception that man and beast lived in harmonious co-existence in pre-colonial East Africa and that neither threatened the existence of the other. This chapter has shown the opposite, namely that man and beast competed for the control of the territory and that the nineteenth century was a period of vanishing wildlife frontiers. The idea of exclusive game reserves was first introduced into Tanganyika with the German ordinance of 7th May 1896 and was motivated by the desire to protect rare species of wildlife from becoming extinct. The ordinance created two hunting reserves, one on the western slopes of Mount Kilimanjaro, and another between the Rubehobeho and Rufiji rivers. The number of reserves was further extended through the Hunting Ordinance (*Jagdverordnung*) of 5th November 1908. The 1896 ordinance also introduced hunting permits and gun licences. A minimum licence fee attached to muzzle-loaders and cost three rupees: the equivalent of the general head tax. A limited hunting permit (*Kleiner Eingeborenen–Jagdschein*) was sold to the local people for ten rupees (*DOZ* 1912). No licence was needed to fight vermin intruding into the settled areas and destroying the village crop. Thus, although the African was not entirely excluded from the noble hunt, it is obvious that this was gradually becoming a European privilege. This development was completed through British legislation (Proclamation No. 16 of 1917, and Game Preservation Proclamation of 1920) which denied a game licence to any native, and made African hunting a matter of special permission by the governor (Copley and Mayer 1934). It seems that exemption from the licensing rules was granted to the so-called 'hunter' tribes only: the Wabahi, Watindiga and Wandorobo, who were allowed to hunt common food animals without formal licence (Thomas 1963). Vermin destruction came within the domain of government and was to be executed through a growing team of game scouts. The cost of gun and game licences effectively foreclosed any legal African hunting. The African who hunted became an outlaw in his own country. By the end of the colonial period, the creation of game sanctuaries 'free from human rights' was advocated as valid strategy for economic development. The nineteenth-century confrontation, with its concomitant system of wildlife-control, ceased and was replaced by a policy which controlled people while leaving the wild animals to roam freely. As wildlife spread, its interaction with the human communities increased and exposed man and his cattle to the dangers of *nagana* and sleeping sickness. I shall return to the particulars of the game policy in connection with anti-sleeping-sickness measures introduced in the 1920s and 1930s. These measures were part of the effort to cope with the ecological disaster that commenced in the 1890s. Before tracing the connection in Chapter 7, we shall in the next two chapters consider some of the secondary economic activities of the nineteenth-century Tanganyikans, their industrial undertakings and their marketing and trading.

CHAPTER 5

The Industrial Supports

No discussion of the pre-colonial economy could be complete without some consideration of its industrial components. These formed an integral part of the traditional economy and contributed significantly to its nineteenth-century expansion. We shall therefore move for some time from the ecological variable to discuss examples of the industrial initiatives. This discussion will lead to an analysis of markets and trading relations which connected supply and demand and acted as a dynamic stimulus to exploit comparative advantages within the indigenous economies.

It seems correct to place particular emphasis on the iron-smelting and tool-making industry which can be seen as directly related to the agricultural initiative. It was a different but related response to the new needs for foodstuffs that arose from the nineteenth-century population pressure. Technological innovations accompanied intensified food production and—as in the case of the iron hoe—were partly responsible for improved agricultural techniques. The second industrial initiative reviewed here, salt-making, is also linked to the agricultural expansion, for it was the prevailing plant diet of the agriculturists which gave rise to an independent demand for inorganic salt. As Bloch (1963) has observed, solving the problem of adequate salt supplies is one of the basic preliminaries for population growth and concentration. Cotton manufacturing—although probably a cultural importation—bears a direct relevance to the agricultural diversification of the nineteenth century and shows not only an important crop adoption, but also a high degree of technical skill. When the White Fathers of Ufipa sought to rescue the local weaving industry, one of their difficulties was the reconstruction of the local looms which were described as 'very complicated and of a delicate construction' (Lechaptois 1913:256).

These three initiatives clearly do not exhaust the technological supports of the pre-colonial economy. Other areas like the production of bark cloth, tanned skins, pottery, weaponry and ornaments have not been reviewed here. This chapter aims at correcting the notion which equates 'pre-colonial' with 'pre-industrial' and seeks to restore technology to its proper and integrated place in the economy of the nineteenth century.

IRON-SMELTING AND FORGING

There are several recent studies of the origin and spread of iron-making in Africa (Chittick 1966, 1967; Fagan *et al.* 1969; Soper 1967, 1971; Shinnie ed. 1971). These studies are on the whole preoccupied with the opening period of 'the Iron Age', a concern not directly relevant to our present study. Of more interest is Fagan's assertion (1965, Fagan *et al.* 1969) that the immediate pre-colonial period was one of industrial decline, due to the same two events that were discussed in Chapter 1—intertribal warfare and slave-raiding. According to Fagan, the Zulu *impis* swept from the south over East and Central Africa leaving death and destruction in their wake. From Zanzibar and Kilwa came the slave-raiders who completed the devastations. By 1850, all was in ruin and there was no more talk about iron. My intention in this chapter is to discuss some of the literature which points instead to a flourishing metallurgic initiative in East Africa in the period prior to European colonialism.

A general review of the literature shows that during the period of our study iron production was a widespread and significant phenomenon in Tanganyika. Blacksmiths were known in practically every tribe, although the iron smelters were less frequent and restricted to the ore-rich communities. Both were skilled craftsmen who sometimes enjoyed extraordinary social and even political prestige. Such a situation has been documented for the Wachagga (Gutmann 1912), the Wapare (Kimambo 1969) and the Warangi (Baumstark 1900). On the other hand, a pariah status attached to the blacksmith (*el konono*) of the Masai, a practice also observed among related peoples like the Tatog and the Somali (Hollis 1905, and Merker 1904). Among the Wanyakyusa the smiths apparently were also given an inferior position (Mackenzie 1925). Baumann (1894:172) wrote about itinerant smiths, the so-called *gidamudiga*, in Turu country. Similarly, Watussi smiths were said to operate most of the industry in some parts of Unyamwezi. In Uzinza, an entire tribe, the Rongo, were known as the smiths and smelters of the region. An interesting division of labour seems to have existed between the sexes with the women responsible for the collection and dressing of the ore and the men taking care of the smelting process proper and of the forging of tools.

Simple but effective iron-making techniques yielded enough metal to satisfy the local demands for raw iron and forged implements. Burton mentions a number of tools manufactured and traded through the regional network. His list comprised field hoes, spears, assegais, arrow-heads, battle-axes, hatchets, knives and daggers, sickles and razors, rings and wire circlets. Bells of different kinds were brought by the caravan carriers probably for resale to the cattle peoples. Pipes with iron bowls and stems entered the trade along with all kinds of pincers or pliers (Burton 1860, II:312).

The most important element in this picture for the purposes of our study is the iron hoe, or *jembe*. The iron hoe was the basic tool among the agricultural peoples and was central in the agricultural initiative. We shall shortly see that the production of the iron hoe was widespread throughout Tanganyika, but there is also evidence that this was a relatively recent break-through, testifying to the growth of the economy and pointing to the agricultural expansion and diversification into more intensive methods of soil exploitation that we have discussed in Chapter 2. Weule (1908) thought that iron hoes had replaced the digging stick as the major agricultural implement of the Makonde, Makua and Yao peoples a few decades prior to the German entry into East Africa. Fülleborn (1906) mentions the occasional use of wooden hoes among the Donde and Konde peoples around the northern end of Lake Nyassa. Similar observations were made from Kilimanjaro (Merker 1904) and from Unyamwezi (Reche 1914). Stuhlmann (1895) found wooden hoes among the Uluguru peoples. These hoes were said to have been in general use earlier and to have survived only for symbolic purposes in that the chief opened the hoeing season with a hoe made from ebony wood. Baumann (1894:200) observed a similar symbolic use of ebony hoes at Ukara island.

Much evidence thus points to a transition from wood to iron as the preferred material for agricultural implements of many peoples in Tanganyika sometime in the early nineteenth century. Stern (1910) dwelt on this likelihood and showed the linguistic connection between wood and iron implements in Unyamwezi where the ebony tree (*Dalbergia*) is called *mugembe* or *mugembija* and the hoe—of whatever make—is called *igembe* and in Kiswahili *jembe*. The change-over from wood to iron was, according to Stuhlmann (1910:58) something that many people could still remember. Where wooden implements were found in active use, the agricultural system corresponded generally to the slash-and-burn type (long fallow) where no extensive field work was needed and the digging stick therefore remained highly functional.

The most important centres of iron production in Tanganyika at the time of the European entry into East Africa are well known (Meyer 1909, I:390). They stretched from Karagwe, Bukoba and Uha in the northwest through the communities of Ussuwi, Uzinza, and Unera southwards to Ukahama, through Unyanyembe into Ukonongo, Ukimbu and Ufipa. In the centre of the country iron works were located in Irangi and in the

Usagaras. Nearer to the coast, iron-making communities were found in the Pare mountains and in the south where the iron exploits of the Wakinga, Wabena and various Songea tribes are well documented. We shall now consider more closely some of the reports of iron production in these different nineteenth-century centres.

Bukoba and Karagwe

It seems natural to commence a survey of the pre-colonial iron initiative with the West Lake Region, where recent excavations have yielded radiocarbon readings of man-made iron dating back as far as 500 B.C. (Schmidt 1974). These readings give greater antiquity to the Bukoba finds than to all the known occurrences of iron at Meroe in the Sudan, and give the material basis for Trigger's challenge (1969) of accepted theories of the spread of the knowledge of iron-making. It seems that iron-making in the West Lake operated continuously until this century when Kollmann (1899), Richter (1900a) and Rehse (1910) observed a flourishing iron initiative in the area and left extensive reports about it. Schmidt contends that smelting came to a complete end only in the 1920s. He connects the peak of iron exploitation to the development of the Buhaya states under their *mukama*, who collected tributes in kind from smiths and smelters. 'Iron was a major part of the redistributive system of the centralized state', writes Schmidt, who thinks that the important quantities of iron that were produced could partly be explained from the state's control of the productive economy (Schmidt 1974:57–58). At one location, in Kangantebbe village in Kianja, Schmidt was shown a slag heap which was 120 metres long, 2–3 metres wide and 2 metres high. Material from this heap had for a long time been used by the local people for the construction of their houses and cattle fences. Mining evidence was equally impressive. Scores of pits were found at Kikukwe village in Kiziba some of which were up to 8 metres deep.

Part of the Bukoba iron demand was satisfied through imports from Karagwe, Ankole and Ussui (Biharamulo) according to Richter (1900a). Karagwe was apparently an important centre of quality iron, and Burton (1860, II:184) claimed that Karagwe weapons and tools were to some extent tempered. Iron implements from this area seem to have been in high demand and were traded widely through the Tanganyika—Uganda caravan network which crossed Karagwe.

Uha

'In the Kibondo area iron smelting is an important industry, particularly in Mabamba and Nyarwonga', reads an entry in the *Kasulu District Book* (Greig 1937a). The smiths produced hoes that were sold to the Warundi and exchanged for Urundi cattle. These were in turn taken to Biharamulo where the cattle were traded for a good profit which made it possible for the Waha to pay their taxes.

Several Waha iron centres were observed by Dantz during his geological expedition in the *Schutzgebiet* (1902:147). The industry survived into the 1930s either because of its remoteness from the main trading networks or because of active revival by the colonial administration during the many campaigns to grow more crops that were launched during the depression years of the 1930s. Further work to clarify such connections is clearly necessary.

Besides iron smelting, work in brass and copper was apparently well established in Uha. The *chef d'oeuvre* of the Waha smiths was reported to be the so-called *mulinga*, a bracelet of great delicacy and fineness (*Kasulu District Book*).

Hans Meyer's work on Urundi indicated that the local Bahutu and Batwa smiths worked imported iron, as no smelting apparently took place in this very populous region where the metal demand may have been very high. Meyer identified the Waha as the main transporters of iron to Urundi from smelting sites in Uzinza and Ussuwi (Meyer 1916:83). Much of this iron also followed the salt trade to Urundi from the Malagarasi River probably from centres further south in Unyamwezi.

Uzinza/Ussuwi

Speke identified perhaps the most important iron-smelting region in all of East Africa in the nineteenth century and indicated 'Iron Manufacturers' across a vast area to the southwest of Victoria Nyanza on his sketch map of Tanganyika. He made the following observation:

> The sandstone in this region is highly impregnated with iron, and smelters do a good business; indeed, the iron for nearly all the tools and cutlery that are used in this division of East Africa is found and manufactured here. It is the Brummagem of the land, and has not only rich but very extensive ironfields stretching many miles north, east, and west (Speke 1864:298).

Thus, Speke seems to have been aware of the continuous chain of iron-producing communities identified earlier as Ussuwi, Uzinza, Mera and Kahama. Central to this initiative were the Rongo people, who by the 1940s had moved—or been moved—southwards to Kahama District where their iron production was studied by Rosemond (1943) during its short-lived revival during the Second World War. Pater Schynse (1892) located the Rongo iron smelters immediately to the southeast of the Emin Pasha Sound in the landscape of Ngulula or Ngalula. At the time many caravans passed through the area to which the traders were no doubt attracted by the flourishing industry of the Warongo. Their activities seem to have involved a fair amount of specialization, with some villages concentrating exclusively on iron production while others occupied themselves with cultivation and cattle-keeping.

Schynse (see also Stuhlmann 1894) stated that iron from Ngalula covered the entire demand of Usukuma, northwestern Unyamwezi and the areas to the west of Uzinza. An important trade also took place to Ukerewe and the areas on the east coast of Victoria Nyanza. The Wakerewe were seen as middlemen in a transaction of raw iron and hoes to the Mara Region where iron was traded to the Washashi and Ngoroine for ivory (20 hoes for 35 pounds of ivory). Also the Arab dhows of Victoria Nyanza regularly called at the Emin Pasha Sound to buy Ngalula hoes for further barter around the lake. Large caravans of Wasukuma came to the area with cattle, goats and trade-goods from the coast in order to obtain field hoes. The result of this exchange was that Ngalula, without being in direct trading contact with the coast, was as well supplied with imported goods, notably cloth, as any of the major carrier tribes (Schynse 1892:39, see also Baumann 1894, and Kollmann 1899).

Some of the iron entering the trading network also came from Ussuwi and Ukumi, two chiefdoms west of Uzinza in present-day Biharamulo. The iron production of this area was first described by Grant (1864:130–31), who gave the name of Walinga to the people specializing in the iron industry. Ussuwi retained its importance into the early years of this century when Meyer claimed that the iron ore smelted there maintained a thriving industry. The area was then seen as thickly populated, particularly in its eastern parts. It was well cultivated with extensive fields of sorghum and sweet potatoes, and the villages were surrounded by banana groves (Meyer 1909, I:295).

Unyamwezi

> *Pwani ja miguwa,*
> *malyoho kwambala*
> *na madebwani kwambale,*
> *galetwe na muwanga.*

This work-song which was recorded by Stern (1910:157) describes Unyamwezi as the land of bellows where good cloth to wear is gained through the charcoal of the *muwanga* tree. The song indicates that iron production had gone beyond the subsistence dimensions of the locality and that the blacksmiths of Unyamwezi were producing for a wider market. Already in the 1850s, Richard Burton (1860, II:311–12) had drawn attention in a lengthy report to Unyamwezi as an important source of iron, although it is not clear on which locality he based his account.

Cameron was equally vague about this subject. Iron was worked in the northwestern parts of Unyanyembe, he wrote, and carried in all directions. Hoes made or traded there were even exported to the east coast by the caravans (Cameron 1877, II:238). Wanyamwezi traders also brought field hoes to Nyaturu country later in the century (Baumann 1894:190).

Broyon-Mirambo identified the Watussi as the real metal workers of Nyamwezi. They were particularly skilled wire-drawers and famous for their production of the so-called *niereres*, 'a kind of ring of the thickness of a millimetre, composed of giraffe hair bound spirally with the metallic thread'. These ornaments were extremely popular and Wanyamwezi could be seen wearing more than a thousand of these rings on each leg, giving the appearance of wearing huge boots (Broyon-Mirambo 1877:31).

Nearly fifty years after Burton's visit, Oscar Baumann found iron working still to be an important activity in Unyamwezi. The professional smelters and forgers were then of the Rongo and Uzinza tribes. Baumann also had praise for the smiths at Urambo, who were able to repair guns and make essential spare parts. Their technical insight and excellent workmanship were quite astounding (Baumann, 1894:232).

Ukonongo

The village of Sara has been identified as the centre of the industrial areas of Ukonongo between Unyamwezi and Ufipa. Iron-smelting was undertaken in high ovens and the wrought iron forged into a variety of tools, hoes, knives, arrow-heads and delicate mouth-pieces for tobacco pipes. Ornaments were produced through well developed wire-drawing techniques. The women also participated in the industrial endeavours with the production of clay pipes, beads and water jars. The entire region seems to have moved towards a high degree of industrial specialization depending on other communities for food essentials. The villages of Ukonongo were accordingly described as 'industrial centres' by Diesing (1909), who compared them to Germany's small-scale industries in Harz and Thüringen.

Irangi

Another centre of iron production was found in Irangi northeast of Kondoa, particularly in the areas of Bussi, Konduzi, and Uriwa. All three communities were well cultivated and supported very dense populations (Werther *et al.* 1898:49, and Baumstark 1900). The Irangi hoes were reported to be of superior quality and to be in greater demand than the hoes coming eastward from Unyamwezi through the caravan trade. The district was an important production and trading centre which supplied most of its northerly neighbours. Iron tools were traded particularly to the Wambugwe, Wassi, Turu, and Ussandaui peoples against cattle, grain and salt.

Usagara/Ukaguru

Last (1883) has given a vivid description of iron-making among the peoples of the Usagara Mountains. To reach the iron smelters, Last travelled through the villages of the Mangaheri peoples where every available plot was cultivated and rice, maize, sweet potatoes, pumpkins, beans and tobacco were produced by the villagers. The influence of the central caravan route, which ran through the district, could be detected in the clothing habits of the people. Nearly all had left the skin-wearing stage in favour of imported cloth.

Progressing south into the Usagara Mountains, Last encountered the iron-smelters who had specialized in their trade to the extent of neglecting cattle-keeping and agriculture. The iron-making was found to be a very compartmentalized affair with ore production as a particular occupation largely undertaken by women. The ore was dressed through gravity methods which made use of the mountain streams skillfully conducted through dugout furrows, where the heavy iron nodules were separated from the soil. Enriched ore was packed in bags made from the fronds of date palms and sold to the professional smelters. When traded, the ore fetched its equivalent bulk in grain. The buyers of the finished ore implements were probably the peasants in the lush valleys of the Usagaras. In these valleys Last found an advanced agricultural system supported by a network of irrigation (see also p. 36). Beidelman (1962a) has claimed that iron from the Usagara Mountains was traded with the Baraguyu, Kamba and Masai peoples. His inference is that these 'raiders' supported the local power structure in the iron-making communities and secured essential weapons in return.

Pare and Kilimanjaro

Decken, accompanied by Thornton, visited the 'iron country of Usangi' in 1859 at a time when the Pare iron, according to these travellers, was 'as famed as Swedish steel' (Decken 1869, II:19). Decken found numerous kilns in active use at the foothills of the Pare mountains and observed a number of women collecting iron-sand from the shallows of the nearby brooks. He thought that a type of magnetite was used in the smelting process which gave raw material for the forging of field hoes, many of which entered the regional trading network.

The iron markets in North Pare are described by Fosbrooke (1954), who timed them as 'Early Iron Age' activities. Characteristic of these markets were a number of flat stones all bearing marks of regularly worked cavities where the iron ingots apparently had been displayed and cut to the demands of the buyer. Fosbrooke's description of a nearby smelting site is of interest for the dimensions it lends to the Pare industry. The hillside below the site was 'a veritable scree slope of broken clay, bellow mouths and lumps of slag', wrote Fosbrooke (1954:102). He found at least 800 bellow mouths exposed on the surface alone and implied that many times this number would be exposed through excavation.

Part of the iron produced in Pare was sold to Kilimanjaro, where Decken again picked up the description of the iron industry. He was particularly impressed by the wire production and the skillful use of drawplates for this purpose. The wire was mostly used in the making of chains that were reported to be popular trading media. Fischer (1884) later found that caravans going into Masailand usually brought with them large numbers of chains and necklaces for barter purposes. Hans Meyer confirmed the high quality of iron workings among the Chagga smiths and singled out Kibosho as the centre of the industry where 'the despot Sinna' had created a school for smiths (1900:210). In another study a decade later, Meyer observed that the Kilimanjaro iron industry was in sharp decline (1909, I:238).

Ukinga

A village called Ku Ndapa—said to mean 'near the iron'—was singled out by Bornhardt (1900:80) as the main smelting centre in the Livingstone Mountains. The village was located at a 2,500 metre altitude in the Hugilo range not far from the German mission of Bulongua. Ore was dug from the mountain sides in pits driving up to five metres into the ground, and smelted in cone-shaped ovens that seldom rose more than one metre over the terrain. Blooms of approximately five kilos were produced from each smelting which lasted two full days.

Elton had earlier written about 'the iron mountain' of the Wakinga and claimed that these tribesmen supplied most of the market for iron and tools among the peoples living to the north of Lake Nyassa (Elton 1879:321). Kerr-Cross told a similar story from his visit to Rungwe in 1893 when he found the area abundantly supplied with iron. He saw people carrying thick 'belts' of iron, copper and brass. These were regarded as money, and the local word for wealth was *ifiera*: iron (Kerr-Cross 1895:118).

Ufipa/Unyika

In the Tanganyika–Nyassa corridor, we encounter the high ovens based on natural draught which seem to have been the main characteristic of the central African iron industry (Money and Kellett Smith, 1897). Kerr-Cross, travelling across the Fipa plateau in the late 1880s, observed numerous smelting kilns which he estimated to be nine feet tall. He thought that each of them would contain half a ton of iron ore (Kerr-Cross 1890:289). Other eye-witness reports are available from Dantz (1900, 1902, 1903), Lechaptois (1913), and Reichard (1892).

An important contribution is Lechaptois' assertion that the Wafipa smelters used limestone as a flux in the production process. It is generally claimed that fluxes were unknown in primitive smelting (Tylecote 1965). If Lechaptois' contention can be proven, it would place the metallurgy of the Wafipa in a singularly advanced position among African iron-makers. Lechaptois raised questions about the survival of the iron industry and reported that many smiths were leaving their work to go into porterage and activities stimulated by the colonial take-over. Most villages continued, however, to have their own blacksmiths. This was seen as a hereditary profession with some opportunities for co-optation into the existing corporation. Lechaptois also noted that the local people clearly preferred their own iron to the imported metal, as the local product was far more malleable and could easily be forged into the desired tools (Lechaptois 1913:247, 250).

Despite such differences in quality, it was the cheap, mass-produced European iron that won the competition in the Ufipa villages. Iron smelting and forging was to all intents and purposes a dead industry when Greig reviewed it in 1937. Although the locally made hoe was still regarded as superior in quality to the imported ones, the price difference was important with local hoes costing four shillings compared with the imported hoe at two shillings. While decrying the loss of a local industry, Greig could nevertheless find solace in the greater logic of the imperial economy:

> It is a pity in some ways to see an established native industry such as iron burning dying out. One cannot help feeling for the craftsmen as they see their prestige lessening and their products being replaced by cheap imported goods. On the other hand the work entailed in producing one hoe is probably greater than that required to grow enough extra food to buy a hoe. Of more importance, however, is the denudation of forest which is necessary for making the charcoal, and if the industry were to continue to flourish the Weald of Kent would have its parallel in Fipa. If the craft is dying out the forests are surviving and there is no doubt which is of the greater ultimate value to the tribe (Greig 1937:80–81).

The centres of iron production discussed above seem to have been the most important and best known in Tanganyika territory in the nineteenth century. This does not mean that iron-smelting was confined to these centres only. Picarda (1886) and Reckling (1942) indicated important forging techniques among the coastal peoples, the Wasaramo and Wasegua. Fülleborn (1906) described smelting furnaces among the Ngoni people of Songea. Lieder (1897) and Bornhardt (1900) found small coned furnaces in various communities along the Ruvuma River. A number of smelting centres located outside of Tanganyika territory may also have been part of its economy through the trading networks. One such centre was located at Seremba or Samia in Kavirondo along the Sio River (Thomson 1885:492, Hobley 1898). Products from this centre were traded to Uganda and probably also to the peoples living around the southern shores of Victoria Nyanza. Several well-known sites were located in northern Malawi and Zambia and were probably part of the southern Tanganyika trading networks. Similar centres may have been located in Mozambique territory. In passing, we should also mention the copper production in Katanga which entered the major trading networks at various points along Lake Tanganyika.

Quantifying the Iron Trade

It is difficult to assess the size of the iron industry in the centres discussed. The production was determined by the demand which undoubtedly fluctuated among the different peoples as a reflection mainly of their agricultural interests. It is also important to consider the population factor as a key to the demand, but this factor is complicated by the trading networks whose boundaries are not always clear. From what has been said earlier about the population in the nineteenth century, it would seem that the combined centres of the West Lake and Unyamwezi must have been the most important of those discussed. The French missionary, Brard (1897) indicated that 30,000 iron hoes were produced in Uzinza each year. Lieutenant Sigl estimated that some 150,000 field hoes, mostly the products of Msalala and Usambiro, were sold annually on the market in Tabora in the 1880s (Sigl, 1892). Sigl confirmed what earlier travellers had written before that the iron hoes were favourite trading objects for the coast-bound caravans and were exchanged for food in Ugogo. Some hoes apparently were brought all the way to the coast. Sigl thought that most Masai and Wahumba (Wahehe) spears were made from iron originally traded as hoes from the Tabora market. Stuhlmann (1910) stated that huge numbers of field hoes were collected as tax in kind from Ngoni tribesmen in Songea around the turn of the century. No exact numbers were indicated. Further research on the earliest tax returns of the different districts might bring more light on the role of iron in the economy of the nineteenth century, and pin-point the size of production in the different centres.

The Magic of Iron-Making

I have deliberately evaded the magico-religious side of iron-making. The interested reader is referred to the works of Greig (1937), Rosemond (1943), Robert (1949), Wise (1958) and Wyckaert (1914) for this aspect. Some of these writers have tended to see the manufacturing of iron as a by-product of the magico-religious needs of the East African peoples. Wyckaert, for example, wrote that his intention in reporting the Ufipa iron production was not to study the smelters and their product from the point of view of an industrial achievement, but to stress the superstitious and religious practices involved in the smelting process (Wyckaert 1914:374). He concluded that 'our smelters seem to attach greater importance to the supernatural influences than to their own work', and saw in the 'purism' of the smelting ritual a sign of suffering souls groping for the light of the true God (Wyckaert 1914:379). Robert (1949:240) characterized the master smelter outrightly as a magician. Wise, following these leads, dwelt on 'the overwhelming importance of the correct performance of the rituals, magical and ceremonial, without which the kiln and all the smith's work will fail. For the successful working of the kiln, the living and the dead, the spirits of the air, wood and rock must work together' (Wise 1958:232).

Such aspects are of little interest here. The important conclusion is that iron was produced in quantities large enough to satisfy the local markets and that its quality was often of quite high standard. Unfortunately, what we may call the 'ritualist school' of research into the East African ironworking has come to dominate the scene. It is therefore important to stress how little emphasis the early observers placed on the ritual aspects of iron-making. To Bornhardt, Dantz, Stuhlmann and others, the magical aspect was a secondary feature amounting, at the most, to a type of trade-union secrecy aimed at maintaining monopoly over an important economic enterprise.

Bishop Lechaptois was a contemporary of the demise of the iron ininiative. Aspects of this phenomenon were the decline of chemical/technical knowledge and the rise of the magical element as a substitute explanation of the metallurgical processes. He wrote:

We are convinced that the present natives are not backward (*arriérés*) as one tends to believe, but that they are rather de-developed (*retrogrades*); that is to say that they do not maintain the degree of advancement that they once possessed. Thus ... they have kept the principles of weaving and the essential elements of iron-smelting. But it is evident that they now apply these principles and rudimentary sciences in a routine and unconscious way. With regards to metallurgy, we are certain that they possess the secrets of smelting which they have inherited from more skilled predecessors, and apply them now without knowing why. When questioned, they are content to tell you that the *dawa* (medicine) is essential (Lechaptois 1913:234).

Bishop Lechaptois' fear, that the Wafipa would be totally crushed through exposure to the technical civilization of colonialism, was well founded. He observed nothing less than a mental de-development following the disruption of the economic initiative. It might be of importance for the contemporary anthropologists to pick up from where the churchman left his clues to a more correct and satisfactory explanation of the magical element than is currently offered by the 'ritualist school'.

SALT PRODUCTION

We have no study of the salt consumption in East Africa that can aid us in quantifying the overall demand for this commodity. Notions about the general supply of salt in the past vary considerably. Burton, who took an optimistic view, claimed that the peoples of the interior of Tanganyika were adequately supplied from the large markets of Ugogo and Uvinza and that they were far better off with regard to salt than 'the more civilized races of Abyssinia and Harar' (Burton 1860, II:402). It was Stuhlmann's opinion, however, that the salt intake of man and beast in the *Schutzgebiet* was deficient and that salt was the possession of the rich people only (Stuhlmann 1910:48). The span of fifty years separating the two observations possibly made both of them right.

In pursuing the nineteenth-century initiative in salt production, we can follow Bunge's original suggestion (quoted in Springer 1918) of a correlation between a diet with a vegetarian basis and a demand for inorganic salt on the one hand, and the absence of such demand among people with animal food as their main nutrient on the other. The underlying reason for this connection is that people relying on a milk and blood diet receive most of their salt needs (calcium, sodium, and potassium) through the food. This type of diet has been commented on by numerous observers of the nomad/pastoral peoples. Johnston (1886) and Merker (1904) have given early observations on the blood diet of the Masai. Baumann (1894) described similar practices among the Watussi rulers of Ruanda. Rehse (1910) wrote about the blood meals of the Hima in Kiziba, and Baumstark (1900) and Fromm (1912) observed the use of blood from live animals among the Warangi and Wafipa respectively.

The pastoralists satisfied their additional demands for sodium chloride through the use of cattle urine. Herrmann (1892:195) commented on this practice in Ugogo. Similar usages were reported from among the Wataturu (Baumann 1894:171), the Masai (Hollis 1802:38), and the

Wakavirondo (Thomson 1885:429). A large part of the salt demands of the peoples mentioned was therefore satisfied internally through the pastoral/nomadic economy. Only a limited demand for additional salt existed. Most of these peoples occupy areas where alternative sources of salt are readily available, and the dietary practice can be seen as a carry-over of older and perhaps common feeding traditions.

We should not overlook the cattlemen's interest in salt for their beasts, however. From Uganda we have reports that the Unyoro king distributed most of the salt received in tribute from the Kibero salt-makers to the Wahuma herders who fed it to their cattle (Casati 1891, II:137–38). The typical cattle people of Tanganyika, the Masai, occupy a terrain par-ticularly rich in natural salt occurrences. Their cattle were regularly treated to salt licks (Eliot 1904:99), a practice which did not, however, add to the demand for manufactured salt. The agricultural Wanyakyusa in-cluded salt as part of the standard diet for their cattle (Fülleborn 1906:291) and probably manufactured this salt either from plant ashes or saline soil.

Demands for salt from sources external to the immediate economy arose with the establishment of settled agriculturists living on a vegetarian diet which, although it contains a great deal of potassium, is largely deficient in other necessary salts. Thus, a demand for man-produced (inorganic) salt and a subsequent industry and trade can be expected to be found largely, if not exclusively, among the agricultural peoples of the nineteenth century in East Africa.

In this section, I shall survey the different sources of salt available to the Tanganyikans in this period. Apart from Morgan's study (1974), no assessment has been attempted of the traditional salt production on a territorial scale. In order to restore this dimension of the pre-colonial economy, I have therefore found it necessary to provide a fairly detailed review of some of the old salt centres and to discuss the literature available on them. While much of the old salt production was intended for home consumption only, some centres of production were clearly of great magnitude. Their activity has correctly been described as an industrial undertaking carried out by specialized salt boilers producing for distant markets and providing the commodity for important transport undertakings.

I shall be concerned only with the salt works which existed inside the modern boundaries of Tanzania. Several works lying on the outside of these borders were of importance to the Tanganyikan peoples in the pre-colonial period. The district of Bukoba, including Karagwe, for instance, received part of its quality salt from the very important salt works of Uganda at Katwe and Kibero (Richter 1900, 1900a; Good 1972). The peoples east of Victoria Nyanza were similarly provisioned from the salt production taking place on the islands in the northeastern parts of the lake. This salt was 'traded up and down the whole east coast of the Nyanza', according to Hobley (1898:366). Another centre, Lake Mweru (Moore 1937) may have been of importance to some of the peoples of southwestern Tanganyika. Before the turn of the century this centre provisioned areas more than 100 miles away and exported 15,000–20,000 pounds of salt per year (Wallace 1899:616). Also, some of the salt centres at Lake Shirwa (Gray 1945) may have included parts of Tanganyika in their trading networks. Finally, the salt-producing areas on Lake Pamolombe, the southern extention of Lake Nyassa (Livingstone 1865), may have extended their trading contacts to the peoples of southern Tanganyika. I shall return to the importance of the trading networks and their commodities in the next chapter.

Salt Lakes

Enormous salt and soda deposits are found in the many lakes that line the Great Rift Valley in East Africa. These deposits have been formed from the sediments of alkaline springs containing varying degrees of sodium carbonate, sodium bicarbonate, sodium fluoride and sodium chloride that have been leached from the recent volcanic rock surrounding the Great Rift Valley. Because most of the lakes have no outlet, natural evaporation in the dry, hot climate has, over a long period of time, concentrated large quantities of salt and soda in the lake regions (Werther *et al.* 1898, Orr and Grantham 1931).

The peoples of the lake areas have since time immemorial made use of these resources, shunning lakes of excessive soda content and concentrating their exploitation in those areas where the purest sodium chloride could be gathered. The local peoples probably distinguished salt lakes by their reddish colour which may have acted as a practical guide to the local salt-makers and aided them in the timing of the salt-gathering season. It also seems clear that the local peoples were able to judge the quality of the salt from the shape of the salt crystals and discriminate between the utility of the different salt lakes. Thus, most reports that I have consulted indicate that the lakes Manyara and Natron (although not neglected) were of limited interest to the surrounding peoples. This corresponds to the fact that both are soda lakes (Orr and Grantham 1931) and therefore of restricted utility for human consumption. The so-called *magadi*, a soda extraction, was apparently utilized only on a smaller scale in the tobacco manufacture and never attracted the large number of salt-gatherers interested in sodium chloride. There are, however, several references to *magadi* trade, and I shall mention some of these later.

From the Great Rift Valley, the salt from Lake Balangda in Mangati was reportedly well sought after, particularly by the Wataturu peoples who brought in into the trade in the form of small cones. They traded the salt for goats and sheep to the surrounding tribes, notably the Wambugwe and the Wafiome south of Lake Manyara (Baumann 1894:138, 246), and to the Watatoga (Kanneberg 1900a: 166). In his article on Turu country, Stadlbaur (1897) identified the Lingida, Gentai, Wassutu and Lalu lakes, and wrote that they were all being visited by the neighbouring peoples for the purpose of collecting edible salt. The Wanyaturu apparently traded salt from Singida lake to Ussure in Eastern Unyamwezi and to the Wassandaui (Baumann 1894:189). Most actively exploited was the Nyarasa (Eyasi) area, both the lake itself and the saline soils in the plains to the southwest of the lake. The neighbouring Waniramba and Wanissansu were said to find salt to cover their demands from this area. The major exploitation was undertaken by the Wasukuma people coming in on well-worn salt roads from the west (Baumann 1894:247). Nyarasa salt was apparently brought all over Sukumaland and to the peoples living on the eastern coast of Victoria Nyanza.

Senior (1938) gives an impression of what this traditional Sukuma salt transport from Lake Eyasi may have been like. The activity apparently gathered in all of Sukumaland up to 150 miles distance from the salt source. Each chiefdom had its *Mundeba* who made the trip to the salt lake several times and acted as manager and organizer of the caravans. Senior reported that the size of such caravans could range up to 300 men and women. He estimated that 'at least thirty thousand people make the journey to Nyaranja annually from the various areas of Shinyanga, Kwimba, Mwanza and Maswa districts . . . The amount of salt which is obtained annually is estimated to be about a thousand tons' (Senior 1938:88, 90).

Two roads were identified as leading from the west towards Lake Eyasi; a northern route existed over Kimali in Meatu and was used by people living in north and central Maswa, Kwimba and Mwanza; a southern route, used by people from southern Maswa and Shinyanga, led through Imala Seko on the Sanga River. The last 40 miles of the road was common to both caravans and led through uninhabited bush. This was an extremely strenuous walk, and Senior claimed that the men carried some 80 pounds of salt in addition to their food and water.

It had been the opinion of Baumann (1894:247) that the large salt deposits of Mangati and Nyarasa were poorly exploited and that no viable trade had developed from these areas. He thought that this situation had been largely caused by the hostility of the Masai and Wataturu peoples to the trading activities. I am inclined to think that the Sukuma salt trade may have been on the same scale as that which Senior reported for a considerable length of time. Sukumaland was clearly one of the most populous regions in Tanganyika before 1890. Given the overall population decline following 1890, it may be that the Wasukuma's demand for salt had not been greatly increased by the 1930s. Although Baumann in his map (1894) indicated Masai territory west of Lake Eyasi, it is difficult to believe that the Masai warriors could effectively have prevented the Wasukuma from obtaining one of their principal necessities of life from this area.

A more effective halt to the local exploitation of Rift Valley salt lakes was made with the proclamation of 4 June 1907 making salt-gathering from Lake Magadi and the surrounding lakes subject to government concession (*Die Landes-Gesetzgebung*, I:570).

Salt Springs

Salt extracted from the saline springs of East Africa seems to have contained fairly pure sodium chloride and to have been of superior taste and quality. This salt was accordingly highly appreciated and widely traded. It is no accident, therefore, that numerous people have taken an interest in the salt springs and that our knowledge about their exploitation is particularly rich.

The springs surrounding the Ruchugi and Malagarasi rivers in the Uvinza area have attracted special attention. This area was identified by Burton as the major centre of quality salt in the territory; the products of Uvinza being 'far superior to the bitter, nitrous produce of Ugogo' (Burton 1860, II:37). The Uvinza salt was accordingly traded over considerable distances, notably north to Victoria Nyanza and west to Lake Tanganyika. Baumann (1894:247) stated that Uvinza salt also went to Tabora, Manyema and Urundi.

About the technique of salt extraction at Uvinza, Fülleborn and Glauning had this to say:

> The salt brine is moved from the salt springs and filled into holes in the ground of 2·30 m diameter and 1·5 m deep. The brine rests there until a sufficient concentration has occurred. The brine is then boiled down in clay jars, the salt given a cylindrical shape, packed in leaves and tied up for marketing. Four such cylinders (called *vahiga*) will make an adequate load for a porter (Fülleborn and Glauning 1900:29).

The salt-boiling colony of the Wavinza was seen by Burton as comprising some 40–50 bee-hive huts constructed on the riverside. The specific reference was probably to the springs at Pwaga (Pawa) as claimed by Sutton and Roberts (1968), but it could have been to a number of the

23 brine springs that apparently are found in the area and were mapped by Haldemann (1958). Cameron (1877, I:234) mentioned temporary villages on both sides of the Ruchugi River. They were deserted at the time (February), undoubtedly because of the long rains which caused flooding in the rivers and put the brine springs under water. When Hauptmann Fonck visited the area in 1896, salt was produced at 7 of the springs. These were identified as Malahi, Kasenga and Pwaga on the Ruchugi River, Labundi (Labundusi), Iambutti, and Nodle on the Malagarasi River. In addition, preparations had been made to start salt-boiling at the Njansa spring where some 200 temporary huts were erected (Fonck 1897:100).

Recent research (Sutton and Roberts 1968) has demonstrated that some of the salt works in the area are of great antiquity and go back to the first millennium A. D. Sutton and Roberts concluded, however, that large-scale exploitation at Uvinza began only in the nineteenth century and was stimulated by growing population, agricultural expansion and the caravan trade. The exploitation was probably at its peak when the German administration took over the country. Lieutenant Ramsey, the first German administrator of Ujiji, found salt to be the town's most important trading article next to ivory and cottons. He estimated the annual production to have been as high as 500,000 vahiga of 25–30 pounds each. In the dry season, thousands of people would come from all directions to Uvinza to boil salt (Ramsey 1896:770). Another observer pointed out that the salt boilers were mostly temporary visitors who would stay in the area only as long as it was necessary to produce a full load of salt. Their stay gave occasion to a vivid trade in wood and foodstuffs. Each interested tribe could apparently boil as much salt as it desired, subject only to a tax in kind to the local chiefs (Leue 1901:63). Dantz found the well-populated areas above the Malagarasi Falls to merit the term *Industriegebiet*, but warned that his statement was not meant in a European, but in a more restricted African sense (Dantz 1902:70). Dantz estimated that 20,000 loads of 25 kilos each were taken from the salt works annually by the end of the century. By this time a military checkpoint (the *Ruchugiposten*) had been erected to enforce law and order and supervise the collection of taxes (in kind) which now went to the colonial administration. Fonck had led an expedition sent out from Ujiji to find out whether the Malagarasi River was navigable and offered possibilities for freighting the Uvinza salt to Lake Tanganyika. In 1903 the Uvinza salt-making ceased to be an African enterprise when the Saline-Gottorp, a branch of the Centralafrikanische Seeengesellschaft was established. By 1905 the production had risen to 22,000 Zentner or 220 tons (Fuchs 1907:186). Vestiges of the traditional salt-making industry remained only in the packing unit which continued to be the *vahiga*, the palm-leaf package. Most of the production continued to go to Uha and Ujiji. Fuchs indicates that 1905 was a good year for the investors in Saline-Gottorp who made a five per cent profit on their shares (1907:186). By proclamation of 16 October 1906 the salt springs of Uvinza were made state property exploitable only by government concession (*Die Landes-Gesetzgebung* I:570).

Saliferous Soils

These salt deposits have generally the same origin as the salt lakes already discussed. Many of the deposits, like the Wembere plains in the Great Rift Valley, have been built up from lactations from volcanic rock. Saline soils can also result from extensive periods of grass-burning when the salts of plant ashes are brought together during the long rains and deposited on undrained flats in areas where clay layers prevent a deep penetration of the salt into the soil. When the water evaporates in the dry season, the salt will appear as a snowy crust on the sand. A third origin would be through the decomposition of salt-containing plants.

A simple chemical analysis can tell us whether the salts are derived from one or the other of these origins. A high presence of potassium and alkali carbonates would indicate a plant origin, whereas the presence of iodine and bromide would point to a marine origin. This difference would be of some importance to the taste quality of the product and eventually to its attractiveness as a trading article. Unfortunately, no such comprehensive analysis is currently available.

Saline soil apparently was the basis for the famous Ugogo salt works during the last century. Becker identified Zingeh in Ugogo as a centre of salt extraction from the soil (Becker 1887, I:448). Burton mentioned Tubugwe east of Mpwapwa and Kanyenye in central Ugogo as important centres; the latter was identified as the origin of the best and cheapest products. This salt apparently played an important role in the territorial trade and Burton stated that 'no caravan ever passes through the country without investing capital in the salt-bitter substance which is gathered in the flakes efflorescing from the dried mud upon the surface of the Mbuga, or swampy hollows' (Burton 1860 I:308). The salt apparently went mostly to western Usagara and to eastern Unyamwezi. This initiative was confirmed by Cameron (1877, I:106) who found the area of Kanyenye to be extensively cultivated with numerous *tembes* spread throughout the countryside.

Arning, writing about the Wahehe, saw the Hehe expansion into Gogo country under chief Mahinja in the 1880s as having some well-defined economic objectives, one of which was to gain control of the Ugogo salt production. The other objectives were to take over Gogo cattle, and to gain control over the central (Ujiji—Bagamoyo) trade route (Arning 1897). By the end of the German period in Tanganyika, the Wagogo produced no salt and imported the required quantities from Lake Balangda south of Mt. Hanang (Scholz 1913).

Salt from saliferous soils was apparently also produced in Uvinza. Cameron visited an area bordering the Lugowa River, one of the tributaries to the Malagarasi east of Ruchugi, where a quite diversified technique of lactation had been developed by 1874.

> A quantity of mud is placed in a trough having at the bottom a square hole partially stopped with shreds of bark, beneath which about half-a-dozen similar vessels are placed, the upper one only containing mud. Hot water is then poured into this topmost trough to dissolve the salt with which the mud is impregnated, and the liquid being filtered by passing through the bark in the holes of the lower troughs, runs out of the bottom one nearly clear.
>
> It is then boiled and evaporated, leaving as a sediment a very good white salt, the best of any I have seen in Africa. If the first boiling does not produce a sufficiently pure salt, it is again dissolved and filtered until the requisite purity is attained (Cameron 1877, I:232).

Even at Uvinza, Leue claimed that saline soils were occasionally added to the spring brine to enhance the salt content (Leue 1901:63).

In Unyamwezi, lactation of saline soil was extensively practised, according to Paul Fuchs (1907:115), who observed the technique in the districts of Ulungwa, Uschyetu, Ubagwe, Luwumbo, and Ussika. An important centre of such production was the 12 kilometre middle section of the *Mongo qua munhu* (salt river) flowing into the Ngombe River northwest of Tabora. Hauptmann Herrmann felt justified in writing about these undertakings as having a fully industrial character. The production took place in the dry season when people from the neighbouring communities collected the saline crusts of the previously flooded areas. This crust was later dissolved, purified and again concentrated over fire. Salt production was reported to be one of the mainstays of prosperity in the district but was running into difficulties 'in this thickly populated and deforested region' (Herrmann 1908:21). Salt from *Mongo qua munhu* satisfied most of the demands of Unyamwezi, including that of Tabora town with its sprawling population of 40,000 people.

During his geological expedition to the *Schutzgebiet* in 1897, Bergassessor Dantz identified some of the major salt-producing areas in Uha. He found numerous salt villages in northern Kibondo close to the eastern reaches of the Malagarasi bend, and judged them to be of particular importance to the populous communities of Uha and Ruanda. Several salt centres were also encountered in the district of Makena in Kihumbi. Finally, Dantz mentioned the south-western edges of the

Kimueni (Kamueni) plains with the salines of the Nyakaro village 'where numerous Warundi arrive for salt boiling after 8 to 10 days' journey from their homes' (Dantz 1902:147). Pater Capus had written earlier from the same vicinity about 'a large population exclusively occupied by salt making' (Capus 1898:185).

According to Dantz and Capus, saline sands mixed with plant ashes were collected and placed in open baskets half filled with grass for filtration. Boiling water was poured over the contents which dissolved and were collected in large clay jars. The brine was later boiled down over fire and a good but somewhat dirty salt was produced. The use of plant ashes in addition to saline soil in Uha was confirmed by Fuchs (1907:176, see also Grant 1925) who observed a large degree of specialization among the Uha salt-boilers. Fully dependent on their trade, they exchanged their product for foodstuffs among the neighbouring peoples. Fuchs described Uha as a thickly populated area where the salt demand accordingly may have been considerable.

Dantz was reluctant to give an estimate of the annual salt production of the Uha villages. He stated, however, that 'by local standards, the production is not unimportant' (Dantz 1902:147). People would come from far away places, even from Urundi, in order to boil salt in these areas. They would stay for around 14 days and return to their homes heavily loaded with the precious commodity.

Saline soils were apparently also exploited in several places in the northern and eastern parts of the country. Close to the volcano Oldonjo Lengai to the south of Lake Natron, Masai people were reported to produce the so-called *magadi* from the soils. Fischer claimed that this article was traded both in Masailand and on the coast. In the Pangani valley, the *magadi* apparently fetched a very high price (Fischer 1884:85). Krapf described a similar trading article among the Wachagga obtained on the Taveta market. This was the so-called *emballa*, 'a kind of earth which they dissolve in water using the liquor for admixture with their food instead of salt, which they have not' (Krapf 1860:245). The origin of this article was the Kahe plains south of Kilimanjaro. By 1890, direct utilization of the saline soils had been replaced in Kahe by techniques of lactation, purification and concentration similar to what has already been discussed. Baumann observed this production and stated that the finished product was packed in banana leaves and traded to the neighbouring peoples, particularly to the Wapare who sent small caravans to Kahe to obtain the soda/salt extraction (Baumann 1894:249).

Related areas of salt-making have been identified in the Pangani Valley at Ugweno and at Mombo along the Mkomazi River (Fischer 1884:44,212). Popplewell described a salt site operated at Makayo village, normally a poor homestead of some 10 families, situated one mile south of Lake Kalamba on the Mkomazi River. The salt flats in the neighbourhood attracted people from the surrounding communities during the 2–3 months' dry season when no cultivation took place. In this period Makoyo village came to life. It was 'crowded with Wapare and Wasambaa, totalling sometimes two hundred men, women and children' (Popplewell 1939:102). The salt flats were apparently regarded as no-man's land, and people from the surrounding tribes were attracted to them. The salt production was mostly brought home by the salt-boilers themselves, but some salt was also sold on the spot where a thriving temporary market—the so-called *gulios*—sprang up attracting traders of foodstuffs to the salt works. We can imagine similar scenes of multiplying activities played out in the other salt centres we have discussed in this survey.

Southern Tanganyika was largely supplied with salt from plant ashes (see next section). At least two centres of salt extraction from saliferous soils have been of considerable economic importance, however, extending beyond family production to the territorial trading network. One such place is Ivuna, immediately south of Lake Rukwa. The water of Lake Rukwa has a high soda content and was accordingly exploited only on a limited scale. It was not used as cooking salt, according to Wallace (1899), but a soda extraction from the lake was added to the locally grown tobacco as a spice. The tobacco, in turn, was widely traded.

The nearby springs of Ivuna provided high quality salt for cooking and eating purposes. The trading circuit of the Ivuna salt was considerable, as the closest comparable saltwork is reported to have been 250 miles away (Spence 1957). We have some indication of the vast dimensions of these salt works in Spence's estimate that some 15 million cubic feet of earth had been removed from the depression surrounding the spring site. Some of this volume had been moved several times, thus multiplying the earth works carried out over the centuries.

When Spence made his observations in the 1950s, only the local people made use of the salt in the form of a strong brine. He found that 'the natives now inhabiting the area are not familiar with the method of obtaining salt by leaching the saline crust and evaporating the brine by boiling' (Spence 1957:27). Excavation had stopped a considerable time ago, and Spence thought it likely that the change in the method of salt-making had occurred with a change of population, during which, supposedly, the art of salt-making had disappeared.

It seems more likely that the disappearance of the production of crystalline salt at Ivuna was directly linked to changes in market and trading relations. Fagan and Yellen have documented the continuous occupation of the Ivuna site by the Iwanda chiefs since the mid-eighteenth century. They also claim that the pans were extensively worked during the nineteenth century when peoples from Nyiha, Nyamwanga, Kuulwe, Wanda, and Bungu tribes 'used to come to the pans to extract salt' (Fagan and Yellen 1968:30). In the beginning of this century, Ivuna salt was still traded to Tukuyu some 100 miles away. Contrary to Spence, Fagan and Yellen claimed that the salt-producing techniques are well remembered by the local people. They reveal that brine was traditionally used for home consumption, whereas evaporation over fire was the standard method for producing salt intended for distant markets. The decline of Ivuna thus seems to fall within the general pattern outlined in this study and is directly related to the decline in population and the stagnation of economic exploits starting with the ecological disaster of the 1890s.

Another centre of great importance is Masasi, where a mission station was founded in 1880, undoubtedly in recognition of the importance of the area. Salt had apparently been produced at this place by the Makua people for a considerable time. The industry was probably of some consequence by the time the Ngoni peoples moved in to establish their hegemony in southern Tanganyika with Songea as the centre. Unlike other peoples who were directly and forcefully incorporated into the Ngoni society and moved out of their old tribal areas, the salt-makers of Masasi were left alone to continue their industry. A system of salt tribute to the Ngoni (Magwangwara) overlords was instituted, however (Lieder 1897:119).

Bornhardt later described the Masasi salt production as 'not unimportant for central-African conditions' (Bornhardt 1900:40). According to him, Masasi salt was traded to the Mozambique side of the Ruvuma River as well as along the river towards Lake Nyassa. Since iron was also produced in the area, it is clear that Masasi must have been an important centre on the main southern trading route. This was the contention of Lieder who compared Masasi's position to that of Kondoa in Usagara for the central (Tabora-Bagamoyo) caravan road (Lieder 1897:119).

Plant Ashes

Whereas saline soils of marine or volcanic origin are found primarily in a steppe environment, salt/potash from plant ashes is normally produced in areas of high rains where little natural concentration of salt would take place in the soil. Traditionally this type of salt production took place in the southern and western parts of Tanganyika. These areas connect with a wider region of plant-ash salts that covers practically all of Malawi, Zambia, Zaire, Gabon, Camerun and Chad (Springer 1918). Stuhlmann (1910:49), on the basis of linguistic evidence, stated the view that plant-ash salt was the original salt product of most Bantu peoples.

Trial and error had provided the various peoples with comprehensive knowledge of the most saline plants in their areas. Thus, Fülleborn (1906:114–15) mentions the use of *Pistia Stratiotes* in southern Tanganyika. Stuhlmann (1910:48) added papyrus and bulrush (*Cypreus alternifolius*), probably from the central and north-western parts of the country. Springer (1918:35) listed water plants like *Vallisneria* and *Patamogeton* as the plants most frequently used in the salt production in Africa generally. Further research in this area would undoubtedly confirm the impression that the plant selection was stratified and in accordance with a plant science of important dimensions.

The technique of production was relatively simple: plants were burnt and their ashes collected. Salt or potash was later extracted from the plant ashes in a waterbath. The resulting brine could either be used directly in the household cooking or be concentrated over fire to crystalline form. The latter technique was used for plant-ash salt entering the territorial trade. This salt would have a strong alkali content (alkali carbonate) and contain very little calcium chloride. An excessive carbonate content would give the salt a bitter taste.

The practice of extracting salt from plant ashes seems to have been widely distributed, but to have given rise to only limited industrial exploitation. As we have seen earlier, this does not exclude the plant origin of some of the saliferous soils exploited in Tanganyika where salt concentration arose as an incidental by-product of major grass burnings taking place over long periods of time. I am dealing here with the cutting and burning of grass for the specific purpose of salt production. This seems to have been a household industry throughout Tanganyika, and may have been retained as a craft into the late nineteenth century only where better quality salt could not be obtained through trade. In many instances, this production went together with the extraction of salt from saliferous soils. Thus, Fülleborn commented that the Konde (Nyakyusa) people extracted their salt from soil as well as from plant ashes (Fülleborn 1906:374). Also the Hehe, Sangu and Bena peoples were reported to gain their salt from plant ashes. In Ubena and Ussangu, Fülleborn wrote of salt extraction as a small-scale industry (*Kleinindustri*) leading to the exchange of Kinga iron against Ubena salt (Fülleborn 1906:253).

An interesting detail is that the plant-ash salt, which is largely composed of potash, may not, in some instances, have been produced purely for salt purposes, but as raw material for soap-manufacturing. Thus, Stuhlmann (1910:49) wrote that a very coarse soap was produced with the help of potash, animal fats or palm-oil in Tabora and along Lake Tanganyika. The soap entered the trade as balls of a grey substance. It was called *kifewe* in distinction to the imported soap which was known under the Arabic name of *sabuni*.

Sea Salt and Salt Imports

The seemingly rich opportunities for salt extraction from sea water were reportedly not extensively utilized in the pre-colonial period. Such exploitation depends for its success on favourable rain averages, high temperature, low moisture, and the presence of natural flats close to the seashore that can be utilized for the evaporation. Reviewing these factors, Springer (1918, see also Stuhlmann 1910) concluded that conditions on the East African coast were naturally unfavourable for solar pans. This, Springer felt, explained what he claimed to be a total absence of solar works north of the Rufiji delta. Today, these supposedly insurmountable obstacles have been successfully overcome, as the string of solar pans at Dar es Salaam, Bagamoyo, Tanga, etc., indicates.

Springer did not address himself to the influence of foreign trade as a possible disincentive for salt production on the east coast. We should in this connection notice that the Rufiji delta was traditionally the centre of the important freight of *boriti*, the straight round-barked mangrove poles of 18-to-24-feet length that went into the floor construction of the multi-storied houses in Southern Arabia (Grant 1939). When the Sultan of Zanzibar claimed sovereignty over the east coast, the dhow skippers from Arabia retained their age-old privilege of free exploitation of the delta forests.

In 1895, Bornhardt (1900:381) found the coastal areas of the *Schutzgebiet* inundated with salt from Arabia, Persia and northwestern India (Kutch), and linked this abundance of salt directly to the *boriti* trade. As the dhow captains were mostly interested in the timber freight, salt was taken to East Africa as ballast. The cost of freight was accordingly negligible, and the price of imported salt could approach dumping levels. Bornhardt felt that local salt works could only be given a fighting chance when protected behind high tariff walls. Besides the economic arguments against such protection, he thought that the Congo Agreements of the Berlin Conference had put the prestige of international law against any such protective devices.

The salt trade was not new, as can be seen from Burton's remarks about the extensive imports from Arabia during his visit to Zanzibar in the 1850s. Nevertheless, Burton thought that the coastal communities were largely self-sufficient with the commodity:

> On the coast the principal ports and towns supply themselves with sea-salt evaporated in the rudest way. Pits sunk near the numerous lagoons and

backwaters allow the saline particles to infiltrate; the contents, then placed in a pierced earthen pot, are allowed to strain into a second beneath. They are inspissated by boiling, and are finally dried in the sun, when the mass assumes the form of sand (Burton 1860, II:402).

Burton was probably correct, and Springer's explanation of the absence of solar works is not tenable. Between the two writers lie some six decades of foreign trading influence on a budding local initiative which in the end was wiped out. Springer's 'scientific explanation' finally buried it. It ought to be an urgent task for further research to restore more fully our knowledge of the early salt works on the east coast and detail their reaction to the growing salt importation towards the end of the nineteenth century. Such investigation might start out with Tangata, south of Tanga town where the Wadigo traditionally extracted salt in solar pans. Before the arrival of the Europeans a brisk trade existed when the Wasambaa of the Usambara Mountains went to Tangata to barter their bananas and maize against the Wadigo salt. Krapf (1860:416) indicated a type of Sambaa sovereignty over the port of Tangata where exports were taxed in co-operation with the Sultan of Zanzibar. The salt works of Tangata were still alive in the 1930s, although the Wasambaa had ceased to trade there by that time (Popplewell 1939).

South of the Rufiji delta several places have been identified as operating solar pans. Bornhardt (1900:382) wrote about salt pans at the Danyanga River 'and on many other coastal points'. He did not further identify the localities. Salt works apparently existed in the Kiswere Creek (Lieder 1897:141–42). Otto Peiper (1926:34–35) described in detail the production technique in use in this area, and added the tidal flats surrounding the Matandu River as a further site of solar evaporation of sea water in the south. I have found no reference to the size of this production and to whether it served the locality or went beyond it to enter a wider trading network. It is likely that the salt to some extent was brought inland along major rivers and caravan routes. Thus, Joseph Thomson, who crossed the Rufiji some 70–80 miles from the coast was told that 'canoes capable of carrying twenty men frequently arrived from the coast with salt to barter for gum-copal and rubber' (Thomson 1881, I:126). We do not know, however, if Thomson referred to salt made on the coast, or whether he skirted the limits of penetration of the salt imported from the Arabian gulf.

COTTON WEAVING

According to Decken, cotton-weaving was the only important handicraft in Zanzibar in the 1850s. Weaving was carried out in the open air and could readily be inspected along the sidewalks of town. Only a coarse cloth was produced, and the industry was rapidly fading owing to increased competition from imported fabrics of American, European and Indian origin (Decken, 1869, I:84). Decken's short account contains the essentials of the history of indigenous cotton production in the nineteenth and twentieth centuries. Scenes of spinning and weaving were recounted over and over again by travellers from different parts of the country. The techniques of production were apparently very similar and so was the finished product. Throughout the area, the industry faced a common threat which should eventually lead to its demise: the competition of foreign textiles disseminated through the expanding network of trade. We shall review some of the material covering the textile initiative in Tanganyika and assess the dimensions of this craft and its geographical locations.

The coastal areas had been first to receive the cotton plant (*Gossypium herbacium*) which—apart from the American variations—seems to have spread from a South Asian source where it was first cultivated (Engler 1895). Stuhlmann thought that cotton had reached the East African coast between the tenth and the fourteenth centuries through the Persian (Shirazi) settlers who built Mogadishu and Kilwa and extended their influence as far south as Sofala. Part of the evidence for this is derived from linguistics where the Persian word *pambak* or *pampa*—meaning a bush carrying wool for clothing—is seen as the origin of the Swahili word for cotton: *pamba* (Stuhlmann 1909:503). Strandes identified Mogadishu, Pate, and Kerimba Island south of Cabo Delgado and its coastal hinterlands as important centres of cotton-weaving at the time of the first Portuguese contacts in 1498. 'There is plenty of evidence' he wrote, 'that spinning and weaving were practised in earlier times along the whole stretch of the coast as far to the south as Sofala' (Strandes 1899:91).

The stone spindles excavated at Kilwa were thought to hail from this early hey-day of cotton production on the East African coast (Stuhlmann 1910:40). This has been confirmed by Chittick, who dated the rich finds of spindle whorls in a recent excavation to the period between the tenth and the sixteenth centuries. These finds indicated a 'great development in the manufacture of cloth, probably cotton' (Chittick 1966:14). From the coast, cotton-manufacturing penetrated inland where the industry started to blossom at a time when the basis of trading relations with the external world was changing from luxury goods for a small elite to mass production intended for the largest possible buying public. Large quantities of foreign fabrics began to appear on the coast and to undermine the indigenous production there. This new type of imports followed the development of mass production in India around 1840 when also machine-produced textiles from Europe and America sought a market in East Africa. Decken predicted the outcome of this trade; later observers confirmed the effect. 'It will not take long before these (home-made) textiles become ethnographical rarities', wrote Franz Stuhlmann (1909:508).

Cotton-manufacturing had not been fully established throughout East Africa at the beginning of the colonial period. In many areas bark-cloth and skins as well as grass and raffia (palm-leaf fibre) fabrics prevailed for clothing purposes. The production of these fabrics was developed to high levels of sophistication as described by Kimwani (1951), Richter (1900a) and Stuhlmann (1909, 1910). Skins and bark-cloth satisfied the local demands in many places, and even on the coast (Tanga) people continued to wear skins in the 1850s according to Krapf (1860). Schurtz (1900) shows, however, a photograph of a 'Waswahili at the Loom' taken at an unidentified location on the east coast. In other areas, neither practical necessity nor moral inhibition introduced through alien religious influences stimulated the production of clothing. Thus, Stuhlmann wrote about the Turu people as covered with beads and bracelets for purposes of decoration rather than out of concern for covering the body (Stuhlmann 1910:38).

Hans Meyer (1909) published a map showing the areas of Tanganyika where locally manufactured cottons were found by the Germans. The data on which the map was based probably derived from the survey undertaken by the German administration in 1901 to ascertain the types of cotton grown and their location (Stuhlmann 1909:508). This was part of an effort to reassess the possibilities for a viable cotton industry in the territory after the disappointing results of 1895–1900. The map shows local cotton-manufacturing south of Kilwa on the east coast, along the Ruvuma River westwards to Lake Nyassa, and in a broad corridor stretching between lakes Nyassa and Tanganyika northwards to Victoria Nyanza. It is likely that the southwestern boundaries of these areas joined neighbouring districts in Mozambique, Malawi, Zambia and Zaire to complete a region of dissemination of the cotton plant as well as techniques of spinning and weaving from entry points on the east coast. We can link this information to the area of the so-called Fixed Heddle Loom which extended roughly from the Mediterranean to the Zambezi River (Ling Roth 1934:63). The observation provided by Fülleborn (1906:511) that in southern Tanganyika the art of weaving was unknown only to the Ngoni people of Songea seems to confirm a southern limit to the area of dissemination. The Wangoni moved into this cotton-manufacturing region from the south and apparently failed to adopt the techniques established there before their arrival.

According to Richard Burton, cotton was abundant in the interior of Tanganyika where looms could be found in every village (1860, I:318). He thought that the East African climate and soil were well suited to cotton-growing and found the quality to be excellent and the specimen to 'rival in fineness, firmness and weight the medium staple cotton of the New World' (1860, II:417). While Burton thus judged the raw material to be of good quality, he had less flattering comments about the manufacturing skills encountered: 'The loose texture of his (the East African's) own produce admits wind and rain', Burton wrote, 'when dry it is rough and unpleasant, when wet heavy, comfortless as leather, and it cannot look clean, as it is never bleached' (1860, II:311). Burton suggested that the relatively poor quality of the locally manufactured material caused an easy preference for imported textiles once these became available in the interior.

Baumann continued the story from Mwanza in the 1890s. A strong black and yellow striped fabric was manufactured in this area and was worn by most people in Sukumaland. This fabric had previously been produced in large quantities throughout Unyamwezi when imported cottons started to be carried up from the coast. Manufacturing of the local material had almost completely stopped in southern Unyamwezi by 1890, and was at the time of Baumann's expedition confined almost entirely to Usukuma (Baumann 1894:232).

Spinning and weaving were also well known throughout Iramba and Ijambi. Whereas the men preferred imported cottons (kaniki) the women were almost all dressed in their traditional costume, a shirt-like garment (kisole) made from locally woven cotton and decorated with glass beads. The hand-spindle was widely used, and weaving was undertaken by people who had made this their trade speciality (Jäger 1913:69). Another report of some interest comes from Bukoba where Richter (1900a:126) stated that the Wahaya had recently learnt the weaving technique from the Wanyamwezi and that entirely new clothing patterns were emerging in the district.

Extensive cotton-growing took place along the east coast of Lake Tanganyika according to Livingstone (1874) and Cameron (1877). As the water level of the lake was something like 20 feet higher in the 1870s than it is today, the cotton fields were not on the flats now bordering the lakeshore, but in the rolling hills and slopes several miles away from the present lake. Livingstone observed:

A very great deal of cotton is cultivated all along the shores of lake Tanganyika; it is the Pernambuco kind, with the seeds clinging together, but of good and long fibre, and the trees are left standing all the year to enable them to become large; grain and ground-nuts are cultivated between them. The cotton is manufactured into coarse cloth, which is the general clothing of all (Livingstone 1874, II:239).

Livingstone had previously seen cotton-growing among the Wafipa, but he had judged their weaving industry to be a dying one. 'Much cloth was made in these parts before the Mazitu (Ngoni) raids began', he wrote, 'it was striped black and white, and many shawls are seen in the country yet' (Livingstone 1874, I:207). Some years later, Joseph Thomson reported extensive cotton-growing and the existence of a small-scale cotton industry among the Wanyiha in the Rukwa Valley. The Wanyiha lived in stockaded villages and wore loincloth of rough home-made cottons said to resemble coarse sacking (Thomson 1881:285). There were two to three looms in every village according to Kerr-Cross (1891). Wallace gives us the following account of cotton production in the Rukwa Valley:

Except the growing of food, the only industry of the people round Rukwa is the making of cloth. In most villages, and especially in those of the Afipa and Awanda, a large portion of the men are engaged in this work, either spinning the cotton or weaving the cloth . . . The men do all the spinning and weaving, using a long spindled spool, and giving the necessary twirl by a smart rub of the spindle between the palm of the hand and the thigh. The loom is a rough frame so arranged that the alternate threads can be raised or lowered past the rest, and cross threads are then passed through on a long wooden lath. The cloth is open and heavy, but strong and much more durable than the cheap calico and coloured prints which are rapidly taking its place. The commonest patterns are white with black striped borders, though checks and black cloths are seen. It is generally made in pieces of about 6 feet by 5, each cloth being sufficient for a dress. All the men and women round Rukwa wear them, but I think there are few now exported, for just to the south on the plateau European calicoes are worn, and a little further south, the Babemba are dressed in bark cloth. A portion is traded to the Afipa on the plateau for iron hoes, and a small quantity even now gets as far as the Mweru marsh for the purchase of salt (Wallace 1899:613).

While cotton weaving thus survived the Ngoni invasion of the area, a more serious challenge followed the entry of imported fabrics into the Rukwa valley. Under this impact 'the cotton industry disappears more and more', Fromm concluded (1912:86) 'and the time is not distant when a *serketa* will become a rarity'. The Rukwa cotton industry defied extinction largely through the patronage of the Christian missions in the area (Lechaptois 1913). It had a temporary come-back during the Second World War when its revival was sponsored by the colonial administration as part of the self-sufficiency efforts of the war economy *(Sumbawanga [Ufipa] District Book).*

SUMMARY

The impression emerging from this chapter is one of industrial agencies in various stages of development, mostly aligning themselves to the expansive course that I have suggested as a general characteristic of the local economies until sometime in the 1890s. Most consequential for our purposes is the iron industry which was widespread and showed a high degree of sophistication and versatility in the smelting techniques and forging. I have pointed to important signs of local division of labour between industrial villages and communities specializing in agricultural pursuits. In this division we may have an important clue to surplus production and novel agricultural techniques discussed in Chapter 2.

One common feature that is reflected in all three industries is the destructive impact of competing commodities entering Tanganyika through the aggressively expanding world trading networks. The graded impact of these imports can best be followed in our discussion of the cotton industry. Here we have seen that an indigenous expansion was still in progress in the interior at a time when the final demise of the industry was fast approaching from the coast in the form of commodities.

I have also mentioned some interesting efforts to revive pre-colonial industries. These efforts merit further investigation. To some extent they reflected the developmental ideas of Christian missions or the eccentric interests of local administrators. But they must also be related to systemic requirements of the colonial economy. Increasingly after 1890 this alien rationale oriented all economic agencies in East Africa and must be brought in to explain changes even at the periphery of the system.

Throughout this discussion, I have stressed quantitative features of the industries to show that the production in the pre-colonial period took place in response to large indigenous demands, that numerous people were involved in these enterprises and that commodities circulated over considerable distances despite the sole reliance on human porterage. It is to the indigenous forms of exchange that we shall now turn our attention.

CHAPTER 6

Markets and Trading Networks

A number of recent studies have pursued the African initiative in marketing and trade (Bohannan and Dalton 1962, Gray and Birmingham eds. 1970, Good 1970, and Hodder and Ukwu 1969). Several disciplines have contributed to build explanatory models of markets in Africa and to bring together empirical data on trading operations in historic times. Unfortunately, in this field there is still little agreement among the authorities, and the case for the African agency is by no means unanimously accepted.

Two contrasting theories of market origin and the spread of trade can be identified. Most of the existing literature falls into either of these. One theory sees the market formation as the outcome of an indigenous polyfocal process, starting with the individual's or group's economic needs and self-interests, and developing through barter in local markets to become externalized and connected to neighbouring peoples via transport operations and regional trading. Features of such a theory will readily be recognized in this chapter.

A second theory sees markets and trade as being implanted in marketless societies through a diffusion process of external origin. Thus, markets in Africa are not held to the *origins* of long-distance trading but rather its *results*. According to Hodder (1965:104), 'the bulk of traditional markets in Subsaharan Africa received their initial stimulus from external, long-distance trading contacts'. Market developments are relatively late occurrences in this model, although the diffusionists are in possession of a theory of infinite regressions and can, when challenged, move to more and more distant contact points for what they can see as the original external impulse leading to trading developments. East Africa has received relatively little attention in research on African trading initiatives, and the tendency has until recently been to endorse Polly Hill's verdict (1963:447) that a marketless eastern half of the continent, in contrast to pre-colonial markets and trade in many parts of West Africa, is 'one of the great geographical dichotomies of Africa'.

A very similar debate on the presence of indigenous markets and trade in pre-colonial Africa—including many parts of East Africa—was settled in favour of the indigenous market agency by Fröhlich (1940) nearly forty years ago. His pioneering work refuted the prevailing notions of closed subsistence economies without trace of markets and trade and built up the case for an indigenous trading development long before colonial contacts had taken place. He also showed that value-loaded concepts and definitions (accommodating the profit motive) often blinded European researchers to the economic agencies of non-European peoples.

Fröhlich's thesis was built on a massive compilation of anthropological material from numerous tribes across the African continent, supplemented by travellers' accounts from the same areas. To this material is now being added the emerging archaeological evidence that confirms the movement of commodities over large distances as part of the cultural totality of the continent dating back to the early iron age. In a review which includes parts of Tanganyika in its source-material, Fagan has claimed that the demands of metallurgists and farmers led to 'contacts between communities living up to several hundred miles apart . . . (and) developed into complicated barter networks extending over enormous areas' (Fagan 1970:37).

Thus, an early African agency seems to be reaffirmed. Later trading impulses—notably the nineteenth-century arrival of overseas initiatives—could build on a ready framework of commodities and routes as well as on a psychology of enterprise growing out of the local situation of economic change. Local and regional trade, particularly in iron and salt, is uniformly seen by recent researchers (Roberts 1970; St. John 1970; and Tosh 1970) as the basis of commercial expansion in the nineteenth century. This chapter will pursue a similar line of thinking. The task here will be to assess the indigenous basis of the late nineteenth-century caravan trade. I shall discuss a number of features of the local food market and insist on its antiquity and indigenous origins. From it developed border markets between neighbouring peoples and special provisioning stations for the caravan trade. Secondly, I shall outline the regional commodity trade and pay special attention to it as a reflection of functional specificity in the nineteenth-century economies.

LOCAL MARKETS

Little concrete information about market institutions has emerged in previous chapters. References to trading have, however, been numerous. This does not reflect an absence of structured marketing conditions, but rather the relative smallness of the markets, which may account for the cursory treatment by many early travellers. It seems also that a number of specialized commodities were traded directly between the particular craftsman and the interested buyer, thus moving the transaction even further out of sight of the passing explorer.

References to local markets are general and add up to a fairly consistent impression of a widespread organizational pattern. 'Foodmarkets are found at known localities all over Pare', wrote Baumann (1891:236). From the western parts of the country where market places could be seen scattered over the entire territories of Ujiji and Urundi, Hore characterized them as 'essentially a native institution' (Hore 1892:70). Grant (1925) indicated the existence of thirty traditional markets in the chiefdom of Heru in Uha, but gave no further information on their character and scope. Karl Peters regarded local trade around Victoria Nyanza as a highly significant activity that 'defies all direct calculation' (Peters 1891:191–92).

According to Fröhlich (1940:238–239), the original African market-system was characterized by: exchange as an intertribal or inter-group performance, exchange of basic food-stuffs and commodities of everyday use, women as the operating market agents, a fixed locality and time sequence (periodicity) and a series of rules and customs regulating market behaviour. The importance of the market in pre-colonial exchange seems to have been grossly under-rated and fresh research to restore the market to its proper place is clearly needed. Uzoigwe's work (1970) from Bunyoro-Kitara in Uganda has commenced the reassessment with a rejection of the idea of a marketless region and the documentation of oral traditions of numerous smaller markets in the district. Similarly, researchers among the Wasambaa (Feierman 1970) and among the Wapare (Kimambo 1969) have stressed oral information testifying to the great antiquity of markets in the two areas. It is likely that fuller evidence of the role of market institutions in the pre-colonial economies will come to light as researchers address themselves more systematically to this problem without the preconceived limits of a diffusionist model.

A fairly comprehensive analysis of one traditional Tanganyikan market system exists for the Wachagga whose experience is probably representative of a number of local situations throughout the territory. In order to gain some understanding of this institution in the local economy, we shall review some of the central observations on the Chagga markets and the impact of the colonial administration on them. Finally, I shall take up the issue of market periodicity and the problem of market origins.

The Women's Food Market

An important feature of the traditional market was its lack of the middle-man element, an element which most European observers would regard as central in any marketing operation. To the European, the middleman assures 'rationality' to the operation and provides it with what researchers (Bohannan and Dalton 1962) have called 'the market principle', i.e. the profit motive. The importance of the traditional market rested, however, in the fact that women met as partners in a total economy to equalize, through exchange, the differences arising from individual production methods. In addition, the exchange provided variety in the diet and disposed of perishable surpluses. Thus, the traditional food market was oriented to distribution, not to profit.

As Gutmann explains it, the market was an institution through which the main features of the communal household could be maintained after collective economic exploitation had been replaced by individualized forms (Gutmann 1926:426). The origin of markets thus clearly relates to structural changes in the mode of production and would seem to be primarily connected with agricultural changes such as we have discussed in Chapter 2. We know that developmental situations similar to those found among the Wachagga existed in several other areas of Tanganyika, and it is possible that the food market was a general and original phenomenon occurring throughout the more advanced agricultural systems of East Africa. We may conclude with Fröhlich that the old market system coincided with the extension of the hoe culture (Fröhlich 1940:306) and possibly formed the nuclei for early exchanges with representatives of other economies or ecological zones such as herdsmen, hunters-and-gatherers, etc.

One of the earliest reports from the Chagga markets comes from Decken's visit in the 1850s. Only women took part in the market transactions, and Decken reported crowds of 400–500 in one such *sangara*. Among the trading articles he noted clay pots, wooden bowls, bananas, beans, peas, sweet potatoes, milk, butter, fat, banana-wine, banana-flour, red earth for colouring purposes and *emballa*, the salty earth coming from Kahe (Decken 1869, I:300). Some of the articles traded were what I have previously identified as commodities (pots, bowls, salt and colour) and indicate that the 'food-market' describes a more diversified commerce than the model term seems to indicate.

Border Markets and Provisioning Stations

We can distinguish two additional developments in Chaggaland externalizing the marketing activity and tying it in with other economic zones and with the coastal trading network. Meyer (1900:186–187) recorded periodic exchanges with the Masai in two border markets, one at Kobonoto with the Masai of Western Kilimanjaro, another at Useri with the Masai of Laitokitok to the east of the mountain. In both instances, markets were held every ten days and attended by women and children who brought the specialities of the two different economies together for exchange.

Another development resulted from the caravan traffic from the coast branching out from Taveta to circle Mount Kilimanjaro en route to Masailand. Taveta was the main provisioning station for these caravans and was in the 1880s a community of some 6,000 people, according to Johnston. It resembled Stanley Pool on the Congo, Dondo on the Quanza, and Khartoum on the Nile, he wrote; it was 'a rendezvous of tribes, tongues, peoples, and nations' (Johnston 1886:210). The impact of this caravan activity was felt among the Wachagga, where Volkens identified two contact points with the caravan routes (in Schira in West Kilimanjaro and at Useri and Kimangelia in the east) where local food markets had taken on features of supply stations (Volkens 1897:240).

Colonial Impact

The non-profit character of the early markets was clearly reflected in the market rules—enforced in Chaggaland by the women themselves through community sanctions. These rules were particularly directed against cheating on quality and volume and against efforts to inflate the exchange prices unilaterally. Gutmann maintained that this system disintegrated under colonial impact due to the ambiguous position of the chief under colonial administration. The chief had previously been the final market authority, but his position broke down and was redefined in colonial *regie*. The result of this change was that 'cheating and falsification of goods spread unhindered in the local markets. Since there is nothing to fear, such practices have taken over the entire market', wrote Gutmann (1926:428–29). 'Undiluted milk can simply not be bought any more.'

Gutmann saw this development as an example of the harm done by European justice and legal practices when introduced into an alien culture. He ridiculed the official stance that people could simply forward their complaints to the authorities and the culprits would be dealt with. The Chagga society did not respond to the new rules, and European justice in the end encouraged practices that quickly eroded the local market institution.

Gutmann pointed out that the colonial order also interfered more directly in the traditional market system when, in 1911, all markets between Marangu and Uru were closed and people were asked to take their produce to a new market centre next to the District Office at Old Moshi. An effective reduction of market-places followed. The longer distances imposed on the marketing activity probably resulted in a disincentive to barter and trade.

Periodicity

By relating the market phenomenon to changes in the mode of production, Gutmann gave the market agency a clearly indigenous origin. This point has been reinforced by studies of African time-concepts which are seen as economically oriented and derived from the local market systems (Fröhlich 1940; Hirschberg 1929). People would come together at fixed market places every 4, 6 or 8 days, depending on the number of such places in the local circuit. This phenomenon gave rise to a time-concept of varied and local nature: the African market-week (*Marktwoche*).

There are examples of a number of different weeks in East Africa. Thus, a four-day week has been reported among the Wakikuyu (Routledge 1910:105–6). Cameron (1877, II:3) reported the existence of a similar four-day week in Manyema in an area which for many years had been a centre of Arab-Muslim influence. From Chaggaland there are examples of a three-day market-week, which reflected the number of markets that could be visited by the local peoples. The days were given names to correspond to these markets: *latumo ja modschi* (market-day in Moshi), *laketela* (market-day in Tela), and *larindimma* (market-day in Kirua) (Fröhlich 1940:259). Eichhorn (1918–22) indicated a five-day week among the Wasambaa, where local markets co-existed with border-markets placed in the meeting ground with the Nyika who were of a different ecological zone. The Wabondei observed a four-day market week, according to Baumann (1891:128).

The examples of Bonde and Sambaa are particularly significant. Both territories lie at crossroads of the northern caravan routes and were probably under strong Christian and Muslim influences that centuries before had brought the seven-day week to the coast of East Africa. The market phenomenon may therefore have predated these external influences. Alternatively, external influences may have been too weak to cause changes in the economic life and organization even in the immediate hinterland of the foreign enclaves on the coast. Particular local market periodicities were in any event operating until the closing years of the nineteenth century, when the seven-day week gradually replaced the older time-concept of economic origin.

COMMODITY TRADE

In the previous chapter, we reviewed the iron-smelting and salt production in the pre-colonial period and located the major industrial centres. As we have seen, many of the peoples engaged in these enterprises were specialists foregoing other economic activities and preferring to barter for foodstuffs rather than grow them. The centre of industrial production accordingly attracted trade as neighbouring or more distant peoples sought to acquire the specialized commodities. Trade seems to have resulted even where the commodity production was seasonal. Thus, the salt-boiling at Uvinza apparently generated two types of supply trade. One group of local people would provide the large quantities of firewood needed for the boiling process; another group, identified by Fonck as people coming from the cattle- and grain-rich Uha, would arrive in 'endless caravans' loaded with foodstuffs to barter for salt. The profit motive was clearly present in this transaction, as one goat would fetch around 20 pounds of salt which could be resold for 2 goats in communities 6 to 8 days' journey away from Uvinza (Fonck 1910:289). The special status of the iron smelters in many communities points to an economic specialization of a similar kind. Some of them lived in close contact with peoples specializing in other types of production and exchanged commodities with them for reciprocal benefits.

It should in this connection be pointed out again that functional specificity was an important part of the pre-colonial economy. If the uneven distribution of certain raw materials like clay, iron, copper, or salt can be seen as the initial incentive for exchange, the development of the *fundi*, the master craftsman, heading guild-like units of artisans protected in their skills by magic and ritual, is another development connected with the specialized exchange economy. These particular masters would concentrate their efforts on the making of a few items, the execution of which would be carried to great perfection. We have given several examples of early explorers marvelling at the technical skills of these *fundi* who were repeatedly compared to the best of European craftsmen. There would be forgers of spears and arrow heads, and makers of shields, specialists in the making of bows and arrows, hoes and tools for field work and the cattle economy. There would be potters, basket weavers and cotton weavers, boat builders and specialists in the making of traps, fish-nets and sails, etc. New needs and opportunities created new types of *fundis*. The arrival of firearms and the need for their repair quite naturally led to the emergence of gunsmiths, wrote Fonck from central Tanganyika. He presented a photograph of a member of this new guild in his book (Fonck 1910:284).

I have stressed specialization and professionalism as part of an indigenous economic momentum. This created not only individual *fundis*, but associated entire tribes and villages with particular trades and handicrafts. To the long list of specialists mentioned above was added the professional elephant hunter, the *Makua*, in the middle years of the nineteenth century. This was a daring and flamboyant profession which fashioned its organization on the many guild-like creations of earlier crafts.

As the ivory hunter represents a continuation of a long tradition of professionalism, the ivory trade must be seen as an extension—not a replacement—of the regional commodity trade. While iron and salt may have been the original and most important trading articles, they by no means exhausted the range of pre-colonial commodity exchanges. As a back-drop to the Zanzibar trading initiative it is important to keep in mind just how extensive this regional commodity exchange continued to be throughout the nineteenth century. A quick look at the evidence seems in order.

Pottery

Since good clay is not found in every tribal community and its quality is most uneven throughout the country, the pottery industry—producing pombe-brewing vessels, saltboilers, household pots and pipe-heads—developed as an important speciality in certain villages and areas. Some of the best-known centres may have been those of the Wakisse on the northeastern side of Lake Nyassa (Fülleborn 1906:415), the Wakonongo (Diesing 1909), and the Wapare (Kälin 1945). Important finds of potsherds both in Uvinza and Ivuna (Fagan and Yellen 1968; Sutton and Roberts 1968) have indicated a close connection between the pottery industry and salt production, and have confirmed reports that the clay jars used for boiling were crushed to remove the crystallized salt. We can gauge the magnitude of the supporting pottery industry from Dantz' estimate (see p. 97) that 500,000 kilos of salt were produced annually in Uvinza in the last years of the nineteenth century.

Cattle

Insistence on the social value of cattle, particularly its position as an item of bride wealth, has overshadowed the commercial role of cattle and small stock in the pre-colonial economy. I have discussed some of these features in Chapter 3 where I have also documented a brisk cattle trade to the coastal areas in the latter part of the nineteenth century. Much of this trade was undoubtedly destined for the meat market of Zanzibar and the many trading centres that had grown up on the coast. Part of the trade was, however, in breeding-animals for the many cattle-keeping communities in the east that I have discussed previously. Suffice it here to indicate that nearly 200 head of cattle were looted from the village of Magogoni outside of Dar es Salaam in 1889 (see p. 189). This was apparently a well-established agricultural community, not a point of trans-shipment of beasts for the Zanzibar slaughter houses. When the Universities Mission attempted to utilize cattle in their transport operations towards Ujiji in 1876, it was the peasants of Sadani who delivered the bulk of the 126 oxen (Hore 1892) from areas that today are declared game reserves.

More important than the coast-bound cattle trade was the exchange taking place between cattle-keeping communities and areas of agricultural and industrial surpluses. Cattle were one of the major commodities traded by the Masai in exchange for Chagga spears (Meyer 1900:238) and grain from the Usambaras (Farler 1882:732), and were similarly used by the Masai in exchange for the iron products of the Usagara smiths (Beidelman 1962a). Wasukuma traders bought cattle among the Wafiome and Iraku peoples (Baumann 1894:178), and we have elsewhere documented an important cattle trade between Ruanda and Uha and Western Unyamwezi (see p. 66).

Donkeys

Donkeys were also traded, both of the Nyamwezi and the Masai breeds (Burton 1860, I:348, II:30; Baumann 1894:251). They were utilized in the caravan transport to move general commodities, but apparently not to carry ivory. A clue to their usefulness is given by Fischer (1884:50) who noted that coast-bound traders loaded their donkeys with *magadi*.

Tobacco

Tobacco has been mentioned in Chapter 2 as one of the spreading crops of the nineteenth century. This was a relatively recent addition to the crops of East Africa and very soon gained in popularity. It gave the impulse to an important manufacturing of pipes which Burton (1860, II:315) and Krapf (1860:114) had already commented on. Thomson praised the excellent quality of tobacco grown in Ukutu south of the Uluguru mountains. Here he met Nyamwezi traders buying up the 'soothing weed' with the intention of selling it in Ugogo and other places where tobacco was not then grown (Thomson 1881, I:163–164). Yao traders coming from the areas around Lake Nyassa marketed more than 11,000 pounds of tobacco in Lindi town between June and September 1890, according to Behr (1892:580). The consumers of this tobacco were Zanzibaris and coastal tribesmen who chewed, snuffed and smoked the *magadi*-soaked product.

Bananas

There is evidence from Kilimanjaro that the Chief of Kibosho organized a specialized trade in bananas to the communities to the east of the chiefdom in exchange for finger millet grown there (Volkens 1897:240).

Coffee

In Bukoba district, coffee developed as a popular trading article. It was grown in the area long before the introduction of the Robusta type which became the only cash crop of the area in later years. In the pre-colonial period coffee was chewed for its stimulating effects and was exported mostly to Karagwe and Uganda (Rehse 1910:79).

Fish

Despite food taboos in some tribal communities, it is likely that fish (dried or smoked) may have been a major item of a trade radiating from fishing communities around the great inland lakes and rivers. During his expedition to Songea in 1893, Tom von Prince observed this trade in the Ruhuhu Valley, where Wangoni from Songea were on their way to Lake Nyassa to buy fish—described as their favourite food. Also caravans of Wanyassa were observed arriving from the lake heavily loaded with fish which they intended to trade for grain among their easterly neighbours (Prince 1914:262). Dried fish (*daggaa*) from Lake Tanganyika was an important trading article in Ujiji (Hore 1892) and was also found on the Tabora market in the early 1890s (Stuhlmann 1894:64).

Grain

As we have seen in Chapter 2, most pre-colonial communities were self-sufficient in foodstuffs and even produced some surpluses beyond the subsistence diet. Barring crop failure there would therefore be a limited demand for regional trade in basic staples. Trade played, however, some part in alleviating occasional local shortages. Hore (1892:249), for instance, makes reference to Nyamwezi grains being carried to 'famine stricken Ugogo'. This was probably a normal occurrence when a rich and prosperous people like the Wagogo were hit by occasional drought and crop failure, and may reflect mechanisms in the pre-colonial economy for solving inter-regional food shortages. Food storage was, of course, widespread in all areas of seasonal cropping (see p. 137). More important is, however, Unomah's documentation (1972:6) of the development of central grain stores in certain parts of Unyamwezi. It is likely that these 'royal reserves' were capable of alleviating local as well as distant shortages when these did not coincide in time.

Another outlet for grain surpluses was found in the caravan trade where Ugogo can serve as an example. In normal years this region was capable of producing important grain surpluses which were traded to the caravans coming through the country. Stanley was struck by the abundance of foodstuffs offered for sale in central Ugogo (Mwumi), and remarked that the Ugogo fields were better tilled than any he had seen nearer to the East Coast (Stanley 1872:177, 181). It was later estimated that 1,200,000 pounds of grain were consumed each year in Mpwapwa district by the caravan porters. Of this volume Mpwapwa produced only 10,000 pounds (Kanneberg 1900:7). The remaining foodstuff was grown elsewhere in Ugogo or traded to the Wagogo from neighbouring peoples, like the agriculturists to the north in Kondoa/Irangi and Singida or to the southeast in the Ulanga Valley.

The Trade Routes

It is probable that these trading foundations explain the rapid spread of the trade in ivory, slaves, gum and copal during the nineteenth century and the relative ease with which the commercial empire of Zanzibar established itself deep in the interior of Africa (see also Smith 1963). The existence of an ordered trading network, barter commodities, and food supplies gives the clue to this success which must be seen in diplomatic terms, not as the result of forced entry through military superiority. Historians have far too readily come to regard the size of the early caravans as an indication of defence needs and ignored that the supply problems must have been considerably augmented with the addition of large numbers of porters to caravans going through supposedly hostile territory. We should therefore remind ourselves of the important prerequisites for taking caravans of up to 5,000 people over vast distances and through several months of uninterrupted porterage. Relative political stability and peace would seem to be indispensable first conditions. Other considerations would be the presence of adequate food supplies and water. Human transportation is economically viable only where the carrier can live by local food barter so that he can be loaded with a maximum amount of merchandise. In this perspective, we can see the impressive size of the nineteenth-century caravans as an indication of a well-developed supply system surrounding the trade routes. Caravans bent on exploration or conquest, however, would not be bound by the normal rules of trading diplomacy and were militarily equipped to make their own law in foreign lands. Thus, Casati's confession (1891, II:284) that it was the superiority of arms and the disrespect of people's property rights that solved the catering problems in Stanley's expedition, is, as a rule, untypical of the trading caravans whose success rested on a dependable supply system. The evidence seems to be that such caravans stimulated in a positive way the agricultural initiative that we have discussed in Chapter 2, both with the introduction of new crops and by providing a regular demand in excess of that made up by the local populations. I have, however, resisted any suggestion that this was a primary cause of agricultural changes in the nineteenth century. Such changes have in this study been more directly connected to population growth as the main initiator.

There is another factor to be pointed out: namely the persistent error of talking about *the* trade route. There was no single and permanent route leading, for instance, from Bagamoyo to Ujiji, or from Tabora to Mengo. Such termini were connected through a network of roads and pathways (*Negerpfaden* in the German literature) centred on all the viable communities found in the general trading direction. This opened the possibility for temporary adjustments of itineraries to local events affecting the supply problems. Tornau (1904) pointed out that several parallel routes existed inland from Kilwa where supply problems were in evidence. Similarly, Kanneberg (1900) pointed to several routes running alongside each other through Ugogo to minimize the possibility of overloading the demand for foodstuffs in particular areas.

Many recent maps on the nineteenth-century trading routes are grossly misleading in this respect. They have been conceptualized on the basis of mechanized transportation, the train or the automobile, and its purely technical premises for the bridging of distances. Caravan transport operated on very different principles. It was human porterage working along an infrastructure of local opportunities for provisioning of barter commodities, food and water resources, and the hiring of substitute carriers. This important feature is partly recaptured in Rochus Schmidt's map of the trade routes around 1890, which is reprinted as Map 6.1. Practically all the major caravan routes of the late nineteenth century fell within the likely trading radius of the centres of industrial production identified in Chapter 5. It is likely that these centres delivered the bulk of barter commodities needed by the coast-bound caravans. This coincidence again underpins the idea that long-distance trading was an extension of local networks and initiatives. It would seem that the important trade routes between Uha and Urundi have been neglected in Map 6.1, probably because relatively little information on the economy of these areas was available to the German administration, which was slow to establish itself in these parts of the country.

The Impact of Trade

As I have pointed out in connection with the grain trade in Ugogo, the activity on the trade routes had a stimulating effect on the surrounding economies, notably on the production of foodstuffs. Ultimately, this resulted in a number of provisioning stations along the trade routes, growing out of existing local food markets or originating through market displacements to suit the caravan demands. A number of these depots

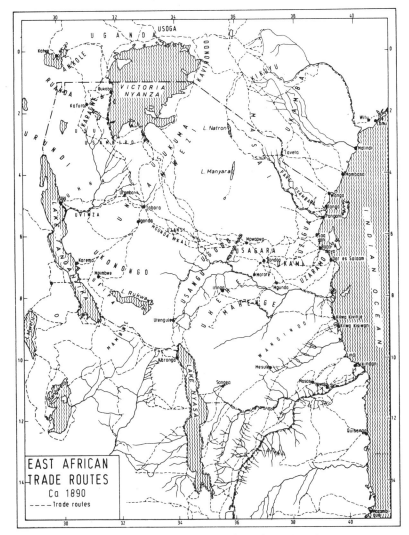

Map 6.1.   The Trading Network, circa 1890. (Based on Schmidt 1892.)

became permanent trading centres often attracting small colonies of coastal entrepreneurs. It is impossible to sort out the relative importance in this development of the coast-bound trade in ivory and slaves and the indigenous economic momentum that has been discussed throughout this study. Blohm (1931:166–72) has pointed to the reciprocal interaction between the external and the indigenous trading initiatives. Roberts gives greater recognition to the Zanzibar-oriented trading impulse—although he does compare it to a very finite goldrush prosperity—which lifted the trading activity from subsistence to support of distant industrial economies. These links with the coast 'brought about a qualitative change in Nyamwezi trade' wrote Roberts (1970:71) who saw the benefits of the link-up in an increase in the volume and flow of trade, and the expansions of existing production. We have partly been able to confirm this in our discussion of the food supplies to the caravans. But this study has not found it possible to make the overseas trading element into an independent developmental factor of momentous impact. Part of the reason for this is the impossibility of extricating it from the rich commodity-trade over long distances that retained an indigenous orientation throughout this period. Although the quantitative evidence of the caravans of overseas inspiration is impressive in terms of carriers, they were certainly dwarfed in comparison to the number of people involved in the local food markets and indigenous commodity trade. The thousands of pounds of ivory brought to Zanzibar becomes a light-weight operation in relation to the thousands of tons of foodstuffs, salt, iron, tobacco and grain that were carried on anonymous shoulders in trading networks not connected to the overseas enterprise.

Also, the evidence is that the overseas trade and its organizers almost without exception remained subordinated to the local economic momentum as well as to the political order (Brown, W. T., 1972, Unomah 1972). One indication of this was the ability of the tribes living across the caravan routes to continue to collect toll (*hongo*) from the passing caravans. The *hongo* institution has probably, as Hore indicates, been unjustly judged by most European travellers, whose unforeseen financial losses unleashed emotional tirades about its abusive evils and destructive impact on all commercial incentive. Hore has given a more balanced view:

> In the countries where it (*hongo*) is demanded the traveller has to pay no other rates or taxes, rents, customs, or fees and in those countries especially he is protected by the local authorities and supplied with water when it is scarce (Hore 1892:51).

Hore compared the *hongo* to customs dues levied in a 'rough-and-ready style' on the nature and quantity of the goods passing through tribal lands. It is possible to see this customs collection as an indication of administrative capabilities as well as the sovereign position of the local peoples *vis-à-vis* the organizers of trade, whether of indigenous or overseas nature.

Moreover, in contrast to the effects of indigenous commodity trade, the bulk of the witnesses presented in Chapter 5 clearly judged overseas trade as a negative factor and saw a direct connection between the decline of local industrial initiatives and the increasing flow of commodities from the coast. The contact areas gradually radiated inland through the very nerve system of the old integrated trading network, first knocking out the more sophisticated of the local achievements like cotton-weaving and wire-drawing and proceeding to undermine gradually the industrial supports of the local economy.

It is increasingly being appreciated that the overseas trading connections represented an illusory source of local development. This has forcefully been pointed out by Rodney, who sees the basis of the overseas trading connection as 'unequal exchange' in the Africans' disfavour, resulting in economic stagnation. 'There could be growth in the volume of commerce and the rise of some positive side-effects', Rodney wrote, 'but there was decrease in the capacity to achieve economic independence and self-sustaining social progress' (Rodney 1972:123). Quite correctly, he sees the result of the overseas trading connections as a stifling of developmental opportunities and the elimination of the industrial half of the local economy.

The destructive impact attributed to the link-up of the industrial economy of western capitalism with the 'traditional' economies of East Africa must in some ways be quantifiable in terms of commodity exchange, trade-route penetration, and people engaged in these operations. Further work is clearly needed in this important field. We shall not pursue the task here because it seems clear that the overseas trading contacts alone did not bring down the East African economies in the 1890s. Their decline was, in a more complex way, due to factors that will be discussed in the following chapter.

CHAPTER 7

Break-down of the Man-Controlled Ecological System: the Causes

In explaining the expanding tsetse belts of the twentieth century in East Africa, colonial authorities stressed the general brutality and lawlessness of the past as causes of the destruction of cultivation and large-scale depopulation. Historians of East Africa have given us ample opportunity to seize upon a similar explanation of the Tanganyikan situation. I shall resist this temptation because the evidence presented so far indicates a different chain of explanations. This evidence has documented the existence of a number of important economic initiatives and the maintenance of an ecological control situation in the period despite internecine wars and slave-raiding. A break-down of the situation occurred at the end of the century and can be linked directly to a cluster of devastations following 1890. It is logical to commence the analysis of this tragic decade with a review of the great Rinderpest. I shall continue the chapter with a discussion of some of the other destructive events, smallpox, jiggers-plague, colonial pacification measures and famine.

RINDERPEST

The great Rinderpest[1] of the 1890s deserves renewed attention by historians since it most likely represents the dividing line between initiative and apathy on the part of a large number of African peoples, particularly in the eastern and southern parts of the continent. It broke the economic backbone of many of the most prosperous and advanced communities, undermined established authority and status structures, and altered the political contacts between the peoples. It initiated the break-down of a long-established ecological balance and placed nature again at an advantage. One searches in vain for any mention of the great Rinderpest in the recent (political) histories of East Africa. Oliver and Mathew (1963) have no index entry either for cattle or Rinderpest.

[1] The Kenya Veterinary Services described Rinderpest as 'an acute contagious virus disease of ruminants and swine, characterized by diarrhoea, nasal and lacrimal discharge and by ulceration of the mucous membrane of the mouth' (*EAAJ* 1939 (5):57).

Ingham (1962) ignores both. *Tanzania before 1900* mentions the Rinderpest twice, but the treatment of this topic is drowned in the military/institutional concerns of the contributors. *A History of Tanzania* makes no mention of the Rinderpest, but indexes Rindi, the Chagga chief of Moshi, nine times.

Mettam (1937) described the Rinderpest as a recent disease in Africa where, prior to 1864, it had been known only in Egypt. It spread to the rest of the continent some twenty years later. Mettam indicated two independent entrance points for the disease to East Africa, *via* Ethiopia and *via* Sudan. Its arrival was in both instances connected with European warfare:

The first recorded outbreak occurred in Somaliland in 1889 and it is generally said that the disease followed the introduction of cattle from India and from Aden for the provisioning of the Italian army during the first expedition to Abyssinia. Once established, Rinderpest spread like wild fire over the whole of East Africa, reaching Lake Tanganyika towards the end of 1890. In the meanwhile the Nile valley as far as Khartoum had been infected by cattle during the British campaigns of 1884–1885. It was held that the disease was introduced by animals purchased in Russia and other Black Sea ports (Mettam 1937:22).

The ravages of the Rinderpest were reported by eye-witnesses from all over East Africa. I shall let them convey their impressions of this 'awful visitation' to Tanganyikan territory through a number of quotations.

Franz Stuhlmann, who travelled with Emin Pasha to Uganda in 1890, met the Rinderpest among the Wagogo. He judged its impact to have been catastrophic and to have reduced the formerly impressive cattle herds to a small fraction of the old size (Stuhlmann 1894:43). A more concrete impression of the destructions can be seen from Vaegeler's claim that individual Wagogo possessed as many as 10,000 head of cattle before the Rinderpest (Vaegeler 1912:76). In 1907, Fuchs thought that the cattle population was less than 10,000 in all of Mpwapwa District (Fuchs 1907:99). Vaegeler's statement falls into line with the description of Ugogo as a land of milk and honey that was given by several early explorers. The Wagogo were then rich and prosperous; they provisioned the trading caravans with surplus grain, salt and meat, and were able to extract the highest *hongo* (toll) of all adjacent tribes. The numerous water ponds reported by Fosbrooke (1957a) to have dotted the areas of southern Masailand, Mpwapwa and Kilimatinde were probably in operation at this time.

The Karagwe kingdom was in full development when Stuhlmann first traversed it and observed the enormous herds of longhorned Sanga cattle that formed the cornerstone of the country's economy. He described at great lengths the techniques of cattle-breeding and reported the use of smoke from cow-dung as a repellent against flies. Many individual owners among the Wahuma rulers possessed thousands of cattle, he wrote, and at one point he estimated the Karagwe herds to exceed 100,000 head. A 'plague' wiped out the herds shortly after his visit forcing the Wahuma (Wahima) to till the soil (Stuhlmann 1894:238). Paul Kollmann, who saw Karagwe in 1896, confirmed the economic ruin of the area where empty cattle kraals could be seen everywhere across the countryside (Kollmann 1899:48).

Travelling south from Bukoba through the districts of Ihangiro and Kimwani, Stuhlmann again encountered the Rinderpest. He admired the large banana groves of the villagers and mentioned the excellent pastures surrounding the settlements. The cattle, however, were gone: 'There are only a few head left in the country from the earlier huge cattle herds', he wrote (Stuhlmann 1894:670). Apparently, the cattle economy was late in reviving. Fosbrooke (1934) reviewed the economy of the Kimwani district forty years later when the people had turned entirely to fishing as their basic livelihood. Gillman's population map (1936) indicated a major sleeping-sickness concentration in the area.

'Stock-breeding in Unyamwezi has suffered enormously from the Rinderpest', wrote Oscar Baumann. 'Almost all of the Zebu cattle died and it is difficult to find any cattle in the area now' (Baumann 1894:238). These losses were reflected on the Tabora market where, according to Lieutenant Sigl, the daily sale of 10–20 head was a normal occurrence prior to the Rinderpest. By 1892, trade in cattle had ceased entirely:

> All trade in cattle has come to a standstill since (the Rinderpest), and will most likely not reach pre-plague dimensions within the next 10–15 years. There are now hardly 100 head of cattle left in all of Unyanyembe from the former herds of 30–40,000. Most of the surviving cattle are bullocks. The situation is typical of all other districts (Sigl 1892:165–66).

Fülleborn reviewed the situation in the southern parts of the country. About the Hehe, Sangu and Bena peoples, he wrote:

> In previous years, the pride and wealth of the Wahehe, the Wabena and the Wassangu were their impressive cattle herds. Elton, for instance, indicated that there were some 10,000 head of cattle in Merere's fortified boma. Bumiller reported that Merere II possessed quite enormous herds in the years prior to the Rinderpest. These herds have become terribly reduced through the Rinderpest and the last years of warfare (Fülleborn 1906:251).

The destruction of the cattle economy also occurred further south. I have already made reference to the situation in Ufipa (see p. 41) where important set-backs occurred. Vast destructions also took place in Konde country (Rungwe), earlier described as an African Arcadia, rich, content and peaceful (Thomson 1881, I:267). Sharpe (1893) indicated that the loss of cattle among the Wakonde (Wanyakyusa) had exceeded 95 per cent. Later, Fülleborn reported:

> The Rinderpest, which raged here in the 1890s, is no longer a danger to the area. The pest severely reduced the vast cattle population and even affected the wildlife. The biggest cattle herds are now found in Konde (Unyakyusa), Untali, Unkika and Ungoni. The excellent grazing grounds of Ukinga have few cattle and along the Ruvuma, Ulanga and Rukwa there are (at least in the parts I know) absolutely no cattle (Fülleborn 1906:364).

The ravages on the Masai herds were catastrophic and caused severe famine among a people who were deprived of their daily food supply: 'Abandoned villages were, almost without exception, the only trace I found of the Masai people', wrote Stuhlmann. 'All their cattle have been wiped out and the surviving people have taken refuge with the agricultural tribes at the edge of the steppe in Ndjoyi, North Ugogo, Nyangana, Hedya, etc. These Masai are on the verge of starvation and quite indifferent. Some have made faint attempts to engage in farming' (Stuhlmann 1892:188).

Oscar Baumann's book, *Durch Masailand,* gives a chilling picture of the destructions caused by the Rinderpest among a pastoral people. Baumann travelled through the territory in 1891 when the impact of the plague was in clear evidence. He first met signs of the catastrophe at Njoronyor (meaning 'reliable water') by the Litema Hills, a place much frequented by the Masai for watering purposes. Here, Baumann observed:

> No human being could now be seen, only an emaciated, half crazy Masai woman staggered with stary eyes through the camp, collecting the refuse of the porters' meals. This was the first sight of the victims of the terrible famine that we were to encounter every day from now on in Masailand (Baumann 1894:19).

From the old Masai settlement in the Ngorongoro Crater, Baumann wrote:

> Large numbers of these woeful creatures (*Jammergestalten*) who now populate Masailand congregated around the thorn fence of our camp. There were skeleton-like women with the madness of starvation in their sunken eyes, children looking more like frogs than human beings, 'warriors' who could hardly crawl on all fours, and apathetic, languishing elders. These people would eat anything, dead donkeys were a delicacy to them, but they would not reject bones, skins, and even the horns of slaughtered cattle. . . . They were

refugees from Serengeti, where the famine had depopulated entire districts, and came as beggars to their tribesmen at Mutyek who had barely enough to feed themselves. Swarms of vultures followed them from high, awaiting the certain victims. Such affliction was from now on daily before our eyes ... (Baumann 1894:31–32).

Baumann estimated that because the Masai were totally dependent on cattle for food, fully two-thirds of the tribe died in the famine. Their entire way of life was changed:

Whereas the warrior somehow managed to survive through hunting and petty thieving, women, children and old people suffered the full measure of the tragedy. The emaciated skeletons of the surviving population trekked across the steppe, feeding on wild honey and half rotten carcasses. All warlike pursuits were doomed to fail. The elmoran were defeated and many times simply failed to return home as starvation overpowered them. Kraals are found only in a few places where people managed to stay alive through hunting and by keeping donkeys and goats. Vast areas of land are abandoned and the Masai live as beggars among the neighbouring peasants (Baumann 1894:165).

Lugard, whose impressions of the Rinderpest were gathered further north, largely in Kenya and Uganda, gave an equally dramatic assessment of its destructions:

The enormous extent of the devastation it has caused in Africa can hardly be exaggerated. Most of the tribes possessed vast herds of thousands on thousands of cattle, and of these, in some localities, hardly one is left; in others, the deaths have been limited to perhaps 90 per cent. In the case of the Bantu (or negroid) tribes, the loss, though a terrible one, did not, as a rule, involve starvation and death to the people, since being agricultural, they possess large crops as a resource. But to the pastoral races the loss of their cattle meant death. The Wahuma, I was told, had perished in vast numbers with their animals. Everywhere the people I saw were gaunt and half starved, and covered with skin-diseases. Not only had they no crops of any sort or kind, to replace the milk and meat which formed their natural diet, but many were unable to accommodate themselves to such a change, and all were completely ignorant of agriculture. The Masai are the same (Lugard 1893, I:525–26, see also 1892).

Contemporary observers like Sharpe (1893) and Stuhlmann (1894) estimated that more than 95 per cent of all cattle died through the Rinderpest. Thus one of the twin pillars of the traditional economy—indeed the only lifeline of many peoples—was suddenly torn away. People were never directly attacked by the epidemic, but suffered the secondary effects of famine. The causal relationship between loss of cattle and famine is fairly clear in the case of the pastoral peoples, and Baumann's account from Masailand may represent a typical situation. But the calamity was not restricted to the pastoral communities. In areas where mixed farming had been practised, the loss of cattle meant inferior cultivation and smaller yields. Further spill-over effects into the agricultural communities were felt when cattle-hungry herders raided the surviving stock of the agriculturists. A third repercussion was felt through the extensive looting of foodstuffs: 'The herders are driven by hunger to break into and sack any community where food is available', wrote one observer (Sander 1893). It is possible that the intense tribal raiding that the Germans experienced in the first years of their stay in East Africa—and to which they reacted so violently—was the direct consequence of economic losses suffered initially through the Rinderpest.

Apart from causing depopulation, the Rinderpest had important social and political impacts. Ford and Hall (1947, see also Kollmann 1899) pointed to the equalizing effect of the disaster in Karagwe where the old ruling clan, the Wahima, was forced after the Rinderpest to depend on the agricultural Wayambo. In other parts of the country, the Rinderpest accentuated the existing social differences. Liebert claimed that far-reaching changes had taken place among the Wahehe where the surviving cattle became concentrated in the hands of chiefs and head-men only (Liebert 1898:27). The overall power position of the East African peoples was deeply affected through the catastrophe. From Kenya, Lord Lugard drew a political conclusion from what he had seen. 'In some respects . . .', he wrote, the Rinderpest 'has favoured our enterprise. Powerful and warlike as the pastoral tribes are, their pride has been humbled and our progress facilitated by this awful visitation. The advent of the white man had else not been so peaceful' (Lugard 1893, I:527).

A territorial cattle census was undertaken by the German authorities in 1902 (Anlagen 1904:69). It showed 460,572 head of cattle in the *Schutzgebiet*, exclusive of Usumbura (Ruanda and Burundi); the latter province was indicated to have 50,000 head of cattle. Assuming that the assessments of losses by Stuhlmann and Sharpe are accurate and that the recovery by 1902 could not have reached more than a 10 per cent level of the pre-1890 cattle herds, we may conclude that the territory which today makes up mainland Tanzania contained *at least* four and a half million head of cattle in 1890. This seems to be a reasonable estimate both in the light of the material that has been discussed so far and the cattle counts that were made later when the herds had been 'restored' in the much reduced tsetse-free grazing areas. Percival's study (1918) of a later cattle plague is of some interest in that it documented a very slow recovery of domestic stock in comparison to a relatively quick regrowth of wildlife.

The Rinderpest marked the beginning of a series of natural and man-made calamities that struck East Africa in the next two decades. Smallpox epidemics, the sand-flea (jiggers) plague, famine and sleeping sickness all occurred within a few years of the great Rinderpest; their exceptional toll was probably linked to this initial weakening of the population. One tragedy reinforced the effect of the other and they were probably all seen by the contemporary Africans as the result of European machinations. 'Nothing was more natural', wrote Rehse from Kiziba (Bukoba), 'than to blame all these calamities on the coming of the Europeans' (Rehse 1910:140).

SMALLPOX

Under endemic conditions, smallpox is a childhood disease. It is known to cause serious infant mortality, but to leave the surviving population with a degree of immunity affording protection against later outbreaks of the illness. The smallpox epidemics that the Germans described in the 1890s, however, attacked the adults as well as the young, and it therefore seems possible to conclude that the disease was re-establishing itself in this period after many years' absence from East Africa. Thus, Fischer who travelled through Masailand in 1882–83, reported extreme caution on the part of the Masai when in contact with the coastal travellers. This was apparently because of fear of smallpox which had earlier been introduced through caravans from the coast (Fischer 1884:89). Harry Johnston also reported that the Masai were apprehensive of foreigners visiting their land because of fear of an illness which he identified as smallpox. The Masai referred to it as the 'White Illness' and associated it with the coming of the Europeans (Johnston 1886:303). This reaction is similar to the attitude of the Ussubbwa/Ussuwi chief, Kassusura, in his dealings with Götzen in 1893. Götzen was an eager photographer and wanted to take a picture of the famous chief whom many European travellers had encountered. The suggestion caused great commotion and the clan elders went into council to discuss it. Finally, a negative answer was given with the reasoning that photographing the chief might aid in spreading smallpox into the country (Götzen 1895:139).

It seems clear, however, that smallpox had been known, at least in some parts of the country, in earlier decades (see p. 24). Thus, Richard Burton referred to smallpox as 'the most dangerous epidemic', that 'sweeps at times like a storm of death over the land' (Burton 1860, II:318). He reported that the Arabs had introduced the practice of inoculation against the disease in their areas of settlement. This was done by the use of live virus from the scabs of infected patients, following a practice that was well established in the Middle East prior to Jenner's discoveries (Dixon 1962).

Reports of smallpox epidemics were quite frequent in the 1890s. Six hundred people died of smallpox in Dar es Salaam in 1893. This was estimated to be 10 per cent of the town's population. Efforts to inoculate against the epidemic were made, but great difficulties were encountered as the vaccine became inactive during the long transport to East Africa from Europe. Particular attention was paid to the troops and the carriers both in government and private trading service. The object was to immunize that part of the population which, through constant movement, was most exposed to the illness and also acted to spread it to the upcountry communities (*DKB* 1891:459, *DKB* 1892:267, *DKB* 1894:338). Lieutenant Elpons, the commander of the Mpwapwa garrison, reported smallpox in that area in 1891. The reference is made in a report on a punitive expedition against a Hehe chief living in Gogo country some five days' march west of Kondoa. Because smallpox had hit the area during the previous year, Elpons desisted from the normal practice of burning the villages where a punitive raid was carried out (*DKB* 1892:285–6).

Katoke mentions a smallpox epidemic erupting in Karagwe in 1892. He writes that 'the outbreak spread throughout the country killing many people including the Mukama himself' (Katoke 1969:203). Ford states that the people of Karagwe associated this smallpox epidemic with the outbreak of Rinderpest two years earlier and used the same word, *mubiamo*, to identify both rinderpest and smallpox (Ford 1971:138). Oscar Baumann's caravan was troubled by a smallpox epidemic among the Waha along the upper Malagarasi River when it returned to the coast from Ruanda Urundi in 1892. This coincided with the encounter of imported cottons, and Baumann concluded that he had entered the northwestern extremities of the Unyamwezi trading sphere. Further west, the people were completely untouched by foreign influences (Baumann 1894:99).

Smallpox epidemics are reported to have delayed the collection of the Hut Tax which had been introduced in 1897. Thus, tax collection was postponed for one year along the coast, in Tanga and Usambara (*DKB* 1899:167). Hauptmann Prince reported that he granted tax-freedom for the year 1899 to a part of Merere's kingdom because the area had suffered heavily from smallpox and drought during the previous months. He reported that the population in the areas around the caravan route from Danjera to Utengule had become severely reduced through this illness (Prince 1899:734).

Further reports came from Kilwa district and the areas across to Donde country and Lake Nyassa where smallpox raged in 1897–98. The reports particularly mention the area of Hangi east of the military station of Barikwa in Liwale as almost totally empty of people due to the epidemic. The station personnel harvested the fields surrounding the empty ghost-towns (*DKB* 1899:659). A similar situation was recorded around the station of Mpande:

> The local people have left their villages and moved into the *pori* (bush) on the assumption that devils (*Schaitan*) have taken over their old quarters and caused the death of their friends and neighbours (*DKB* 1899:659).

As I have pointed out in Chapter 1, early explorers reported the frightful scenes of smallpox epidemics breaking out in the trading caravans. Dr. Becker (1899) held caravan transport to be the major factor in spreading smallpox throughout the country. He failed, however, to explain why smallpox suddenly became rampant in the 1890s when the caravan trade was sharply on the decline from the previous peaks of trading activity. His description of the caravan routes in a period of epidemics is of some interest as it supports the point made earlier about communicable diseases as the possible origin of some of the most chilling reports about the slave-raiding. 'During an epidemic', wrote Becker, 'it is common to see the unburied bodies of the plague victims lying along the caravan routes. A great number of bodies are found particularly in the vicinity of the wells and resting places' (Becker 1899:761).

Most important for an overview of the destructive impact of smallpox on the population of German East Africa is the estimate of casualties provided by Becker. It is not easy, he wrote, 'to provide exact annual figures of victims of smallpox and dysentery. I believe, however, that I understate the case when I say that the *Schutzgebiet* last year alone (1898) lost more than 150,000 people through these two illnesses (Becker 1899:761).

THE SAND-FLEA PLAGUE

The arrival of the sand-flea or jigger-flea (*Sarcopsylla penetrans*) in Africa has been dated to 1872, when the British ship *Thomas Mitchell*—in ballast from Rio de Janeiro—called at the Angolan port of Ambriz (Pechuel-Loesche 1882:297). From there, the insect spread rapidly across the continent, aided by the caravan traffic which brought it from one trading station to the next. This development has been well documented by Hesse (1899). A quarter of a century after its first contact with African soil, Oscar Baumann (1898:165) could report that the sand-flea had arrived in Zanzibar, thus completing its trans-continental move. It left enormous sufferings in its wake, as this sketch of the Tanganyikan situation will indicate.

Baumann had observed the sand-flea ravages in the Congo in 1885. He met the insect again when travelling westward through the *Schutzgebiet* in 1891–92. From the iron-producing area of Ugulula (Ngalula) in Uzinza, he wrote about people suffering the universal liability of a disease which is introduced for the first time into a population which is either non-immune or ignorant of appropriate counter-measures:

> Those who keep the feet clean and look after them daily to extract the jiggers have little to fear from this plague. But left to themselves, the sand-flea larvae will grow to the size of a pea and finally break out into sores. When these appear in large numbers, they can cause blood poisoning and death. Particularly in areas where the sand-flea occurs for the first time, and where its treatment is unknown, its impact can be devastating. We saw people in Uzinza whose limbs had disintegrated. Whole villages had died out on account of this vexation (Baumann 1894:72).

The latter observation is most important: where people encountered the flea for the first time, and knew nothing of the methods to combat it, the impact of the jiggers was extraordinary and often resulted in the loss of lives. The sores caused by the flea remained unattended to, became infected and resulted in gangrene and death. Götzen wrote about terrible sores resulting from neglect to remove the larvae at an early stage. In some extreme cases which he observed among the Rongo iron workers in Msalala, the sand-flea had infected the hands and arms of the helpless victims (Götzen 1895:94, 111).

Rehse, who saw the jigger in Kiziba and described its ravages as an unbearable public calamity, did not think that the sand-fleas alone could have caused the very high number of deaths that apparently were occurring in the district. He thought that only the combined impact of the Rinderpest—causing famine—and the sand-fleas could possibly explain the high mortality rate (Rehse 1910:140). Similarly, the destruction of the Karagwe people was seen by Herrmann as resulting from the joint impact of smallpox and sand-fleas: 'This is a warlike and populous people', he wrote, 'but at present decimated by smallpox. Moreover, the sand-flea attack of 1892 was so vicious that the harvest had to remain in the fields because no labourers could be found' (Herrmann 1894:58).

The German station at Mwanza was particularly exposed to the sand-flea attack, and the soldiers were constantly plagued by the fleas. At one stage, half of the men were reported to be unable to walk on account of jiggers, and the commanding officer seriously thought of moving the station to more hospitable surroundings (Herrmann 1893). The people of Nyegezi, the area surrounding Mwanza, simply gave up their economic pursuits and migrated out of the area in large numbers (Werther 1896:86).

Hans Meyer observed the sand-flea ravages among the Masai settlers at Laitokitok on the northeastern slopes of Mount Kilimanjaro. He called the jiggers 'the most fearful calamity that has ever afflicted the East African peoples' (Meyer 1900:119–20). He gave examples of people who were unable to walk and were seen crawling around on all fours groaning with unbearable pains.

The situation in Ufipa in the south western part of the protectorate showed many similarities. Fromm reported that people unable to walk on account of the jiggers were a common sight. Their feet had simply rotted away. Fromm blamed this on the indolence of the people in dealing with the jiggers in an early and purposeful way (Fromm 1912:81). Finally, from Lindi District, Weule observed the end of the trans-continental spread of the sand-flea and presented a number of photographs of the leg-stumps that were the typical result of a serious jigger attack. 'It is quite common', he wrote, 'to see natives of this place with one or two toes missing; many have lost all their toes, or even the whole front part of the foot, so that a well-formed leg ends in a shapeless stump' (Weule 1909:252, see also Berg 1897).

As Rehse indicated, the original sand-flea attack was probably not a killer disease. But coming at a time when nutritional conditions were critical and the people's resistance was low, the impact of the sand-fleas was disastrous. The jiggers plague undermined people's mobility and work efforts and threatened their ability to maintain the local economy. It added to the number of tragic events of which the 1890s in East Africa abounded.

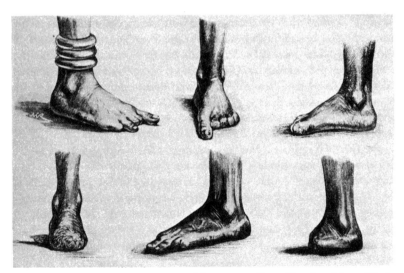

Figure 7.1.   Sand-Flea Destruction of the Human Foot. (Reprinted from Weule 1908:Plate 58.)

FAMINE

The early explorers, both in their writings and in the pictorial material they produced, leave no doubt that the peoples they visited operated well-planned households. Amazement is often expressed at the number and size of food storages for basic staples like maize, millet, rice and sorghum. Baumann, for instance, wrote about large cylindrical storage baskets— more than one metre tall—that were kept by the Wabungwe inside of their *tembes* (Baumann 1894:184). Cameron described storage houses that reached the height of 20–25 feet on the west coast of Lake Tanganyika. In Unyamwezi, he saw grain bins made from Londo-bark that would contain dozens of bags of grain (Cameron 1877, I:293).

Against this background, the question of the repeated famines in the 1890s is a puzzle which the argument of 'the native's laziness' that was advanced at the time does not fully explain. As Fülleborn argued the case: 'The Negro lives in the present. In prosperous years he never reflects on the need to provide for leaner years ahead. He follows the old customs and transforms his surplus into *pombe* (beer)' (Fülleborn 1906:43). The geographer Hans Meyer argued in similar terms: 'It is only under exceptional circumstances that the East African puts aside the surpluses of a good harvest to provide for the coming year and safeguards against the frequent famines. He prefers to turn his produce into *pombe* and imbibe it—oblivious of the future' (Meyer 1909:397).

These views are almost certainly historically incorrect and overlook the rich material on granaries and food storage techniques which earlier travellers have produced. A more fruitful line of argument (than the one represented by Fülleborn and Meyer) is to link the famines that occurred in the later years of the century to the calamities that I have already discussed: the Rinderpest, the smallpox epidemics, and the jigger-plague. Such a connection has, to some extent, been anticipated throughout. Three additional factors, directly related to the establishment of the *Schutzgebiet*, must be considered. These are firstly, the effects of the 'pacification' policy and secondly, the procurement practices of the German administration. A third element is the labour recruitment policy, a policy which greatly affected the economic well-being of the people and their production of foodstuffs. All three factors can be identified as essentially man-made reasons for famine. In addition, natural catastrophies like drought or locust swarms must be considered. It is difficult to sort out the relative impact of this variety of causes on the making of famines. I shall not seek to do that, but shall briefly give an overview of famines in the 1890s before turning to a further consideration of pacification, procurations and labour recruitment.

The 1890s were a decade of famine. German reports mentioning this fact exist in abundance, although some of the earliest observers may not have understood the signs of famine and misread the situation. Götzen, for instance, dismissed the rumours of famine in Ushirombo when he travelled through the area in 1893. To prove his point, he photographed five young boys who, he wrote, in no way gave the impression of being undernourished (Götzen 1895:101). The picture, which is reprinted as Figure 7.2, is a good illustration of the young survivors of severe food shortages; it shows the protruding bellies which are one of the classical signs of protein malnutrition—Kwashiorkor.

Figure 7.2. Kwashiorkor in Ushirombo, 1893. (Reprinted from Götzen 1895:101.)

While food shortage in Ushirombo was probably related to the effects of the Rinderpest, the locust plague of 1893–95 caused severe food shortages in many agricultural communities. Outbreaks of red locusts (*Nomadacris septemfascinata serville*) are conditioned by specific ecological and climatological factors and are, in East Africa, geographically restricted to three centres: the Rukwa Valley and the Malagarasi Basin in Tanganyika and Lake Mweru in northern Zambia (Gunn 1956). Successful locust-breeding seems to be dependent on a constantly favourable moisture level in the soil where the eggs are hatched, and is associated with a moderate rainy season. The seriousness of a locust outbreak is related to the size of the area of breeding. This is controlled by the general water level in the particular outbreak area where alterations of drought or rains can turn vast areas into potentially favourable breeding grounds.

Locust plagues of different intensity have probably followed with some regularity in the past, although the plague of 1893–95 is the first recorded calamity of this nature. Gunn has sought to correlate locust outbreaks with reports of the water level in Lake Rukwa and thinks it possible (although not certain) that the locust plague of the 1890s originated in this area. Wissmann (*DKB* 1893:494–95) reported that the Rukwa area suffered severely from locusts in this period. Of some importance is the fact that there was no memory of an earlier drought period among the people then living in the lake area (see p. 77). They apparently attributed the draining of Lake Rukwa to the thirsty spirit of Kaiser, the German explorer who had been buried in Ukia in 1882 (Gunn 1956).

The red-locust plague of 1893–95 is well documented and was a matter of considerable government concern (Sander 1902). It struck simultaneously in many communities, wiped out the possibilities for local self-help in food supplies and brought a number of peoples face-to-face with starvation. A government proclamation of 1895 indicated that the districts of Kisaki, Kilosa, Mpwapwa, and Ulanga had been badly ravaged by the locusts and needed the special attention of the authorities in the form of seed-grains and other aid measures to recommence crop production (*DKB* 1895:100–101). Other reports mentioned Tabora, Tanga, Pangani and Kibosho on Kilimanjaro as areas where considerable destruction had taken place (*DKB* 1895:12, 212, and 253). Oscar Neumann's expedition found locusts among the Wakwafi of Nguruman in the present Mara Region. All fields had been razed to the ground and serious famine raged in the area (Neumann 1894:422). A report from Bondei near Tanga indicates the seriousness of the locust attack:

> The young locusts were all over the country during Easter week. They destroyed everything in sight. Not even the hard leaves of the pineapple and the palm-trees were left untouched. The fields of maize and rice were totally devoured. The wells had to be covered against the locusts and the houses tightly closed against them. For half a year the people lived on imported foodstuffs (*DKB* 1894:489).

The major staples of the period, rice, maize and sorghum were particularly exposed to the locusts and were in most instances totally destroyed. In Kisarawe, near Dar es Salaam, the locusts reportedly turned the fields into deserts (*DKB* 1894:489). Also sugarcanes were badly razed. Groundnuts, sweet potatoes and cassava apparently resisted the insect and were introduced as relief crops in several places.

The export statistics of the 1890s, presented in Table 7.1, give some indication of the seriousness of the food situation. Falling food production was not caused uniquely by the locust plague, however. The German 'pacification' measures also destroyed agricultural opportunities and the prohibition of slavery spelled the end of production on many coastal plantations and their reversal to bush. Fitzgerald (1898) has documented this development between Malindi and Mombasa, and it seems likely that the plantation network along the east coast of Tanganyika was similarly affected.

TABLE 7.1.   *Crop Exports from German East Africa*

| | Quantity in 000 English pounds | | | |
	1892	1893	1894	1895
Coconuts	3,924	3,963	4,849	5,407
Sesame	1,750	1,652	2,728	2,511
Rice(unhusked)	1,804	2,400	726	2
Rice(husked)	1,332	5,074	752	6
Maize	734	878	126	10
Sorghum(Mtama and Mawele)	4,902	9,256	5,966	59
Chiroko beans	134	255	138	670
Other beans	127	82	13	414
Sugar, syrup	2,483	2,468	1,575	354

Sources: 1892: *DKB* 1893:344–47; 1893: *DKB* 1894:542–45; 1895: *DKB* 1896:362–65; Sander (1902).

The table shows the catastrophic decline in the production of the major staples like rice, maize and sorghum. It also shows some surprising export increases in 1895, notably of coconuts, sesame seeds, and beans. According to the Governor's Annual Report, these changes were the direct result of the people's increasing impoverishment. Larger coconut exports did not stem from new plantings or higher yields, but from denied consumption traded for cash in order to buy back cheaper survival foodstuffs. The increased export of beans has a similar explanation (Sander 1902).

The resulting famine conditions, particularly in the interior, became so serious that the German authorities feared that political unrest might follow and threaten the security of the territory (*DKB* 1894:574). Primarily for such reasons, the administration started to import rice for distribution to avert any major catastrophe. In fact, the famine was made into a useful occasion for the administration to gain labour for its many 'projects of civilization'. As the peoples from the interior were being driven towards the coast by the spreading famine, they were absorbed in road construction and farm work. The policy of *quid pro quo* was proudly proclaimed:

> The Governor does not intend to distribute the food free of charge, but rather to sell it cheaply or to exchange it against work performance. He hopes to generate some good results from this approach and to considerably increase the contribution of the local people to useful endeavours like road construction (*DKB* 1894:406).

There were, however, strict physical limits to Government aid, even when paid for by the receiver. Transportation was by porterage and it was reckoned that the carrier would consume his own load of grain (average of 50 pounds) in 30–40 days' walk. Any rescue operation at more than 15–20 days' distance from the major depots of the coastal towns was therefore ruled out for cost and physical reasons (Becker 1899).

A second administrative response to the famine conditions was to grant tax exemption to the hardest-hit areas. König (1910) reveals that Governor Schele had already made suggestions for the introduction of a taxing system in 1895, but that this had been postponed because of widespread hunger conditions throughout the colony. When Hut Tax (*Haus und Hüttensteuer*) was introduced in 1897, its effective collection was initially hampered through continued famine conditions in many places. The famine was undoubtedly connected with the protracted period of drought and another outbreak of locusts in 1897–98.

The famines before and around the turn of the century took large tolls. Fülleborn indicated that 3,000 persons died in Lindi District in 1900 after a severe famine that reduced the people to eating roots and the bark of trees (Fülleborn 1906:43). On the upper Ruvuma, a similarly large number of casualties was reported by Busse (1902). Malcolm (1953) documented the famine in Unyamwezi in 1900 which can be compared in severity to the one reported from Lindi. The local people called it the hunger of the *miombo—nzala ya mitundu*—to indicate that the bark of trees constituted the main nutrient. There had been a famine in Usambara in 1899 following serious drought during the previous year. Several thousand people were reported to have died (Meyer 1900:37). Similar conditions were reported from Tanga District where a recorded population of 123,300 in 1897/98 had been reduced to 61,300 in 1898/99. 'Half of the population has been either eliminated through the famine or has left the district in desperation', wrote Hans Meyer. 'Also the other coastal districts have suffered tremendous losses of human lives through the drought and the ensuing famine. In addition, locust destructions and the smallpox epidemics have caused great havoc' (Meyer 1900:264). An overall assessment of famine casualties was made by Dr. Becker (1899) who thought that ¾ million people had died of hunger during the five years 1894–1899. As we shall see in the following sections, German policies—apart from the limited famine relief—added to the natural calamities of the period to make the 1890s a turning point in the economic life of the Tanganyikan peoples.

PROCURATIONS

Kuczynski, reviewing the evidence surrounding the great famine of 1898–99 in Kenya, pointed out that its extraordinary impact was due partly to man-made factors stemming directly from the recent arrival of the Europeans. Their procuration of foodstuffs for military purposes or in connection with the railroad-building greatly contributed to the calamity (Kuczynski 1949, II:199). In some instances, the African producer was tempted by the new market opportunities; he took a chance on the future and sold off more of his surpluses than he was normally accustomed to. In other instances he had no say in the matter. Whatever had been harvested would be taken away through forced deliveries or punitive raids. Clarke Brooke (1967) has made a similar connection between man-made factors and the severity of food shortages in Central Tanganyika.

Evidence of famines that arose as part of a deliberate strategy of warfare—not as its accidental by-product—will be reviewed in the following section. But also a 'peacetime' procuration policy pursued by the colonial authorities may have contributed to acute food shortages at different stages throughout the *Schutzgebiet*. The Europeans' attitude to the local economy and their limited understanding of surplus and trade in East Africa contributed to a strained food situation. There seems to have been little immediate appreciation by the incoming foreigners of the devastations suffered by the economy in the early 1890s, and reluctance to trade on the part of the Africans was seen as a sign of commercial retardation—as a backward cultural trait that had to be stamped out, if necessary by force.

An interesting glimpse into the mind of a future administrator can be found in Götzen's book *Durch Afrika von Ost nach West*. The author recounted his travels through Ugogo where, as usual, the caravan depended on the local markets for their foodstuff. The time was 1893, and the ravages of the Rinderpest had passed through shortly before. Götzen indicated no awareness of this, although he reported that there were few cattle around. The local peoples were unwilling to trade and completely ignored German offers (Götzen 1895:33). Götzen reasoned that the unwillingness to trade was a simple reflection of the non-commercial mentality of the people and that the occasion was ripe to give them a first lesson in the benefits of trade. The available stock was accordingly rounded up, the best selected, and when the scared owners later showed up they were paid in cash and given a sermon on commerce and its mutual advantages to buyer and seller. Götzen later philosophized on the incident:

> It would be very much easier simply to seize the foodstuff wherever it is found with the right of the strongest. But if one feels justified in the penetration of an uncivilized country because one is the carrier of a higher culture, then certain obligations—among them the introduction of the native to the basic practices of civilization—are tied to this right. The exchange of products and objects of value is among these basic practices (Götzen 1895:34).

Götzen's epistle is, of course, a stupid man's soliloquy in a situation he did not fully understand. But the misunderstanding was not as much complete as it was deadly. The colonialist, through his practical teaching of commercial virtues, also removed the margin of surplus security of stock or storage that separated the East African peasant from famine in the eventuality of crop failures during the next planting season.

COLONIAL WARFARE

The recent research into the early German period in East Africa has concentrated on the Maji Maji wars and their aftermath. It has been a central effort of these works to link the uprisings to the chain of protest that culminated in the nationalist movement and Independence in 1961. Bell (1950:38) opened this argument with a characterization of Maji Maji as 'a national war of independence'. To Gwassa and Iliffe (1968:3) the Maji Maji war is 'the national epic of Tanzania'. This is the 'enlargement of scale' theme: the manifestation of intertribal co-operation and the ideology of resistance to a common enemy cementing the different peoples taking part in the uprising. Also, Maji Maji represented an important setback to the German occupation, and showed the options of simple techniques of warfare and organization against one of the world's leading military powers (Iliffe 1967). Nationalist historians have thus given positive interpretation to the military encounters because of their contribution to the sense of 'nationhood'. Colonial historians, on the other hand, have seen active warfare as part of the civilizing mission of European powers. Economic questions have seldom been raised. One exception is Henderson (1943) who stressed the World War I period in Tanganyika as a high-water mark of economic self-reliance.

I am interested in the destructive element of the military encounters and the way in which this added to the forces of economic decline already identified in this chapter. This perspective is new, so that little support can be drawn from already existing research. I have therefore found it necessary to provide a relatively detailed account in this section to substantiate the contention that colonial warfare must be seen as a major cause of the destruction of the local economies of Tanganyika.

I shall briefly discuss the superior weaponry and destructive capacity of the German troops, the *Schutztruppen*, then go on to review the political situation which the Germans sought to control and the way in which this situation called forth battle tactics that were particularly destructive to the local people and their economy. Thirdly, I shall present some of the available quantitative data on the early wars and finally review the impact of the First World War in Tanganyika territory.

Arms

The standard weapon of the *Schutztruppen* was the M/71 *Jägerbusche*, a single shot breech-loader used in Europe for big-game hunting because of the large calibre and the half-mantled bullets filled with lead (dum-dum) that broke on impact. The M/71 had an excellent stopping effect at short range, and was ideally suited for storming. More up-to-date hand-weapons, like the repeating rifle Mauser M/97 with a smaller bore and complete steel-mantled bullets, were used by the German officers. Nigmann, discussing the advantages of the different guns, concluded that the relatively old-fashioned M/71 gave to the *Schutztruppen* an absolute superiority in a situation where antique muzzle-loaders were the most advanced weapons found among the adversary (Nigmann 1911:96). A breech-loader was a true rarity among the Africans and has been reported only in connection with peoples who had easy trading connections to markets supplied by British arms. Sinna of Kibosho reportedly was in possession of a number of breech-loaders that made the storming of his boma very complicated (Schmidt 1892:248). On the other hand, Mkwawa, who captured an important supply of European weapons including field-pieces, machine guns and numerous M/71s, was apparently unable to utilize these in the defence of Iringa; they were stored in the main arsenal of the boma (Prince 1914:302). Even during the coastal fighting in 1888–91, where Swahili trading elements with excellent international connections took part, the muzzle-loader was the predominant type of gun. It seems likely that the fortified boma which developed in this period was built in response to a situation where the muzzle-loader was gaining entrance. It was against these strongholds that the superiority of the faster breech-loader was repeatedly demonstrated as panic soon broke out at the approach of the rapid-firing ranks of the *Schutztruppen*. In most instances, such storms were supported by machine guns and field-pieces of 4·7 to 6·7 cm. calibre. Tom von Prince claimed that one troop column could deliver between 2,000 and 3,000 shots per minute and that the accompanying machine gun would add 500 more (Prince 1914:161).

In open terrain, such a formation could take on very superior numbers of spear-throwing warriors who would normally have to develop their attacks at less than 150 metres' distance. At this remove, the African formations were exposed to frightful losses. An early encounter of the *Schutztruppen* with Mafitte warriors who were unaccustomed to European weaponry was described by Nigmann:

> The Mafitti attacked again and again with furious anger, and the bodies of the wild and courageous attackers kept on piling up around the troops. The body count showed 400 dead (Nigmann 1911:13).

Heavy fire-power gave a clear military superiority to the *Schutztruppen*. Other important elements were their maximum use of discipline and surprise. These three factors composed the offensive strategy which made it possible for approximately 2,500 *askaris* and officers to control a territory which could muster one and a half million warriors in scattered bands under independent leaders.

Scorched Earth

The German officers were well aware that their superior fire-power could be neutralized by the terrain. Three punitive expeditions against the Yao chief Machemba in the hinterlands of Lindi gave no decisive military result. Machemba's people were never seen, their muzzle-loaders were fired from the deep bush and their constant harassment caused moral confusion in the troops. The porters disappeared or were shot, and the ammunition was wasted in ceaseless firing against a vanishing enemy. The troops became extremely vulnerable in retreat (Schmidt 1892).

Machemba provided the first practitioner of the *Kleinkrieg*, the guerilla warfare which caused the greatest concern to the military leadership and against which new tactics had to be developed. These tactics were the scorched-earth policy and the resulting man-made famine. Such means had initially been used to remove the local support from the chiefs of resistance in the early coastal fighting. The systematic razing of villages between Sadani and Mandera, for instance, depleted all local supplies and finally brought the followers of Bwana Heri to surrender (Schmidt 1892:155). This became the strategy relied upon almost entirely during the Maji Maji wars where the vastness of the war zone and its natural advantages for guerilla tactics made any decisive military confrontation practically impossible. The man-made famine was a cruel but useful ally which the *Schutztruppen* should not refrain from putting to use, wrote the standard military handbook (*Anleitung* 1911:23; see also Götzen 1909).

The lack of unity among the African peoples was an important element that to some extent aided the German designs, although recent researchers have probably under-played the degree of early (pre-Maji Maji) ethnic co-operation in warfare against the colonial intruder. German historians commenced this trend when describing their occupation of the east coast between 1888 and 1891 as the response to an 'Arab revolt', thus singling out a supposedly alien element for attack and implying that the German military presence was that of a liberator of the African masses from the oppressor (Bülow 1902). This ideology had developed out of the political situation in Germany where the christian/catholic *Zentrum* needed a crusade in order to support colonialism. It was with a moral commitment that the German *Reich* entered East Africa to cope with the military defeat of the *Deutsche Ostafrikanische Gesellschaft* (DOAG). Thus, the *Reichstag's* vote for 2 million marks which sent Hermann von Wissmann as *Reichskommissar* to East Africa to organize the *Schutztruppen* was officially aimed at suppressing the slave trade. The securing of German interests in the area was his second objective only. Writing his memoirs some years after the *Reichstag* vote, Wissmann fell into line with the general ideology to declare that 'the deliverance of Equatorial Africa from the thraldom of the Arabs has become my life object' (Wissmann 1891:186).

In the real situation, the German faced not an isolated alien oppressor, but a concerted resistance which cemented coastal and inland peoples around an initial Arab and Swahili element. This element may have been important mainly in the early stages, as pointed out by Müller (1959; see also Bennett 1961). But as Table 1 in the Appendix indicates, the participation of the African peoples in the early fighting is overwhelming, as is also the number of tribes co-operating. Thus the most formidable adversary in the early fighting was probably not Bushiri who could be isolated because he stuck too closely to his ethnic *confrères* along the central caravan route. He was hanged to instill fear as he was useless as a medium to draw supporters to a lasting settlement. A more formidable opponent was Bwana Heri, the Segua chief, who expanded his intertribal contacts as the fighting was going on. Rochus Schmidt stated that Arabs, Baluchis, slaves, Wasegua, Wanyamwezi and representatives of all possible tribes (*alle möglichen Stämme*) followed Bwana Heri when he came to make peace in Sadani in March 1890 (Schmidt 1892:180). He thus demonstrated his vast following even in defeat. A contingent of 600 men was even then on its way from Ujiji and Tabora to reinforce his troops, and he had earlier struck alliances with the Mafitti (Wangoni) of Ulanga, the Wadoe, the Wanguru, the Wadigo and the Wazaramo. There were rumours of contacts with Simbodja of the Wasambaa and with the Wahehe.

Resistance was born on the coast where the initial contacts with the German forces were made. It spread inland with the German penetration to affect the Wayao in the south where Machemba organized the people, to Ugogo and Uhehe. By 1891 the resistance had become mainly an African affair and the symbol of resistance shifted to the Wahehe and their chief Mkwawa after their routing of the Zelewski expedition at Lugalo. It took three years of carefully planned isolation of the Wahehe from their possible allies before a direct strike was carried out against Iringa in 1894. This involved the building of a cordon of military stations along the central caravan route at Mpwapwa, Kilosa, Lusolwe, and Kisaki. A second aim of these stations was to secure the caravan traffic and put an end to the local *hongo* practices and place the authority of levying duties squarely with the colonial officers at the points of import/export.

The isolation of the Wahehe also involved a number of preliminary battles, the defeat of Isike of Tabora, who was a potential ally, and the destruction of Chief Kimaraunga near Lake Rukwa. Tom von Prince had no doubt that Kimaraunga's routing finally convinced Merere, the Wasangu chief, that neutrality was the best policy in the coming encounter. Tom von Prince's expedition to Songea in the last part of 1893 was directed to seal off any support for the Wahehe from the famous Wangoni war-machine (Prince 1914:258, 260).

Thus, despite the multitude of socio-political entities present, the situation in Tanganyika did not lend itself easily to divide-and-rule operations. Manipulation was not one of the real options of the Germans. They readily recognized this: 'There are no tribes on which we can rely unconditionally', asserted their military handbook (*Anleitung* 1911:15). Individual tribes and chiefs were living in great suspense over the options of taking sides. A decision to come forward to make *shauri*, receive the *Schutzbrief* and the German flag usually followed defeat in battle or clearcut lessons taught to neighbouring peoples that were too overwhelmingly realistic to be neglected. Every German defeat heightened the uncertainties and brought rumours of concerted risings. The defeat at Lugalo caused stirrings along the central caravan route and even as far away as Moshi where Chief Meli was encouraged to commence his own rising (Prince 1914:177). Every German victory clarified the options and the risks. Battles were therefore delivered with the clear aim of teaching lessons of new power relations to undecided peoples. This may have added to the degree of brutality and wantonness in the fighting, the reports of which, for instance, seldom mention the taking of prisoners.

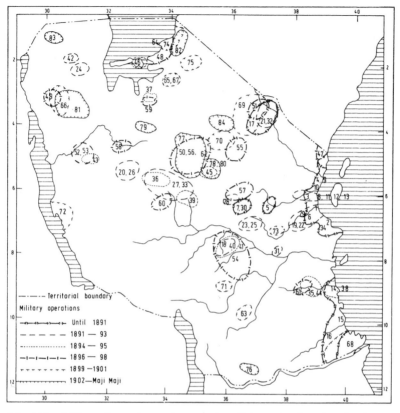

Map 7.1. Military Operations prior to Maji Maji. (Based on location sketches in Nigmann 1911.) Numbers refer to leaders, location or tribe identifying the military operation. The numbers are in approximate chronological order.

1. Bushiri—Bagamoyo	17. Sinna—Kibosho
2. Dar es Salaam	18. Wahehe—Lugalo
3. Sadani	19. Mafitti—Songomero
4. Pangani	20. Siki—Tabora
5. Mafitti at Somwi	21. Meli—Moshi
6. Mafitti at Jambo	22. Mafitti—Mhunzi
7. Mpwapwa	23. Kondoa by Kilosa
8. Sadani—Mandera	24. Kisiba
9. Pangani	25. Wahehe—Munisagara
10. Bushiri	26. Siki—Tabora
11. Bwana Heri—Mlembule	27. Wagogo—Kilimatinde—
12. Bwana Heri—Mlembule	Unyangwira
13. Bwana Heri—Palamakaa	28. Wahehe in Ugogo
14. Kilwa Kiwindje	29. Wasegua
15. Lindi	30. Quamba near Mpwapwa
16. Machemba	31. Mabuena—Gerengere

On the side of the African resisters, similar objectives were pursued as destruction became a means of forcing fence-sitters to take sides and of isolating the military stations through the devastation of the surrounding countryside (Prince 1914:78–79).

The Impact of Pacification

In order to gain an overall impression of the magnitude of the early colonial wars in Tanganyika, I have compressed some of the available material in Map 7.1 and in the Appendix: 'Early Colonial Wars' (on pp. 188–92). The map is based on original location sketches drawn by Nigmann (1911) and covers the period from 1888 to the Maji Maji uprising. Altogether 84 locations are shown on the map, corresponding roughly to the operations which, according to Section 23 of the Imperial Act of 27th June 1871, qualified as a *Feldzug* and gave rights to state pensions to the German participants. In the Appendix, I have made a partial reconstruction of the quantitative evidence of human and material destruction available on the battles shown on the map.

32. Meli—Moshi	59. Wasweta
33. Nondoa	60. Ukimbu
34. Mafitti at Nserekere Lake	61. Watumbi
35. Warudje	62. Iraku—Ussandaui
36. Ujansi	63. Upogoro
37. Bulima	64. Suma and Wiga—Shirati
38. Kilwa Kiwindje	65. Watende
39. Konko	66. Urundi
40. Iringa	67. Waburungi—Wagaya
41. Mage—Iringa	68. Machemba
42. Kisiba	69. Arusha—Meru
43. Limueme—Usenje	70. Mbulu—Iraku
44. Hasan bin Omar	71. Lupembe—Ubena
45. Gonga Mountains	72. Wabende
46. Lukonge—Ukerewe	73. Uluguru
47. Moa	74. Ussaya—Shirati
48. Waruri	75. Ikoma
49. Urundi	76. Matengo
50. Turu—Irangi	77. Iramba—Issansu
51. Meru	78. Ussandaui
52. Luassa—Uha	79. Msalala
53. Uvinza	80. Ussandaui
54. Uhehe	81. Urundi
55. Wahumba—Masai	82. Wassanaki
56. Ussandaui	83. Wawudi
57. Mpwapwa district	84. Masai mountains
58. Urambo	

A number of observations can be made from this exercise. First, it is clear that armed conflict must be seen as a continuous tradition in the German colonial period. Colonial battles and skirmishes were fought throughout the country from 1888 onwards often against a number of different tribes that acted in co-ordination against the foreign occupant. Armed resistance and intertribal co-operation did not commence with the Maji Maji wars, but were further expanded and brought to greater perfection in these wars than during the earliest encounters. Secondly, important losses of manpower were suffered by the different peoples through the 'pacification' measures. The casualties, which are probably under-reported in the Appendix, were made up of the young tribesmen, who represented an important labour potential in the local economies. Their removal could not take place without serious repercussions on the local level. Thirdly, 'pacification' measures were usually accompanied by systematic destruction of houses, crops and storages, as well as by the capture of available stock. Fourthly, the 'pacification' measures were trained on some of the major peoples of the nineteenth century and continued over a number of years as in the case of the Wahehe, Wagogo and the peoples of the Arusha-Moshi areas. The local economies thus suffered repeated disruptions and made reconstruction a difficult task.

Neither map nor table covers the extensive Maji Maji wars, which caused extraordinary havoc mainly due to the scorched-earth policy pursued against the warring tribes. The military command found that famine was its most useful weapon (Götzen 1909:132). The guerilla tactics of the tribes made it impossible to inflict significant losses in battle and the theatre of operations was too vast to permit a concerted military response. Instead the attention was trained on the civilian population. Kozak has detailed these events in Ngoni territory where Hauptmann Johannes' troops never pursued the Wangoni forces, but were stationed in strategic food-producing locations to prevent any farm activity during the main seeding periods. The local people were faced with the cruel choice of surrendering or facing death by starvation (Kozak 1968). This practice continued even after the formal surrender of the Wangoni chiefs. 'From Songea (the district headquarters) the people were prevented from cultivating their fields anew', wrote Father Häfliger at the Kigonsera Mission. 'Upon my remonstrations I was answered: "The people should know what it means to stage a rebellion"' (quoted in Kozak 1968:104).

The total loss of lives during the Maji Maji wars is a matter of conjecture. An early official population estimate indicated that 166,000 people lived in Songea District in 1902/3 (Anlagen 1903:7). Häfliger thought that no more than 20,000 were left after the Maji Maji wars. The difference does not, however, represent absolute deaths, since many people fled or migrated to other areas due to the military presence and the continuing food shortages. By August 1907, when the military operations had ended, the German Reichstag received the information that a total of 75,000 Africans had died during the war (quoted in Iliffe 1969:21). Hill (1957, II:93) puts the total figure at 120,000 dead, mostly from famine. Father Büttner (n.d.:31) claimed that nine-tenths of the Pangwa tribe of 30,000 had been wiped out. In 1908 there were only 70 children in all of the Upangwa area.

It was with particular reference to the Maji Maji wars that Moffett—paraphrasing Tacitus' verdict on the Roman warfare in Germany—wrote that 'the Germans in East Africa made a solitude and called it peace' (Moffett 1958:76). I have sought to point out that large-scale destruction took place through colonial warfare from the year 1888. An entirely new dimension of destructiveness was added to military operations at this point. No amount of native savagery could have had a similar impact on the general economy and on the population. The contrast between the old and the new barbarism is brought out in one of the songs recorded by Weule at Masasi in 1908 by an old bard—Sulila—who had experienced the transition:

> Let us be brave, we elders. They asked: What is war? They say: 'Mr. Sulila is not yet born.' Then comes (the war) of the Mazitu (Ngoni); guns are fired; then they ran away. But the Germans came; it was dangerous to see; the bush was burnt, the goats were burnt, the fowls were burnt—the people were finished up altogether; the tax came up (they had) to bring a hundred jars (of rupees). They were not satisfied. (Their) heart was frightened. Mr. Sulila telegraphed to the District Commissioner: 'He may skin me to make a bag for his money.' Now I am tired (Weule 1909:173–74).

The First World War

The area where the Maji Maji wars had been fought became ten years later the major theatre of operations for Lettow-Vorbeck's guerillas in the drawn-out East African Campaign. I shall complete this section on European warfare in Tanganyika with a brief review of the impact of the First World War on the local economy.

It is quite evident that the people of Tanganyika bore the brunt of this campaign and that their economy suffered heavily. Indirectly, large sections of the population were affected through the procurations policy of the warring armies which reduced local stores to mere survival rations. Also, a more limited portion of the people were drawn directly into the campaign as beasts of burden moving supplies for the two armies, building their roads and doing general camp work. Lettow-Vorbeck (1920:21) indicated that 'hundreds of thousands of carriers worked for the troops', but gave no precise figure for the German recruitments which were largely by forced conscription. Most sources are equally vague about the numbers involved. The Germans kept up a heavy demand on local manpower throughout the phase of traditional warfare, that is until the end of 1916. The main carrier corps was then dismissed and guerilla warfare commenced with a vastly reduced team of Africans following the German troops. By this time the Allied forces had experienced their own difficulties with mechanized transport in the East African rains, and had come to rely increasingly on local carriers. In early 1917, the Allied carrier corps was estimated by Fendall to have reached somewhere between 125,000 and 135,000. He thought, however, that at least double that number had at some stage been engaged by the Allied forces (Fendall 1921:206). While the Allied carrier recruitment initially had taken place in Kenya (Savage and Munro 1966) and West Africa, recruitment in Tanganyika seems to have dominated from late 1916 onwards. It seems possible to conclude from the two sources quoted above, that upwards to one-half million Tanganyikans were at some stage engaged by the troops to take part in the war effort. According to Fendall, the conditions under which the carriers laboured were 'appallingly difficult', particularly during the operations along the rivers of southern Tanganyika. But already the German rescue operations of 1916 bringing food supplies from the Central Railway to the troop concentrations at Kilimanjaro had shown the predatory wastages in the carrier corps. Some 10,000 carriers had been recruited to move supplies to the nearest connecting link on the Usambara railroad. Their work was extremely strenuous and the health conditions precarious. Lung illnesses and dysentery ravaged the ranks. Some 2,000 carriers died during this operation (Schnee 1919:144).

Fendall's experience with the carrier plight was along the Rufiji River where the porters worked for whole marches up to their armpits in water. 'The wastage was dreadful. The motor drivers lasted a few weeks at the outside. As for the porters, they went sick and died at an alarming rate' (Fendall 1921:92). British intelligence reported that the German conscripts deserted in large numbers and that the carriers therefore were tied together in camp at night (Buchanan 1919:153). Conditions in the Allied quarters were hardly any better. Writers from both sides deplored that it was impossible to keep the carriers on more than half-rations even during some of the most exhausting supply movements (Schnee 1919:238; Fendall 1921:206).

By and large, it was the produce of their fellow countrymen that the porters were moving along to the troops. With the coastal towns blockaded by Allied ships, the German army was entirely dependent on local food supplies. The survival of the army was the primary objective, and it is likely that these supplies were acquired under duress and cut into the normal survival margins of the local food stores and cattle herds. Schnee indicated that European plantations were quickly re-oriented to produce for war purposes, but that 90 per cent of the foodstuffs collected came from the African producers (Schnee 1919:142). As the German campaign increasingly turned to guerilla techniques, formal supplies were dispensed with along with the carrier corps. The army started to live off the land and organized its own units (*Erntekommandos*) that were charged with bringing in sufficient supplies from the neighbouring communities. A similar practice had been used earlier in the campaign whenever supply lines had broken down. This was the case in central Tanganyika in 1916 when the troops—both German and Allied—harvested the native fields. 'Subsistence depended almost entirely on the stuff the forage-parties of the companies were able to bring in', wrote Lettow-Vorbeck from Kondoa-Irangi. 'In this extremely rich Kondoa country the troops could obtain a variety of food in abundance' (Lettow-Vorbeck 1920:139). Feeling the pinch of disrupted supply lines, the South African troops entering Mpwapwa in 1917 resorted to similar practices. They 'scoured the country for food of any kind', according to Collyer (1939:185).

The campaign south of the Central Railway Line was fought almost entirely on a guerilla basis by the German defenders. Schnee seems to indicate that their movements were largely determined by the availability of food (Schnee 1919:270), and it may be a question whether Lettow-Vorbeck's guerilla tactics were forced on him by the supply situation or whether they were selected on military/logistic grounds. The transition to the new tactics took place in Rufiji in January 1917 under near-famine conditions when it became imperative to reduce the number of unproductive mouths in the German ranks. In February the troops left the Ulanga Valley because of acute food shortages in the area. Under these circumstances the civilian population of the war zone suffered enormously. Schnee recognized the severe hardships inflicted on the sparse population, living without cattle in an area which, even in peacetime, had shown difficulties in producing a viable surplus. In many instances, the war-time experience would seem to have been the beginning of the hunter-gatherer existence of some of the southern peoples in recent times. Conditions became so precarious, wrote Schnee, that people left their houses and fields and took refuge in the bush. Only occasionally and at night time would they steal back to search for food in their own *shambas* (Schnee 1919:271–72).

LABOUR RECRUITMENT

The German administrators and settlers were quick to identify the labour problem as the key to colonial success. The early importation of Chinese and Javanese workers was a temporary solution to the problems raised by the local economy which did not generate a proletariat for labour exploitation. In addition to this general problem, two factors aggravated the chances for successful labour recruitment. One was the seasonal character of much of the early European demand, notably on the plantations, which coincided with the planting and harvesting seasons of the local peasants. A second feature was the heavy geographical concentration of the labour demand basically in two areas, Tanga-Usambara and Lindi districts. A less concentrated demand arose in connection with the Central (Dar es Salaam—Kigoma) railroad construction. Some appreciation of the geographic location of the labour demand can be seen from Map 7.2 which indicates German plantations and settlements around 1908.

Against these difficulties, a situation of greater responsiveness to labour recruitment had to be engineered. The Tax Ordinance (*Steuerverordnung*) of 1 November 1897 introducing the Hut Tax into the *Schutzgebiet* was the first public effort in this direction (Bursian 1910). The tax could be paid in produce, work or cash. It was replaced by a further tax ordinance of 22 March 1905 which considerably increased the tax rate and changed the system from the hut model levied on the entire family to the head tax which hit the individual as a potential worker. It is the impact of these legal manipulations aimed at creating a work force that is of interest here. In the following section, I shall briefly outline: (1) the growth and size of the African labour force, and (2) the result of labour recruitment on the local economies and populations.

The African Labour Force

We do not possess a full labour survey for the German period in Tanganyika. Some scattered information is available on the new initiatives like railroad-building, construction of military and administrative *bomas*, and plantations. Much less is known about the development of domestic services, porterage and sea-transport, and about the transfers of workers from older professions to fill the newly created labour demands. Table 7.2, which is compiled from occasional listings in the annual reports from the *Schutzgebiet*, is, therefore, a tentative outline only. It can bring some initial light on the problem, but lacks precision as a basis for accurate appreciation. It shows the very rapid expansion of the colonially oriented labour force from a few thousand around 1900 to more than 170,000 in the years preceding the First World

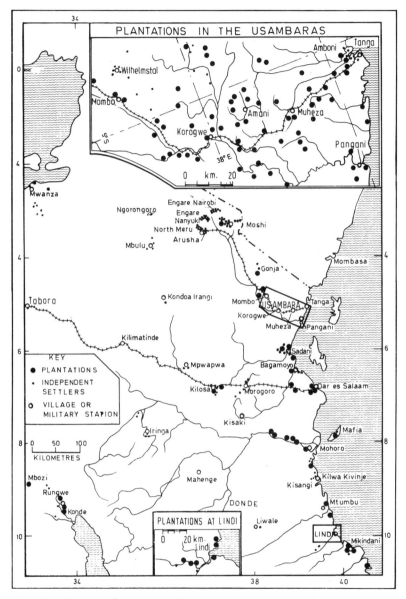

Map 7.2.   German Plantations and Settlements, ca. 1908. (Based on Meyer 1909.)

TABLE 7.2. *The Tanganyika Labour Force, 1900–1913*

Type of Labour	1900–01	1901–02	1902–03	1908–09	1910–11	1911–12	1912–13
Plantation labour	4–5,000	4,500–5,050	10,000–11,500	36,126	57,526	80,290	91,892
Mining and Industrial Labour					3,260	2,235	2,966
DSM—Kigoma Railroad (construction)				14,200	8,500–14,500	11,000	18,000–16,000
DSM—Kigoma Railroad (operations)					2,707	3,671	3,090
Rebuilding DSM—Morogoro railbedding							2,400
Tanga–Usambara Railroad (construction)					6,900	5,400	655
Tanga–Usambara Railroad (operations)					684	684	877
Harbour construction, Tanga							100
Workers on Government stations							5,000
Employees with European traders							2,500
Caravan carriers in European employment							5,000
Mission employees						1,000	3,000
Domestics in European service						8,000	9,000
Askaris in military and police service						6,000	6,000
Caravan carriers for non-Europeans						20,000	15,000
Workers and domestics in Arab and Indian service						10,000	10,000
Sailors						1,000	1,200
Total in salaried employment (permanent)						156,000	172,000

Sources: 1900–1909—*Janresbericht*
1910–1913—*Die Deutschen Schutzgebiete in Afrika und der Südsee*

War. We do not know exactly where these workers came from, what age-group they represented, etc. Further work in this area is clearly needed.

Impact on Local Economies

It seems likely that much of the early colonial labour force resulted from a gradual absorption and transformation of previous part-time workers like the carriers in long-distance trading. The great caravan trade was drastically altered by the colonial impact. The Kilwa trade route had practically folded up by 1900 (Fuchs 1905) as a result of the activities of the African Lakes Corporation which began supplying the areas bordering Lake Nyassa and Lake Tanganyika from the east coast via the Zambezi and Shire rivers. A second development was the creation of a Belgian colony in the Congo. This sealed off most of the Manyema trade from reaching Tanganyika.[1] Thirdly, the completion of the Mombasa railroad to Victoria Nyanza in 1901 reoriented the trading patterns around the Lake and deeply affected the trading and transport activities of the Wanyamwezi and the Wasukuma. While the Germans deplored the overall loss of trade, they welcomed the release of labour which they hoped could be quickly absorbed into their own enterprises. Thus, the Dar es Salaam–Kigoma railway was created with the double purpose of re-establishing the former trading axis through central Tanganyika and releasing further manpower for colonizing purposes.

The long-distance trading of the Wanyamwezi is a well-documented enterprise. Already Burton had described them as 'the only professional porters of East Africa' (Burton 1860, II:29–30). Meyer (1909, II:391–92) estimated that some 200,000 carriers passed annually through Tabora at the height of the trade. This was a seasonal undertaking that had extended from the Unyamwezi and related economies, and was still intimately tied to the planting and harvest seasons when the Germans arrived. Burton reported that caravans did not set out from Unyanyembe during the rainy season and that the men seldom left their fields between the months of October and May (Burton 1860, I:339). Broyon-Mirambo, the Swiss sailor-trader who became the son-in-law of the famous Urambo chief, indicated that this pattern had changed little toward the end of the 1870s despite the enormous expansion of the caravan traffic during the intervening twenty years:

> The Wanyamwezi, although they are travellers and traders, generally remain at home at seed-time and harvest; they are for the most part good agriculturalists,

[1] While 208,000 kilos of ivory had reached the coast in the peak year of 1892, the average annual trade fell to 20,000–25,000 kilos after 1900 (Stuhlmann 1909:792).

and for this reason provisions are always abundant in their country (Broyon-Mirambo 1877:36).

A report written from Tabora during the short rains in 1892 indicated that not a single carrier was available during this period because every man was at work in the family *shamba* (Sigl 1892:166).

By 1900, conditions had changed, for the *Jahresbericht* for that year reported that the 'industrious' Wanyamwezi—were finally being 'persuaded' to enlist for longer periods of work in the Usambaras and on the coast. Some evidently took up permanent residence (*Jahresbericht* 1900/1901:15). Tax exemption, which initially existed only for contracts longer than six months, undoubtedly contributed to this change. Increasingly, therefore, the men from the interior cut themselves off from the home economy and commenced a proletarian existence on the coast. Some of the results of this development could be seen by 1910 and have been documented in a series of reports on village life in Unyamwezi.

The absence of men was a striking feature throughout Unyamwezi in this period, and only women, children and old people could be seen in the villages. Under their care, agricultural production and cattle-keeping was in rapid decline. From surplus production in the early 1890s, the province was on the verge of poverty in 1910: 'This country-side which was once the granary of the interior and a showcase of agricultural enterprise, has completely deteriorated under the impact of the labour migration (*Sachsengängerei*) of able-bodied men which has been going on for years', wrote the *Koloniale Rundschau* (1910).

In 1910, Hans Meyer travelled through Ushirombo where, for lack of any male labourers in the villages, he was forced to hire women to relieve the sick porters in his caravan. He wrote about general economic decay in the area and stated that he had never, during his wide travels in East Africa seen such poorly-kept houses and fields as in Ushirombo (Meyer 1911:356). The Central Railroad was approaching Tabora at this time, and Meyer made some interesting observations on rural and urban changes:

> Complete changes are taking place in Tabora with the approach of the railway . . . Numerous trading spots, stores, bars and hotels have already opened their gates and await the stream of business which the railroad is supposed to bring . . .
>
> Unfortunately, the district of Tabora has had no share in the upswing which Tabora town is enjoying. The migration of a large part of the male population to coastal plantation areas and to the railroad acts like a cancer on the central regions whose people are correctly regarded as the most industrious and motivated workers of our colony (Meyer 1911:357).

A year after Meyer's visit, a White Father, Burgt, who had lived in Ushirombo since 1892, confirmed the decline of agriculture in the district and pointed out that in areas where the majority of the men had gone to work for the Europeans, the independent local economy was deteriorating. He stressed that the continued sapping of the labour force from central Tanganyika was fraught with great dangers. It caused not only the ruin of the indigenous economy, but exposed the entire province to the very real dangers of depopulation. The author estimated that there might have been as many as one million people in the four major tribes of the province, the Wasukuma, Wagwe, Wirwana and the Wassumbwa, in 1890 (see also Buder 1899). By 1912, he reported, 'the population of Unyamwezi has declined enormously and will soon disappear completely. Abandoned or half-empty and decaying villages (*majaja*) can be met everywhere; everywhere are the signs of old cultivations' (Burgt 1913:706). Burgt thought that the population had been reduced to less than 500,000. In 1893, there had been 120 villages in Ushirombo chiefdom, some of which, like Igulwa, the chief's headquarters counted more than 1,000 people. By 1912, there were hardly 5,000 people in the entire chiefdom. The birthrate had decreased, and there were few children in the villages. A survey of 840 married women revealed only 702 children; the majority of the women having only one child or no children at all. Burgt warned that the unrestricted labour recruitment would have to stop in order to prevent a major demographic catastrophe (Burgt 1913; see also Löbner 1914).

The author challenged as outrageously false the notion that working with the European planter was a school of civilization and an education to work, and that the Nyamwezi worker therefore would return from the coast better equipped to 'develop' the local economy. Burgt reported that not even one in three of the men came back to the villages. Those who did return, brought with them less cash than *kaswende*—venereal disease. He thus pointed to the appalling health conditions in the early labour camps and to the workers' easy exposure to epidemics and prostitution. These conditions have been discussed in detail by Otto Peiper (1920) who recorded a 50 per cent mortality among the plantation workers. Those who survived became the carriers of venereal diseases to the interior which may have been relatively untouched by these illnesses at the time. Thus, Burgt stated that there was no syphilis among the Wanyamwezi until the intensification of the long-distance trade on the coast.

Bösch (1930) also blamed the migrant workers for the spread of the disease to Unyamwezi. A review of the *Medizinal-Berichte* of the early German period confirms that venereal disease became a major problem after 1900. It was described variously as a '*Landeplage, algemeines Volksleiden*, and *Haupt-*

volkskrankheit', thus indicating the seriousness of a problem regarded as relatively new.

Unyamwezi was not unique in being a labour-recruiting area. Several labour pools were created, and other peoples from Kigoma, Ruvuma, Singida, Mtwara, Ufipa, etc., were at some stage affected by the European penetration and drawn into the labour market. The resulting development in Ufipa showed clear parallels to what had happened in Ushirombo. During large parts of the year all male hands were absent working on European plantations or in the railway camps, and Ufipa was full of 'spinster villages' (*Frauendörfer*) where authority rested with wretched old men who were unable to work (Fromm 1912:93).

The forced hiring of porters during the 1914–18 campaigns has already been reviewed. It was a different but related chapter in the uprooting of the Tanganyikan husbandman and the destruction of the local economy.

Much of the early patterns of labour migration, whether forced or voluntary, still remain and can be seen in a recent publication by Claeson and Egeroe (1971). Not all labour pools were as badly affected as Ushirombo and Ufipa, although features of their experience can probably be traced in all labour-exporting areas throughout Tanganyika. In most of them, economic recovery remains an agenda for the future.

SUMMARY

We have seen that the great Rinderpest of the early 1890s practically eliminated cattle from the traditional economies. In considering the fate of the people, we have documented a number of natural and man-made calamities that undermined the people's health and well-being. It is in this period we find the demographic break and the commencement of depopulation that I suggested in Chapter 1.

Man and beast combined to maintain an ecological control situation throughout the nineteenth century. With the removal of cattle and the weakening of the population, this hold on the environment started to slip. We shall see the result of this in the following chapter where I shall pay particular attention to sleeping sickness (trypanosomiasis) as the direct result of the deteriorating ecological situation. We shall also consider the policy measures invented to combat trypanosomiasis and pursue their overall relation to the question of ecological control.

CHAPTER 8

The Ecological Collapse: Results and Remedies

The result of the interlinked tragedies discussed in Chapter 7 has been anticipated throughout. In a short period of time they led to the collapse of the man-controlled ecological system of the nineteenth century. With fewer people to till the fields and fewer cattle and goats to graze the ground and keep the bush at bay, and with imperial laws prohibiting grass-burning and hunting, nature was quick to commence its recovery. The managed culture became overgrown by shrubs and trees. Wild animals, recovering from the Rinderpest, soon moved in to establish grazing grounds in old cultivations. In their wake, the tsetse fly spread to put vast domains of land beyond the reach of economic activity.

I have earlier pointed to the connection, made in German reports, between the depopulation of the Tabora region and the advance of the fly-belt there. Similar observations from other localities indicate a country-wide pattern of ecological transformation. Bursell reviewed the situation around Songea:

> The areas which have recently been invaded by tsetse appear to have been well populated during the last century; from local evidence it seems that they were deserted about the time of the Maji-Maji rebellion, early in the present century. Owing to the somewhat primitive methods of cultivation practised in these parts of Songea, conditions for regeneration would be favourable once the cultivations had been abandoned. The original vegetation has been able to re-establish itself without reverting to earlier stages in the plant succession, and at present the vegetation has reached the dry sub-climax characteristics of the greater part of Southern Tanganyika. This sub-climax is the *Brachysteiga Pseudoberlinia* woodland, locally known as '*miombo*' (Bursell 1955:590–91).

The ecology of the Lupa Goldfields in Chunya was discussed by Grantham in 1932. The area was then uninhabited and covered with *miombo*. Grantham thought that the area had been previously cultivated probably by a small and shifting population (Grantham 1932:2). From Uzinza, Burtt reported on his first flight over the area: 'We observed that much of the Northern part of the Uzinza hinterland in the chiefdoms of Buchosa and Karumo were clothed with a very open form of *Combretum* woodland, greatly resembling regeneration on old cultivation'. Burtt also confirmed an older report by Napier Bax who had written from the area west of the Geita Hills of 'great islands of old cultivation in all stages of reversion to bush' (Burtt 1937). Culwick wrote from Bukoba (Kbwera and Bugeni) of former agricultural areas that had become overgrown by trees and shrubs. This had led to the eastward expansion of the fly-belt 'making it impossible to keep stock in places where cattle formerly flourished' (Culwick 1938:33). In southern Uha, Grant made these observations:

> In earlier times the mountains of Ushingo and parts of the lowlands, as for instance Masengi, Mitundu, Mulalo, Sabaga and Kalimungoma, were cattle districts, the cattle having died from rinderpest some time before European administration. The loss of stock caused the people to move, the one-time cattle areas becoming re-forested, and the tsetse has returned ... Sabaga is of peculiar interest: what was, within the memory of natives still living, an open grassy plain dotted with cattle, sheep, and goats is today a vast deep papyrus swamp full of hippo, sititunga, crocodile, wildfowl, etc. (Grant 1925:412).

A similar transformation took place, not only in the open grass-steppes and *miombo* woodlands but also in the highlands. Karagwe, for example, underwent in a somewhat longer time extensive ecological changes. The situation was reviewed by McMaster:

> No longer could a depleted population, with few cattle, maintain the open grasslands. The bush grew away from them and created a habitat favourable to invasion by the tsetse fly (especially *Glossina Morsitans*) which advancing by way of the central depression and the Kagera Valley, was not slow to enter the domain. Such is the delicacy of ecological balances that the subsequent condition of high Karagwe was in some ways worse than its original state before the entry of man. Early man had the advantage of virgin soils, and it is reasonable to assume that the Bahima entered into tsetse-free pastures. Today the reclamation of high Karagwe faces greater difficulties; the problems posed by the tsetse fly and soil depletion are accentuated in the presence of a disintegrated human society (McMaster 1962:88–89).

An illustration of this widespread ecological transformation can be seen in Figure 8.1. It shows the reduction of the open and cultivated land in four western districts of Tanganyika: Biharamulo, Kahama, Tabora and Ufipa. By 1929, the man-controlled areas of these districts are mere isolated islands in the vast expanses of tsetse bush.

In 1913, the German administrators produced the first comprehensive map of the tsetse fly situation in Tanganyika. It has been reproduced as Map 8.1 on p. 164 and shows approximately one-third of the country covered by the fly-belts. Although a number of reservations could be made with regard to the minute accuracy of survey maps of this nature, the map provides the general outlines of the danger-zones at the time. A later sleeping-sickness officer with the British government held the map to be 'a surprisingly poor product', omitting important tsetse-belts with which, he thought, the Germans would certainly have been familiar (Napier Bax 1943a:42). His judgement was probably wrong. There is little doubt about the important advance of the tsetse belts in this period, although it was discussed far more freely in confidential reports than in public announcements. The East African Commission on the Tsetse Problem in Tanganyika Territory warned in 1924 that the fly-areas were expanding and would, if not dealt with, soon cover three quarters of the entire territory (*TNA 2702, II*).

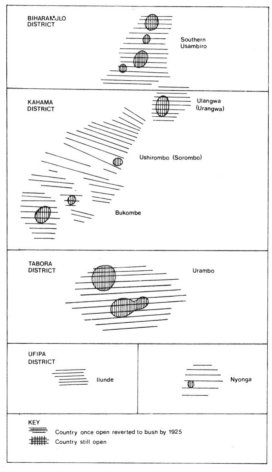

Figure 8.1.   Diagram to Illustrate Reversion from Open Country to Tsetse Bush in Different Districts. (Redrawn from Maclean 1929.)

Map 8.1.   The Tsetse Belts of 1913. (Based on *DDS* 1912/13.)

The tsetse situation of the inter-war period is shown in Potts' map reproduced on p. 165. It shows approximately two-thirds of the country occupied by tsetse flies. A comparison of the two maps confirms the advance of the fly which was common knowledge among the administrators in the German as well as in the British period. It was nevertheless hard to admit to an almost complete failure to check the spreading tsetse after years of research and reclamation measures. It was equally difficult for the colonial mind to conceive of an important African initiative—including successful ecological control—prior to the coming of the Europeans.

The African achievement, as well as an account of the complex factors leading to its decline, has been brought out in the evidence in the preceeding chapters. On the strength of this evidence, it seems possible to conclude that the two maps portray fairly accurately the deteriorating situation where bush and fly were on the advance driving the peasantry

Map 8.2.   The Tsetse Belts of 1937. (Based on Potts 1937.)

and their cattle to retreat before them. At a crucial stage in this decline, a new ecological balance was established in which man was no longer in control and where he suffered the consequences of this through *nagana* and sleeping sickness which erupted in epidemic form in East Africa at the beginning of this century.

SLEEPING SICKNESS

In 1901, Dr. Albert Cook reported a mysterious new disease from different localities in Busoga, Uganda. This was sleeping sickness. By the end of 1903, 90,000 people had died from the illness. By 1906 the death toll had risen to 200,000 (Bell 1909, 1910). It was believed that the illness had entered the Protectorate through infected soldiers among Emin Pasha's troops who had been rescued from Wadelia on the Albert Nile by the Stanley/Tippu Tib Expedition. Sleeping sickness was thought to have spread to Wadelia from old endemic foci in the lower Congo during the first years of existence of the Congo Free State when the country was 'opened up for trade and enterprise' by European initiative. Epidemics were held to be the unwitting result of civilization which created avenues for the spread of the trypanosomes to new populations. Cruel loss of lives was the initial price of the trypanosome's adaptation to a new human environment. The outbreak of sleeping-sickness epidemics could thus be explained through a migratory thesis by tracing connections between areas of epidemics and the known historic foci of the illness (Fairbairn 1948; Morris 1963; Ormerod 1961).

When sleeping sickness was discovered in Tanganyika along the shores of Victoria Nyanza in 1904, the *Medizinal-Berichte* reported that the illness had travelled with migrant labourers who had become infected while working in Uganda (*Medizinal-Berichte* 1908–1909:26). Outbreaks along Lake Tanganyika and in Ruanda and Burundi were thought to have resulted from sick people coming in from the Congo. When sleeping sickness erupted along the Ruvuma River in 1910, the investigating doctor was able to trace the source of the epidemic to a house-servant who had become infected in Mozambique territory when he visited there with his master (*Medizinal-Berichte* 1910–11:62–63). An independent focus of the illness was thought to have been established in the Zambezi Valley from the Congo and spread northwards to Mozambique and Ruvuma. Again, when the Maswa epidemic broke out in 1922, it was attributed to sick Congolese soldiers who were said to have brought the illness during the First World War. The Maswa focus was seen as the origin of several later epidemics (Fairbairn 1948).

This migratory thesis is increasingly being discredited as an entomological endorsement of the tendency among colonial administrators always to blame calamities on neighbouring countries and communities. Instead, there is growing interest in a theory (ecological thesis) which explains conditions of epidemic sleeping sickness from specific ecological imbalances, as 'a consequence of quantitative changes in the relationships of three of the five populations involved—man, his domestic livestocks, and the wild fauna—and the effects of these changes upon the remaining two populations, the trypanosomes and the tsetses' (Ford 1971:494). All these populations have had a long presence in East Africa. What has been changing over time has been the relative frequence of their interaction. The original establishment of man's ecological control of the area undoubtedly exposed the first pioneers to the acute dangers of trypanosomiasis. As man's control became established we can imagine that the danger of interaction with the vectors was reduced. Individuals undoubtedly continued to contract sleeping sickness and occasionally to die from the illness, but no records were kept and the frequency of cases was too low to give rise to extensive tribal lore. On the whole, endemicity did not hinder economic exploitation and development.

Mild endemicity erupted into epidemics due to factors which affected the population, predisposed it to the onslaught of the illness and increased the frequency of interaction between man and vectors. These are concrete historical factors. Their joint impact altered, in a most fundamental way, the very basis for the East African existence, namely man's ecological control. This control situation was not broken until 1890 but in many areas of East Africa recovery is still a matter for future generations to achieve.

It lies beyond the scope of this study to explain the entomological advances that substantiate the ecological thesis. The interested reader is referred to the works by Hoare (1972) on trypanosomes and by Ford (1971) where the ecological thesis has been explained and illustrated with case studies from well-known epidemics. On the strength of his evidence, Ford believes it possible that the Ugandan tragedy of 1901 'grew out of a long-standing endemic condition' (Ford 1971:243), thus cutting the umbilical cord of the migratory thesis which, until recently, has explained all later epidemics in East Africa through a Congo/Uganda connection.[1]

Tsetse and trypanosome research led to a number of discoveries which, in due time, influenced public policy measures intended to combat sleeping sickness. One such measure resulted from Robert Koch's discovery of the crocodile as the favourite feeding ground of *Glossina papalis*. Consequently, a plan was conceived to starve out the flies by depriving them of their favourite food. In the British-German Treaty of 27th October 1908 on the Combat of Sleeping Sickness in East Africa, the contracting parties declared an all-out war on the crocodiles. Soon the local population was engaged in egg collection and apparently waged a successful campaign. 'One saw hundreds of thousands of crocodile eggs piled up at the headquarters in Mwanza during the days when the

[1] Dr. Feldmann of the German medical corps seems to have had early doubts about the migratory thesis. His own research on Ukerewe island and at Ikoma convinced him that sleeping sickness had manifested itself in the area previously. The Wakerewe described an illness called *Ruti* and *Msiro* which Feldmann thought might have been sleeping sickness. In Ikoma he obtained information of an illness which was said to have occurred approximately 100 years earlier and caused depopulation in several districts. The illness had originated through the bite of flies. The flies had entered the country along with herds of buffaloes that had been displaced inland because of heavy flooding in the two rivers Ruwana and Mbelegiti. The buffaloes did not become sick, and after their return to old grazing areas the illness also subsided (*Medizinal-Berichte*, 1905–6:63).

stipulated collector's premium was paid out', read an account of the operation (Steudel 1928:28).

A few years later, Bruce made suggestions to the Desart Committee to make complete wildlife elimination a part of the sleeping-sickness campaign (Desart 1914). Similar solutions, which focused on the importance of the permanent host in combat measures, were expressed by Dr. Davey in connection with the Maswa epidemic in 1924, as I have discussed in Chapter 4. They were disregarded because of the prevailing logic of the migratory thesis with its preoccupation with the man–fly relationship.

A programme for mass evacuation of populations at risk was embarked upon to save lives during the Uganda epidemic. The entomological understanding at the time was that the human trypanosomes were transferred mechanically on the proboscis of the fly from one person to the other. It was thought that the transfer of the illness could be broken by the isolation of the sick and the separation of the healthy people from the infected vector. People were therefore moved to safe areas away from the fly population to await a time when the infected flies had died and the home areas could be reoccupied at no further risk. This intention was nullified by the discovery that tsetse flies could remain infectious for generations, a discovery which motivated the policy of total tsetse eradication contained in the Desart Committee's report in 1914. In practical terms, this policy led to the establishment of permanent population concentrations and clearings. The Desart approach directly affected the ecological control situation by surrendering the land and by removing human beings and domestic animals from the lines of confrontation with the insect vector of trypanosomiasis.

Dr. Maclean (1930) pointed to differences between this approach and that taken earlier by the Germans in Tanganyika. Their strategy—apart from erecting treatment centres where sick people could be isolated and attended to—was apparently to concentrate on reclamation work to clear bush and shoot wild animals in the field. The population at large was left alone to take up the challenge of the invading tsetse in their home areas. With the British entry into Tanganyika, the concentration policy came to prevail there also.

THE PERIPHERY IN COLONIAL DEVELOPMENT

Sleeping Sickness Concentrations

The British continued some of the German initiatives, but expanded them through the Desart policy of large-scale concentrations. Single families or individuals living scattered in tsetse-infested forest country were brought together to areas which were deemed to have fertile soils and permanent water. These areas were cleared of bush for permanent settlement. 'Provided the site is suitable', wrote Maclean (1930:122), 'the bigger the population the greater the prospects of success'. The aim was to achieve a population density of at least 100 people per square mile in the clearings. At this level it was thought that the people, by their own efforts, would eradicate all traces of the fly and keep the settlements in a risk-free condition. One thousand families were seen by Maclean as a reasonable minimum for a viable concentration.

The concentrations were intended to facilitate internal development as centres of education, health, water and conversion. A trained dresser would be present in all of them to detect possible outbreaks of sleeping sickness. It was further planned to bring in new methods of agriculture and husbandry to improve the general economy of the affected areas. Maclean's 'Hexagon Scheme'—based on a rotation system and six years of fallow—was introduced in a first effort to regiment peasant agriculture at the lowest level (Maclean 1930).

Through the implementation of this scheme it was calculated that a total of 8 to 12 acres of land could be kept under effective control by each family in the settlements. It was seen as an essential step towards proper utilization of land. On paper, its prospects of success seemed at the time quite as self-evident as the later schemes of block-farming, village settlements and *ujamaa* villages.

The scheme assessments were initially favourable. The resettlement of scattered Waha of Kibondo/Kasulu 'marks something like a revolution in their tribal life', stated one report. It 'will make easier the task of changing a disease-ridden and backward horde of savages into a disciplined and prosperous community' (*PCAR* 1933:77–78).

Moffett described the concentration schemes as necessary consolidations for renewed human advance: 'Since one or the other, man or *Morsitans*, had to move', he wrote, 'it was perforce man who did so. He moved; but it was not a mere ignominious retreat, rather it was a tactical manoeuvre to enable him to take up a better defensive position' (Moffett 1939:35). The people affected by the move were 'happy and content' and 'genuinely pleased with their new surroundings' (Moffett 1939:37). The particular site discussed by Moffett—who was the officer in charge of operations—was Urambo where the concentration of 1,000 families was carried out in 1936–37. People were moved from a number of scattered Urambo homesteads and villages to the Nchemba concentration area some 40 miles northwest of Tabora on the Tabora–Isehangazi road. The grave sites of Mirambo—the 'Bonaparte of East Africa'—and of

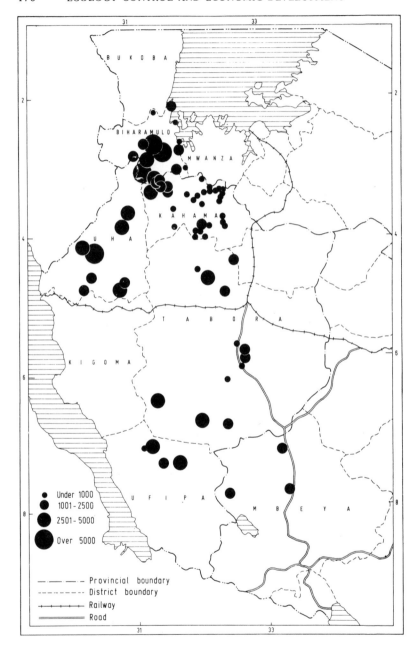

Map 8.3. Sleeping-Sickness Concentrations (until 1934). (Based on Gillman 1936.)

Mpendeshalo, his brother and successor, were left when their people were undertaking their 'strategic retreat'. Today, the Unyamwezi tribal land has become the home of refugees from Ruanda at Ulyankulu where a town of 30,000–40,000 peoples has been cleared in the bush-remains of Mirambo's old empire.

Gillman's population map of Tanganyika based on data from the 1931 Census and district supplements up to 1934, identified the different sleeping-sickness concentrations then in existence and indicated their approximate population. The location of the settlements has been presented in Map 8.3, and the numbers of resettled people have been worked out in Table 8.1.

TABLE 8.1.   *Sleeping-Sickness Concentrations in Western*
Tanganyika—until 1934 (after Gillman 1936)

District	Total population (1934 figures)	No. of people in sleeping sickness settlements	Percentage of people concentrated
Kahama	76,000	32,200	43·5
Biharamulo	90,700	37,600	41·5
Tabora	154,300	22,200	14·5
Uha	181,500	22,800	12·5
Ufipa	92,800	9,800	10·5
Mbeya	106,400	5,400	5·0

The table shows that almost half of the populations of Kahama and Biharamulo districts (43·5% and 41·5% respectively) had been moved into sleeping-sickness settlements by 1934, and that important concentrations had taken place in Tabora (14·5%), Uha (12·5%) and Ufipa (10·5%) districts.

Information on the concentrations undertaken in later years is given by Fairbairn (1943, 1948) and has been collected in Table 8.2. The move to concentrate people continued throughout the 1940s and 1950s, particularly in Liwale and Kilombero. Material on the latter settlements has not entered the table. The information is incomplete due to the disappearance in the National Archives of Tanzania of a number of relevant files. It is difficult therefore to provide a full survey of the sleeping-sickness schemes, their magnitude in terms of people involved and expenses in relation to the Government's total welfare and agricultural development schemes.

The Urambo example indicates that the concentration schemes failed as nuclei of economic reconstruction. A review from Singida of Maclean's

'Hexagon Scheme' in 1942 showed that the rotation system had broken down and only the immediate surroundings of the settlements were maintained as cultivated land. Eighty-five per cent of the people of the scheme then lived in and effectively controlled only one-third of the original terrain scheduled for one such scheme. Further concentration of the people was therefore recommended (Minutes, 3–4. 6.42, *TNA* 30600). Another review was made by Staples, a botanist with the Veterinary Department, who visited 27 concentrations in western Tanganyika. Staples pointed to their deficiencies as economic entities. The absence of cattle in most settlements forced people to rely on shifting cultivation and frequent soil exhaustion and erosion were seen as resulting problems (*TNA* 31351). In a more recent evaluation, Apted wrote about a 'static' economic situation in the concentration areas: 'The incidence of the disease was kept down and the threat of epidemic outbreak was minimized, but at the same time there was little chance of development and vast areas of land, much of it of potential value, had to remain unused' (Apted 1962:19). Besides keeping much land uncultivated and ungrazed, the removal of the population turned vast tracts of land over to the inevitable invasion of bush, wildlife and tsetse, causing in a number of instances, a need for second and third concentrations to be undertaken. 'These

TABLE 8.2. *Sleeping-Sickness Concentrations in Tanganyika Territory*

Year	Area	Tribe	Number of taxpayers moved	Total population moved
1933	Kibondo-Kasulu	Waha	11,320	37,300
1933	Biharamulo	—	4,113	13,600
1933	Geita	Wazinza Warongo	1,541	5,400
1936	Urambo	Wanyamwezi	1,251	3,253
1937	Utowa-Bugomba-Bweru	Wanyamwezi Wasumbwa Waha	1,500 150	5,000
1940	Itaranganya-Mpunze	Wasumbwa	461	1,659
1941	Mahenge	Wangindo-Wapogoro	1,680	7,000
1941	Madaba	Wangindo-Wapogoro	166	846
1942	Ruaha	Wangindo-Wapogoro	1,440	5,760
1944	Babati	—	420	1,372
1945	Liwale	—	2,000	8,000

Sources: Fairbairn (1943, 1948).

settlements', wrote Apted, 'were maintained only at the cost of constant vigilance by the Settlement Officers engaged for that purpose' (Apted 1962:18). The administrative files give some of the reasons for the failures. I shall discuss only two of these: the lack of local support due to the hardships associated with the settlement maintenance, and most importantly, the failure to give a positive place to the African and his development in the schemes.

Lack of Local Support

First of all, few settlements enjoyed local support, although they were formally made under the Native Authority Ordinance through local chiefs and headmen. In most instances, neither the sense of urgency for action nor an understanding of the measures proposed seem to have been present in the affected populations. Most concentrations came about through the pressure of district and provincial administrators as instances where it was 'necessary to save the African from himself' as the phrase repeats itself in the official correspondence (*TNA* 31351). In most instances, the people involved were eager to return to their old settlements and to the grave sites of their forefathers and peg themselves to the ground in surroundings they knew and understood.

I have already referred to Moffett's opinion on the Urambo Settlement (see p. 169). As an implementing officer, he was perhaps bound to exaggerate the popularity of the move to concentrate villages. It is revealing, though, that the Provincial Commissioner conceded that the Urambo move had depended for its success on the availability of transport and that the people had such large quantities of food, in addition to the rest of their belongings, that it was impossible for them to move unaided. (Letter to Chief Secr. 4.12.36, *TNA* 23892). Also disestablished through the Urambo move was a newly-built Moravian church.

The administrative files thus reveal that viable communities—not scattered homesteads—many times were being uprooted and brought into what Apted judged to be 'static' economic conditions. Moreover, the viability of the communities may have taken a turn for the worse as the cycle of local economic activities was broken and the planting seasons disrupted as the result of negligence among the implementing officers. A circular from the Department of Agriculture deplored such occurrences:

> Agricultural work is not like some other work; it cannot be put off without risk; you must not miss the planting rains, and foresight is very important. Get that well into the heads of everyone connected with this concentration work as well. It is no use moving people just too late to plant enough to keep them through the year (Circular No. 163. Dept. of Agric. 10.10.33, *TNA* 21709).

A more permanent factor which caused large-scale opposition to the concentrations was the communal bush and forest clearing associated with their maintenance. It was initially attributed to famine when several gangs of Warangi flocked into Arusha in 1927. Further investigations convinced the Labour Commissioner that the move had been caused by dislike of the communal bush cuttings initiated by the Tsetse Department. 'These people went to Arusha, not as workers, but as refugees', he wrote (Letter to Chief Secr. 10.10.27, in *TNA* 11341). A recent paper (McHenry 1974) has suggested that cattle-owning chiefs had vested interests in some of the clearing measures and that an alignment of interests arose between the reclamation officers and the local chiefs. But the chiefs were apparently also deeply concerned by the fact that people were leaving the tribal land in protest against the harassment and the forced reclamation measures. The P.C. Central Province was well aware of the hardships inflicted by inflexible reclamation schemes and the adverse reactions they caused in the local population:

> These continual calls for labour have made both chiefs and people wonder when they will be allowed to devote themselves—undisturbed for a spell—to the care of their own flocks and herds and the preparation and cultivation of their shambas. Neither the chiefs nor the government can regard such a position with equanimity as—if we cause the resident population to move from the fly front—the work of reclamation can only be evanescent (Letter to Chief Secr. 23.11.27, *TNA* 11341).

Various reports complained that concentrations were being deserted by the best manpower, and that efforts to arrest and prosecute were inefficient measures to stem the tide. In some places in the Central Province as much as 15 per cent of the concentrated people—mostly the young and middle-aged men—absconded (P.C. to Chief Secr. 8.6.43, *TNA* 28446). Thus, although labour recruitment was formally prohibited for one year after concentration was completed, these settlements nevertheless produced a willing proletariat which was rapidly drawn out of the local economy.[1]

[1] A few scattered figures from the Provincial Commissioners' Reports indicate the magnitude of the clearing operations.

Communal Bush Clearance

Year	Place	Workforce	Worktime
1929[*]	Kwimba, Maswa	5,600	10 days
1930[**]	Kwimba	9,600	10 days
	Simiyu	12,000	10 days
	Maswa (Ubinza)	12,500	10 days
	Usega	1,200	n.a.
1935[***]	Mkalama	20,000	n.a.

Sources: [*]*Provincial Commissioners' Annual Report, 1929.*   [**]*Provincial Commissioners' Annual Report, 1930.*   [***]*Provincial Commissioners' Annual Report, 1935.*

The Role of Africans

Failure to consider the African positively at the centre of administration and development is part of the colonial legacy. The peripheral place allocated to people can be seen in some of the concentration measures undertaken—not for the purported health reasons—but for reasons of labour recruitment, soil conservation and wildlife protection. In many instances the motivations were interlinked and can be understood only from the point of view of colonial biases. One such bias concerned the African as an inept farmer and husbandman causing soil erosion, water shortage and the general impoverishment of the land. Against this understanding, it was possible to regard the spreading fly-belts and the accompanying depopulation as positively good. 'Animal trypanosomiasis has been by no means an unmixed curse', wrote Kirkpatrick. 'Soil erosion, even though it has only recently become "news", has been, is, and will continue to be, one of the greatest problems of Tropical Africa. Nothing that has so far been done to combat the menace of soil erosion has been so effective as the work of the tsetse-flies' (Kirkpatrick 1936:411). Getting rid of the tsetse would simply mean enlarging the areas open to destruction through wasteful native practices. Although Kirkpatrick suggested combat measures against the tsetse fly, the idea that the fly was holding the land in trust for future more enlightened generations was widespread. By 1962, the idea had cropped up in the prestigeous U.N.-sponsored Food and Agricultural Organization (FAO). One of its pamphlets, dealing with the developmental obstacles posed by the tsetse fly, reads: 'There is perhaps some benefit in the fact that infected areas are protected from improper use; and it is to be hoped that when they are eventually exploited it will be within the framework of proper land-use plans' (FAO 1962:97). Given this basic ambivalence *vis-à-vis* the Africans, concentration measures could be given a positive interpretation even when they had the effect of simply moving people off the land and turning it over to the insect trustee.

By the 1940s, labour recruitment became actively associated with the concentration measure. Forces were at hand in this period to abolish the old centres and create new ones that would be connected to the more dynamic pools of development created by a number of foreign enterprises in the interior of Tanganyika. The interdepartmental Sleeping Sickness Committee made a partial review of some of Maclean's old schemes in 1948. It had this to say:

> These settlements are small and isolated and while reasonably effective in controlling human trypanosomiasis they cannot be regarded as capable of achieving any great degree of economic or social progress. It is borne in mind

that they were made in the presence of a serious outbreak of sleeping sickness some twenty years ago and that while they afforded the most practical solution to the medical and administrative problems posed by the epidemics of 1928 they no longer accord with the economic and other developments of the present time.

Government could properly be advised to abolish the settlements . . . and resettle their inhabitants in proximity to areas being developed which are in need of workers and food products. At the same time all unauthorised bush settlements should be effectively controlled by the appointment of a sufficient number of settlement officers (Minutes, Sleeping Sickness Committee, 11.2.48, *TNA* 23892, II).

The areas considered as being in need of a reorganized population were Mpanda District, with important mineral (maica) developments, and Tabora and Liwale districts, where the groundnut schemes of the Overseas Food Corporation were to be located. In the case of Mpanda, it was recognized that the mining interests (both Uruwira Minerals and the Department of Lands and Mines) were pressuring for resettlement of old concentrations. 'It appears', wrote the Director of Medical Services to the Member for Agriculture and Natural Resources, 'that from an economic point of view and for the prosperity of the mine, such concentrations of population would be of great advantage to Messrs. Uruwira Minerals, both from the provision of local source of native-grown food and a nearby pool of casual labour' (Letter 16.7.48, *TNA* 23892 II).

The proposed location of a groundnut scheme in Nachingwea also changed the fortune of Liwale District where extensive concentrations had been recommenced by the P.C., Rooke Johnston, in 1946. The groundnut scheme gave a new meaning to these operations as they provided necessary labour forces for the expected groundnut boom.

Wildlife Preservation

A general bias in favour of game preservation permeated large parts of the British colonial administration in Tanganyika and accounts for the creation of some of the large game and forest reserves in the territory. Wildlife was given a free license to spread into the vast areas abandoned by people in the concentration moves. In several instances, the two policies were intentionally linked and people were moved out in order to create wildlife sanctuaries. These moves involved thousands of people and square miles of land at the periphery of economic exploitation. With their concentration, the domains under human control were significantly contracted, thus continuing under government auspices the process of ecological transformation that had been at work since the 1890s. We have discussed wildlife in a previous chapter and shall now give only a few examples of the planned disestablishment of the human agency at the frontline of the man-controlled ecosystem.

One of these instances related to the Chimpanzee sanctuary at Gombe stream in Western Kigoma. Chimpanzees were discovered in the area in 1942, and a complete reserve was established in the following year. It included, in addition to about 50 families of monkeys, around 500 people living from fishing in the lake and cutting firewood for curing purposes in the hillside. As the woodcutting was thought to disturb the chimpanzee population, the D.C. received approval to have the people removed from the area in 1944. Wrote the D.C.: 'The number of taxpayers is only 28, and that small strip of country would seem to be of more value to chimpanzees than to these few humans' (D.C. to P.C. Western Province, 25.10.44, *TNA* 31317).

Gombe stream was no isolated incident. The Mbulu Game Reserve was reported to comprise native grazing land extending to thousands of acres and native settlements with a population of about 10,000 people. It also enclosed the entire township of Mbulu and the administrative centre there (D.C. to Director of Game Preservation, 7.9.27, *TNA* 11234).

In 1931, the township of Dodoma and its surroundings were gazetted as a game reserve for the purpose of preserving a herd of greater Kudu after the construction of one dam and the improvement of others in the vicinity of the township had greatly improved conditions for wildlife.

When border adjustments in 1937 enclosed several thousand people within the gazetted game reserve of Lake Rukwa, the Superior of the White Fathers' Mission at Zimba saw the need to 'protest against such ordinance enclosing a great Catholic Mission in the middle of a reserve'. He pointed out that the villagers already found it difficult to cope with wild animals. During the previous year more than 200 domestic animals—cattle, goats and sheep—had been killed by lions, leopards and wild dogs. The Superior felt certain that the extension of the game reserve would aggravate the situation: 'After some years that (*sic*) will be impossible to have cattle or donkeys in my mission' (A. Bigot to D.C., 24.4.37, *TNA* 21210).

No people were moved out of the Lake Rukwa area in order to accommodate wildlife interests. Compulsory movement of people was, however, associated with the creation of other game reserves, like the Katawi Game Reserve in Mpanda (D.C. to P.C. 17.6.31 *TNA* 11234, II), and the Sabi River Reserve south of Manyoni where, after the people had been moved out, 'the sanctity of the game is well shown by the utter desolation of the country' (P.C. to Chief Secr., 16.7.31, *TNA* 11234, II). In Liwale, 40,000 people scattered in small family groups over thousands of square miles were moved out to make room for the world's largest game reserve in the Selous. The man in charge of the operations, Rooke Johnston, the P.C. of the Southern Province, held that development depended on the eradication of all human rights and interests in the areas. '*Delenda est Liwale!*' he wrote. 'And with this goal in view I went all out to achieve what I had conceived in 1931 to be the only solution to the betterment of Liwale District and its people, namely its elimination (Letter to Chief Secr., 21.11.45, *TNA* 31796). The policy was upheld as late as in 1969 in a major review of the Selous Game Reserve:

> The Selous Game Reserve is the largest tract of land in East Africa, and probably in the whole of the African continent, which is free from human rights. It is one of the finest game areas in the world, and the game is increasing . . . The program of the Selous Game Reserve is of vital importance, for not only can the successful implementation of our plans be of great value to the country, but will also create the impetus for other areas to be developed and utilised along similar lines (Nicholson 1969).[1]

The Development of the Periphery

The institution of population concentrations has never been properly evaluated by people without clear career and prestige investments in the implementation of the schemes. Another difficulty is that the rationale for the schemes has changed over time from a single-purpose health measure at the time of their inception to multi-purpose developmental units in the terminal days of British administration. This fact has blurred the opportunity for assessment, although the material operation as well as the ecological results of the schemes would seem to be constants. This lack of any thorough evaluation has contributed to the retention of villagization as a core idea in the developmental thinking of the country from the colonial period until the present.

Towards the end of the British period, population concentration had clearly taken on a developmental rationale. Health reasons continued to be quoted when people were forcefully being moved, but assorted other motives such as administrative expediency, labour recruitment, soil preservation, and game conservation explain why the concentration measures retained their popularity among administrators. Throughout the 1940s, therefore, the concentration measure was positively advocated as an administrative device to be pursued for reasons of 'development'.

An effort to establish this policy as a general strategy for the whole country was launched by Rooke Johnston in a memorandum on 'Closer Settlements' to the Provincial Commissioners Conference in 1945. Harking back to Maclean's old schemes, Rooke Johnston here described the concentrations as focal units for purposeful government action, services and initiatives aimed at quickening the pace of what was now iden-

[1] I am grateful to Mr. Audun Sandberg for this reference.

tified as economic advancement. Thus the concentrations were described as centres of medical aid, education, agricultural extension work, veterinary services and marketing organizations. Most importantly, the scheme was judged to be psychologically acceptable to the people, as 'the movement into large settlements would not be a departure from, but rather a return to, tradition'. Rooke Johnston had described the pre-colonial settlement pattern as consisting of large nucleated villages built for defence purposes against marauding tribes and slavers. European pacification had broken up this pattern. Now, a more enlightened breed of colonial representatives would restore the historic continuity in the form of 'closer settlement'. 'I am convinced', Rooke Johnston concluded his memorandum, 'that the policy of closer settlement can be beneficially applied to large areas of Tanganyika and that it is indeed a condition precedent to real progress on the part of the African population. I even go so far as to suggest that it should become part of the declared policy of Government, and an integral part of post-war development' (Memorandum to Chief Secr., 3.5.45, *TNA* 31351).

The provincial commissioners unanimously agreed to these sentiments, and R. de Z. Hall, the P.C. of the Central Province, later put their ideas into a draft bill 'to Provide for the Removal of Natives from their Homes in Circumstances of Emergency' (*TNA* 31351). The measure would have put concentration measures in the forefront as a government responsibility, while at the same time it would have enhanced the discretionary powers of the provincial commissioners. It was probably the latter feature which caused the Governor, Sir W. D. Battershill, to have second thoughts about the bill and eventually to drop it: 'he does not like it a bit' read the Chief Secretary's note (Notation 3.9.47, *TNA* 31351).

Fiske (1927) had raised doubts about the concentration measures in Uganda both on entomological and economic grounds. His views were never heeded by the policy-makers who indirectly came under criticism from his views, and it is generally believed that the concentration policy on the whole worked well: it saved lives and may have forestalled major epidemics. In ecological terms, however, the policy weakened man's mastery of the land. The policy controlled the people—not the land—leaving the flies to rule the terrain, the fields for agriculture and grazing which are the primary assets in the economic development of East Africa's masses. Ideally, the concentrations were to represent a stage of consolidation from which the people—buttressed by the benefits of government-sponsored health and education measures—would soon commence their reconquest of the land. As it happened, no such advancement was generated and the sleeping-sickness concentrations remain a forgotten lesson in East Africa's developmental history.

Conclusion

This study has moved away from the political focus which has characterized much of the recent writing on the Tanganyikan past and has sought to make a preliminary contribution to the economic history of the area. We have described the production side of the pre-colonial economies and given full weight to their dynamic and integrated character. Agriculture was not simply a subsistence undertaking, for example, but exhibited a great variety of innovations and adaptations, probably in response to population pressures on the resource base. We have also discussed the flourishing cattle economy, operated partly as a pastoral undertaking, partly as a mixed system where domestic animals supported the agricultural initiative.

Three industrial enterprises have been identified underpinning the local economies, the production of iron, salt and cloth. Iron-making in particular developed individual and group skills of considerable advancement. In the discussion of iron production, we called for further research to assess the degree of technical sophistication and metallurgical insights attained during the nineteenth century. In addition to the industrial efforts presented in detail, the pottery industry, basket-weaving, bark-cloth production and the tanning of skins contributed to the total craft pattern. Functional specialization seems to have characterized all these crafts; the high degree of division of labour resulted in interdependence in the production system.

We have also traced the existence of local trade in commodities and food, exchanges between tribes, and the development of supply operations to the trading caravans and emerging urban centres. The emphasis has been on production rather than trade, which has been fairly well covered by historians as the organizationally most complex and impressive of East African economic initiatives. The point that emerges from this study is that trading over long distances characterized the activities surrounding local commodities like iron and salt long before the emergence of 'long-distance trading' of ivory and slaves centred on the east coast. The mass involvement in local barter was the significant exchange phenomenon on which externally oriented trading networks were later superimposed.

Most importantly, this study has shown that the pre-colonial economies developed within an ecological control situation—a relationship between man and his environment which had grown out of centuries of civilizing work of clearing the ground, introducing managed vegetations, and controlling the fauna. The relationship resulted in an 'agro-horticultural prophylaxis' (Ford 1971), where the dangers of tsetse fly and trypanosomiasis were neutralized and 'Africa's bane' (Nash 1969) was made a largely irrelevant consideration for economic prosperity. The contrast to the twentieth century, when the tsetse fly has been 'one of the major obstacles to economic development' (Ormsby-Gore 1925), is clear.

A proper understanding of this perplexing contrast in the very conditions for economic activity between the late nineteenth and early twentieth centuries has necessitated a re-evaluation of pre-colonial history. In meeting this challenge we have presented evidence which has so far only to a limited degree been used in the historical writing on the area. Extensive use has been made of untapped German material as well as the findings of many different disciplines like demography, ecology, entomology, geography and medicine. This use of an interdisciplinary approach has added new dimensions to our understanding of Tanganyika's economic development which political economists have tended to explain from relationships of commodity exchange only.

The eruption of tsetse-borne sleeping-sickness epidemics in East Africa at the beginning of this century is an event of which many historians have not realized the full significance. We have shown that the epidemics resulted from a relatively sudden human and cattle depopulation and the attendant loss of control over the environment. This ecological explanation puts into perspective what in comparison is the smaller impact of earlier events like slave-raiding and intertribal warfare, to which historians have given so much attention.

On the whole, our findings have supported Burton's impressions that 'comfort and plenty' characterized life among the major peoples of Tanganyika in the latter part of the nineteenth century. This impression of the period is in stark contrast to early colonial writers who saw in East Africa nothing but 'blank, uninteresting, brutal barbarism' (Eliot 1903). These writers experienced the African economies at a point of extreme crisis and mistakenly judged the conditions of life in this period to represent the height of East African development. Their understanding of the past was fixed by their own experiences and their writings left little recognition of an African agency capable of important achievements.

The implications of this study are less clear with regard to the current writings of the 'development of underdevelopment' orientation. Writers of this 'school' have sought the roots of African underdevelopment in the pre-colonial contacts of unequal exchange with trading elements of mercantile and feudal formations. These writers, and the colonial historians that preceded them, ascribe a fundamental importance to trade although the verdict on the impact of trade differs diametrically. Where one set of historians sees trade as a tool of diffusion for European achievements and development to Africa, the other judges trade as the vehicle for underdeveloping the periphery of an economic system. Both schools of historians would seem to give to the external trading phenomenon a penetrative impact it did not have. The externally founded trading enclaves on the East African coast have undoubtedly fluctuated in importance throughout the centuries, but at no time prior to the period of Euopean imperialism did their contacts with the hinterlands have the ability of subjugating the East African economies and depriving them of important developmental opportunities. A second common assumption has been that the East African economies were virtually without any production base and that their material weakness predisposed them to the foreign trading penetration. Quite to the contrary, this study has shown the strength of the material basis of the economies until the 1890s when their destruction hastened the establishment of foreign rule.

The general features of the pre-colonial economies remained largely untouched by these externally induced commercial initiatives. This study has suggested that the impact of the slave trade in East Africa may have been less fundamental than what is usually assumed about the Tanganyikan theatre, and urged a follow-up of Sheriff's efforts (1971) to locate and assess the demand for slaves. The market situation in East African slaves was different from that of the western half of the continent and should be more clearly reflected in the historical evaluation.

Also, it seems that the more 'legitimate' long-distance trade was successfully handled by local economies without causing their disruption. One of the peoples most thoroughly enmeshed in this trading and transport activity, the Nyamwezi carriers, remained tied to the local economy even in the closing years of the nineteenth century. They might, as Raum has suggested (1965:169) have had their feet in two economies—one local and one external—yet when the planting season arrived in Unyamwezi they would be next to their women in the family *shamba*. The seasonality of their agricultural system set the limits of their participation in the international trade, not the other way round.

Alpers' recent work (1973a) along the caravan routes from Bagamoyo and the East Coast confirms that the impact of overseas trade was limited to the immediate coastal hinterlands where a 'peasantization'—dependence on external economic forces by local husbandmen—was found to have taken place. I have indicated a similar change in a number of coastal communities in the discussion of the agricultural systems (pp. 30–1) but judged the local strength of these economies to have outweighed their dependence on external market factors.

It was different with the budding East African industries that succumbed under the impact of trade. In this area, however, we are also faced with a geographically restricted and fluctuating impact of the external trading contacts, not with a massive flood of commodities inundating the entire area. We have shown that cotton-weaving ceased to operate in Zanzibar in the 1850s. It died out in Unyamwezi in the 1870s and was just getting started in Bukoba in the 1890s when trade goods from the coast were flowing in sufficient quantity to destroy the infant craft.

Salt production came to a standstill on the East Coast with the arrival in Zanzibar of cheap salt from India and the Arabian gulf probably in connection with the important freight of mangrove poles. In Uvinza, the African initiative was foreclosed through colonial legislation in 1903. In Uha, salt production was prohibited in the 1930s due to ecological changes and the dangers of sleeping sickness which the salt boilers were exposed to during their long treks through tsetse-infested bush (*TNA* 3517). Thus the external impulses of trade (and later of politics) had clearly limited spheres of penetration, the extent of which changed over time and expanded with the approach of formal colonization. This changing impact of the external agency and the build-up of external control variables call for further investigation by economic historians. The backward projection of Lenin's theory of imperialist exploitation to pre-colonial economic formations is only a substitute for this much-needed assessment. The Marxist position is, of course, to make a distinction between pre-colonial plunder for reasons of 'primitive accumulation' of capital in centre-periphery relationships on the one hand, and the systemic exploitation which characterized the imperial contacts on the other. This later exploitation was judged by Lenin to have become possible only through the technological and transport advances that accompanied the move into industrial capitalism.

Our study falls into line with this position, although a large part of it has dealt with the disruption of local economies and the complex reasons for this, rather than with colonial exploitation directly. I have emphasized the 1890s as a decade of disasters and pointed to impersonal forces marginal to the colonizing effort, as well as to the colonial impact, which destroyed numerous local economies. Thus, the extractive stage of colonialism in Tanganyika was immediately preceded by a period of extensive destruction of the material base and the disintegration of social structures and economic agencies. As a general summing up of this decade, we can venture the suggestion that the conditions for economic life deteriorated and brought many tribes back to a frontier situation where the conquest of the ecosystem had to recommence. These developments make the contrast between pre-colonial and colonial periods a necessary and valid dichotomy for purposes of economic analysis of Tanganyika and possibly other East African situations. It is evident, however, that in maintaining this contrast we challenge the notion of an inferior status imputed to the pre-colonial period.

Little has been said about the organizational features of production and consumption in this study. An analysis of such features is a logical next step which future research will undoubtedly pursue. If this study has succeeded in questioning the conventional idea that pre-colonial economies reflected nothing but indolence and sloth, a starting point may be to re-explore the idea that the traditional economies were embedded in political structures and processes, the 'traditional' nature of which prevented innovation and change. In Marx's writings, it was the smashing of the unprogressive nature of the social and political formations of pre-colonial societies that was seen as a redeeming task of European colonialism. Meillassoux (1960) has adapted West African material to this model and shown the role of the chiefly element in containing economic change by manipulating structures and values serving the maintenance of established power relationships. We do not at the moment know whether the political element in East Africa fits this description. There seems, however, to be a clear connection between political authority and economic activity. We have referred to traditions of the chiefs of Bukoba ordering the creation of positive agricultural conditions through massive mulchings on laterized soil. The spread of the chiefly office has in some places a connection with the introduction of the longhorned cattle in East Africa. Many tribal founder myths point to the chief as the instigator of markets or as a master craftsman, commanding allegiance because of his possession of certain rare economic skills, like hunting or iron-making. Much further work is needed in this area to bridge economic and political aspects of the pre-colonial societies before the local evidence can yield conclusions of comparative value.

Our insistence on change and adaptation—indeed an insistence on economic calculus—in 'traditional' economies makes it necessary, however, to question older assumptions about the unadaptive nature of the political element, and to trace possible impacts of economic variables on political changes and state formations. Another question which stems directly from the idea of the 'traditional' economy's being embedded in social structures and processes relates to the system of distribution and seeks to detect the major benefactors, whether individuals or groups, that are maintained through the structural features. This problem has not been tackled with any succinctness in the Tanganyikan situation and may be a fruitful next field of enquiry by historians.

Systemic exploitation presupposes an economy that yields surpluses that can be raked off. To find and/or establish such situations was clearly the aim of the colonizing power whether it was 'the official mind' proper which caused the scramble for colonies as Robinson and Gallagher (1961) maintain or whether this was caused by the pressure groups of capital, industry and trade as discussed by Hobson (1902) and Lenin (1913).

The constructive achievement of German colonialism has been reviewed by Eberle (1960) and Henderson (1943). The exploitative features have been taken up by Müller (1959) and Tetzlaff (1970). The British period has been analysed by Iliffe (1971), with particular reference to the development of African cash crops through agricultural improvements following the 1930s. The particular interest of this study has been with the periphery of the colonial economy where the battle for ecological mastery was lost in the first decades of the twentieth century and an effective halt was placed on human agencies and the indigenous rationale regarding resource exploitation. We have described the total dehumanization of the decision-making processes from the point of view of the local husbandman who found his claims to a livelihood overruled by concern for wildlife protection or other Europe-centred undertakings. It is tempting now to see the Tanganyikan conservation programme as a distant replay of the enclosure acts in British history when it was said that the sheep ate the people and the poor were made to sacrifice for the pleasure or necessity of an economic system that was not theirs anymore. While tsetse flies occupied vast parts of old settlement areas, the official mind (see pp. 175–6) expressed satisfaction that the land was 'held in trust' by the insects until a new breed of African agriculturists—educated to European expectations—would be forthcoming.

Today the economic initiative is again thrown back to the people of Tanganyika in a policy of self-reliant development. 'Development means the development of people', writes President Nyerere (1973:59) under whose leadership Tanganyikans have been restored as masters of their own destiny and participants in decisions affecting their own lives. Yet, while an assorted multitude of external experiences daily influences the current development concerns, important biases against past achievements of the peoples of Tanganyika still prevail. It is important, therefore, to renew the efforts to seek out and popularize the valid lessons of past achievements to inspire the current transformations and the popular agencies that will carry them to success.

Appendix: Early Colonial Wars

In the following table, I have made a partial reconstruction of the quantitative evidence of human and material destruction available on the battles shown on Map 7.1 (see p. 148). The material is collected from three sources: *Deutsches Kolonialblatt* (*DKB*), Nigmann (1911), and Schmidt (1892). Identification numbers coincide in map and table and make cross-reference an easy possibility.

A number of difficulties should be mentioned in connection with the material utilized. First, the table is a fragmented account, covering the period between 1891 and 1896 only. Most military encounters in this period were given an extensive public reporting and the *Deutsches Kolonialblatt* presented information of a quantitative nature including the number of troops participating, ammunition distributed and spent, types of arms utilized, lootings and burnings, prisoners taken, and even body counts. After 1896 this detailed reporting stopped, and it has not been possible to follow up the information through the confidential military reports now in the Potsdam archives. Tanzanian historians may at some future stage like to revert to this important source material to establish more accurately the human and material ravages which their communities were exposed to through the so-called 'pacification'.

Secondly, the published reports dealt with the warfare as clean-cut military affairs and suppressed information on the killing and wounding of non-warriors.[1] Such casualties may have doubled or tripled the purely military losses, particularly in connection with the fighting in the African strongholds in which the entire population was usually drawn together for safety. Prince revealed the heavy losses of women and children at the storming of Sinna's fortress at Kibosho and he made similar observations about *tembe*-fighting in central Tanganyika. Women and children would normally remain in the *tembes* throughout the fighting and usually succumbed there in the general tumult (Prince 1914:57, 118).

---

[1] Mr. Loren Larsen has called my attention to this discrepancy in the published data, and indicated that the original military reports, which he consulted, contain detailed information on civilian casualties also.

A third problem relates to the number of wounded, and their chances of recovery which would seem to have been practically nil. Given the standard of medical care in the African communities, we can safely conclude that most wounds were liable to serious infections that probably ended in death. Similarly, indirect losses that followed the routing of the communities are not revealed in the official reports, but could in some instances—as is evident from the Maji Maji wars—have multiplied the casualties. One should therefore accept that the available casualty figures probably suffer from gross under-reporting.

Finally, the standards for selecting the battles indicated in Map 7.1 and the following table are those of the Imperial Act of 1871. These may not necessarily coincide with the most relevant standards for selecting the battles that caused the greatest devastations to the African peoples and economies. Villages were burnt and people shot as a routine matter by military patrols to enforce the new principles of law and order. Incidents of this nature are not part of the following survey. Such an important omission, for example, would be the raid carried out against Sultan Sengrema in the Urima area of Usukuma in 1891. The raid took place in a locality where village followed village for an uninterrupted distance of five hours' march by the troops. All housing quarters with the exception of 500 huts were burnt (*DKB* 1892:330). Tom von Prince's expedition against the Wambuga people south of Kisaki is another example. An arrow had been shot against a German patrol, and 250–300 huts were burnt to the ground as a punishment (*DKB* 1892:422). Similarly, the survey does not cover the extensive fighting that took place in the Rukwa Valley against Chief Kimaraunga. Also, the military encounters of the scientific/diplomatic expeditions of Baumann, Stokes and Emin Pasha are not accounted for. The exploratory nature of the survey should therefore be underlined, and the need for further research in this area reasserted.

COLONIAL WARFARE, 1889–1896

Ref. No.[1]	Date	Place, tribe, leader	Tribes partici- pating	Destruction	Body count
1.	8.5.1889	Bagamoyo Bushiri's camp	Arabs, Baluchi, Swahili, Wasaramo	*Boma* burnt	106 dead
2.	10.5.1889	Magogoni by Dar es Salaam	Arabs, Baluchi, Swahili	Village de- stroyed, 170 cows, many goats and sheep taken	8 dead

[1] Reference numbers correspond to those of Map 7.1.

3.	6.6.1889	Capture of Sadani	Segua, Wadoe, Nguru, Swahili, Wakami	Town and several strongholds destroyed	105 dead
4.	9.7.1889	Capute of Pangani	Arabs, Swahili	Town partly destroyed	30 dead 50 wounded
5.	4.9.1889	Bushiri followers at Somwi	Mafitti (Ngoni)	Village and camp destroyed	30 dead, many wounded
6.	16.9.1889	Mafitti near Jambo	Mafitti (Ngoni)	Several camps destroyed, cattle taken	Huge losses
7.	Oct. 1889	Mpwapwa	Wagogo	n.a.*	n.a.
8.	9.11.1889	Bwana Heri supporters, Sadani-Mandera	Wasegua	All villages destroyed	Huge losses
9.	—	Pangani	n.a.	n.a.	n.a.
10.	Nov. 1889	Nguru, Bushiri camp	Arabs, Swahili	n.a.	30 dead
11.	2.12.1889	Bwana Heri's camp	Wasegua, Arabs, Swahili	n.a.	50 dead, masses of wounded
12.	4.1.1890	Bwana Heri, Mlembule	Wasegua, Swahili	*Boma* destroyed	Very heavy losses
13.	9.3.1890	Bwana Heri, Palamakaa	Wasegua, different tribes	10 villages destroyed	40 dead
14.	4.5.1890	Kilwa Kiwindje	Arabs, Swahilis	Town partly destroyed, cattle taken	30 dead
15.	10.5.1890	Lindi	n.a.	n.a.	n.a.
16.	Oct. 1890	Machemba Stronghold near Newalla	Wayao	Several villages destroyed	Heavy losses
17.	13.2.1891	Sinna's Stronghold Kibosho	Chagga	*Boma* and village destroyed 4,000 cows, 5,000 goats and sheep taken	200 dead
18.	June– Sept. 1891	Uhere, Lugalo (Zelewski Expedition)	Wahehe	*Tembes* burnt in many districts	700 dead
19.	Aug.–Sept. 1891	Mafitti in Songomero	Mafitti, (Ngoni), Mahenge, Wahehe, Wangwangwara	Numerous villages destroyed	n.a.

* n.a. = not available.

20.	6.6.1892	Siki stronghold near Tabora	Wanyamwezi	Village destroyed	60 dead
21.	10.6.1892	Meli at Moshi	Chagga	n.a.	n.a.
22.	27.8.1892	Mhunzi	Mafitti	Village destroyed	More than 200 dead
23.	10.10.1892	Kondoa	Wagogo, Wahehe	n.a.	100 dead
24.	7–14.11.1892	Kisiba	Wahaya	Cattle and ivory taken	94 dead
25.	8.12.1892	Munisangara	Wahehe	11 villages destroyed	23 dead
26.	10.11.1893	Siki's stronghold near Tabora	Wanyamwezi	Town destroyed	250 dead
27.	18.2.1893	Kilimatinde–Unyangwira Road	Wagogo	*Tembes* destroyed	20 dead
28.	10.3.1893	Mdaruru in Ugogo	Wahehe	n.a.	50 dead
29.	13.3.1893	Maamanda	Wasegua	Village destroyed	30 dead
30.	3.5.1893	Quamba near Mpwapwa	Wakaguru	n.a.	Many dead
31.	12.7.1893	Mabuena in Gerengere	n.a.	n.a.	n.a.
32.	12.8.1893	Meli's Chiefdom, Moshi	Chagga	n.a.	135 dead
33.	28.8.1893	Nondoa	Wagogo	n.a.	All dead
34.	3.12.1893	Nserekere Lake	Mafitti	n.a.	More than 100 dead
35.	11.6.1894	Warudje Valley, Kilwa	Warudje	Villages burnt	15 dead
36.	13.6.1894	Ujansi,	Wajansi Wahehe	Villages burnt	Numerous losses
37.	July, Aug. 1894	Bulima, Usukuma	Wasukuma	n.a.	n.a.
38.	7.9.1894	Kilwa, Kivindje	Wavudje	n.a.	More than 37 dead, lots of wounded
39.	13.10.1894	Konko	Wahehe, Wangwana, Wanyamwezi, Wakimbu	Several villages burnt	Many wounded
40.	30.10.1894	Iringa	Wahehe	Town looted and destroyed	More than 300 dead
41.	6.11.1894	Mage	Wahehe	n.a.	30 dead
42.	18.7.1895	Mutatembwa of Kisiba	Wasiba (Wahaya)	Village looted and destroyed	40 dead
43.	10.8.1895	Chief Taragalla, Usenje	Rugarugas	Village destroyed	All dead

44.	Oct. 1895–	Hassan bin	Swahili,	Village	n.a.
	Jan. 1896	Omari	Warudje	destroyed	
45.	26.11.1895	Gonga	Watataru	n.a.	n.a.
		Mountains			
46.	November	Chief	Wakerewe	1,000 goats,	40 dead
	1895	Lukonge,		40 cattle	
		Ukerewe		taken	
47–53.	n.a.	n.a.	n.a.	n.a.	n.a.
54.	December–	Uhehe,	Wahehe	n.a.	400–500 dead
	July 1896	Iringa			and injured

Bibliography to 1977 Impression

See also Additional Bibliography 1977–1995 page 209

The following abbreviations of names of publications frequently referred to will be observed: *DKB—Deutsches Kolonialblatt, EAAJ—East African Agricultural Journal, MDS—Mittheilungen (von Forschungsreisenden und Gelerhrten) aus dem Deutschen Schutzgebieten,* and *TNR—Tanganyika/Tanzania Notes and Records.*

Acker, Pater (1908), 'Die Erziehung der Eingeborenen zur Arbeit in Deutsch-Ostafrika', *Jahrbuch über die Deutschen Kolonien* I : 117–24.

Adams, P. A. M. (1898), 'Uhehe und das Land bis zum Nyassa-See', *MDS* XI : 246–250.

—— (1898a), 'Vom Nyassa-See nach Upogoro und Donde', *MDS* XI : 251–253.

—— (1899), *Im Dienste des Kreutzes*, Augsburg: Literarisches Institut.

—— (1902), 'Das mittlere Flussgebiet des Lukuledi', *MDS* XV : 133–138.

—— (1903), *Lindi und sein Hinterland,* Berlin: D. Reimer.

Ainsworth, Commissioner (1905), 'Reports Relating to the Administration of the East African Protectorate', Africa No. 6. Cd. 2740, London: HMSO.

Allan, W. (1965), *The African Husbandman,* Edinburgh: Oliver and Boyd.

Allnutt, R. B. (1942), 'Rice Growing in Dry Areas', *EAAJ* VIII : 103—108.

Alpers, E. A. (1967), *The East African Slave Trade,* Nairobi: East African Publishing House.

—— (1969), 'Trade, State and Society among the Yao in the Nineteenth Century', *Journal of African History* X : 405–420.

—— (1973), 'Rethinking African Economic History', *Kenya Historical Review* I : 163–188.

—— (1973a), 'Peasantization and Differentiation in Eastern Tanzania During the Nineteenth Century: An Aspect of Rural Class Formation', University of Dar es Salaam: Department of History (Seminar Paper, Typescript).

—— (1975), *Ivory and Slaves in East Central Africa*, London: Heinemann Educational.

Anlagen—Anlagen zum Jahresbericht über die Entwicklung der Deutschen Schutzgebiete in Afrika und der Südsee (Beilage zum Deutschen Kolonialblatt), Berlin: Mittler und Sohn.

Anleitung—Anleitung zum Felddienst in Deutsch-Ostafrika (1911), Dar es Salaam: Deutsch-Ostafrikanische Rundschau.

AMR—Annual Medical Report, Dar es Salaam: Government Printer.

Apted, F. I. C. (1962), 'Sleeping Sickness in Tanganyika, Past, Present, and Future', *Transactions of the Royal Society of Tropical Medicine and Hygiene* LVI : 15–29.

Arning, W. (1896), 'Die Wahehe', *MDS* IX : 233–246.

—— (1897), 'Die Wahehe', *MDS* X : 44–60.

Ashcroft, M. T. (1959), 'A Critical Review of the Epidemiology of Human Trypanosomiasis in Africa', *Tropical Diseases Bulletin* LVI : 1073.

—— (1959a), 'The Importance of African Wild Animals as Reservoirs of Trypanosomiasis', *East African Medical Journal* XXXVI : 289–297.

Austen, E. E. (1903), *A Monograph of the Tsetse-flies Genus Glossina, Westwood based on the Collection in the British Museum*, London : British Museum (Natural History).

Bagshawe, F. J. (1930), 'Tribal History and Legends: Waluguru, 15/4/30', *Morogoro District Book*.

Bald, D. (1970), *Deutsch-Ostafrika 1900–1914. Eine Studie über Verwaltung, Interessengruppen und Wirtschaftlichen Erschliessung,* München : Weltforum Verlag.

Baum, E. (1968), 'Land Use in the Kilombero Valley', pp. 21–50 in Ruthenberg, H. (ed.) (1968).

Baumann, O. (1891), *Usambara und seine Nachbargebiete*, Berlin : D. Reimer.

—— (1894), *Durch Massailand zur Nielquelle,* Berlin : D. Reimer.

—— (1898), 'Der neueste Afrika-Durchquerer', *Petermanns Geographische Mittheilungen* XLIV : 165–166.

Baumstark, Leutnant (1900), 'Die Warangi', *MDS* XIII : 45–60.

Baur and Le Roy (1886), *A Travers le Zanguebar: voyage dans l'Oudoe, l'Ouzigoua, l'Oukwere, l'Oukami et l'Ousagara*, Tours : Mame et Fils.

Becker, J. (1887), *La vie en Afrique*, 2 vols., Paris : J. Lebègue.

Becker, M. (1899), 'Ueber Bahnbau in Deutsch-Ostafrika', *DKB* X : 760–63.

Behr, H. F. von (1891), *Kriegsbilder aus dem Araberaufstand in Deutsch-Ostafrika*, Leipzig : Brockhaus.

—— (1892), 'Geographische und ethnographische Notizen aus dem Flussgebiet des Rouvuma', *MDS* V : 15–20.

—— (1893), 'Die Völker zwischen Rufiyi und Rovuma', *MDS* VI : 69–87.

—— (1893a), 'Die Wakuasteppe', *MDS* VI : 40–60.

Beidelman, T. O. (1962), 'A History of Ukaguru: 1857–1916', *TNR* Nos. 58–59 : 11–39.

—— (1962a), 'Ironworking in Ukaguru', *TNR* Nos. 58–59 : 288–89.

Bell, H. H. (1909), 'Report on the Measures Adopted for the Suppression of Sleeping Sickness in Uganda', Colonial Reports—Miscellaneous No. 65, Uganda, Cd. 4990. London : HMSO.

—— (1910), 'Sleeping Sickness in Uganda', *Scottish Geographical Magazine* XXVI : 478–485.

Bell, R. M. (1950), 'The Maji Maji Rebellion in the Liwale District', *TNR* No. 28 : 38–57.

Bennett, N. (1961), 'The Arab-German War of 1888 on the Tanganyika Coast', New York : African Studies Association, Annual Meeting.

Berg, Bezirksamtmann (1897), 'Das Bezirksamt Mikindani', *MDS* X : 206–222.

Berry, L. (ed.) (1971), *Tanzania in Maps*, London : University of London Press.

Bloch, M. R. (1963), 'The Social Influence of Salt', *Scientific American* CCIX : 89–98.

Blohm, W. (1931), *Die Nyamwezi, Land und Wirtschaft*, Hamburg : Friedericksen, De Gruyter & Co.

Bohannan, P. and Dalton, G. (eds.) (1962), *Markets in Africa*, Evanston, Ill., Northwestern University Press.

Boileau, F. F. R. (1899), 'The Nyasa-Tanganyika Plateau', *Geographical Journal* XIII:577–95 (with map).

Bornhardt, W. (1900), *Zur Oberflächengestaltung und Geologie Deutsch-Ostafrikas,* Berlin: D. Reimer.

Bösch, F. (1930), *Les Banyamwezi, peuple de l'Afrique orientale,* Münster: Bibliotheca Anthropos.

Boserup, E. (1965), *The Conditions of Agricultural Growth,* London: Faber.

Brard, Pater (1897), 'Der Victoria-Nyansa', *Petermanns Geographische Mittheilungen* XLIII:77–80.

Brass, W. *et al.* (1968), *The Demography of Tropical Africa,* Princeton, New Jersey: Princeton University Press.

Braun, E. (1968), 'Land Use in the Kilombero Valley; from Shifting Cultivation to Permanent Farming', pp. 21–50 in Ruthenberg (ed.) (1968).

Braun, K. (1906), 'Der Reis in Deutsch-Ostafrika', *Berichte über Land-und Forstwirtschaft in Deutsch-Ostafrika* III (4):167–217.

Brehme, Dr. (1894), 'Bericht über das Kulturland des Kilimandjaro und dessen klimatische und gesundheitliche Verhältnisse', *MDS* VII:106–131.

Brett, E. A. (1973), *Colonialism and Under-development in East Africa,* London: Heinemann.

Brock, B. and P. W. G. (1965), 'Iron Working among the Nyiha of South-Western Tanganyika', *South African Archeological Bulletin* XX:97–100.

Brode, H. (1911), *British and German East Africa, their Economy and Commercial Relations,* London: E. Arnold.

Brooke, C. (1967), 'The Heritage of Famine in Central Tanzania', *TNR* No. 67:15–22.

—— (1967a), 'Types of Food Shortages in Tanzania', *Geographical Review* LVII:333–357.

Brown, W. T. (1972), 'The Politics of Business: Relations between Zanzibar and Bagamoyo in the late Nineteenth Century', *African Historical Studies* IV:631–644.

Brown, B. (1972), 'Muslim Influence on Trade and Politics in the Lake Tanganyika Region', *African Historical Studies* IV:617–630.

Broyon-Mirambo, P. (1877), 'Description of Unyamwezi, the Territory of King Mirambo, and the best Route thither from the East Coast', *Journal of the Royal Geographical Society* XXII:28–36.

Buchanan, A. (1919), *Three years of War in East Africa,* London: John Murray.

Buder, Hauptmann (1899), 'Bericht über die Shirambo-Expedition', *DKB* X:473–475.

Bülow, H. von (1902), *Deutschlands Kolonien und Kolonialkriege,* Dresden and Leipzig: F. Pierson's Verlag.

Burgt, J. M. M. van der (1913), 'Zur Entvölkerungsfrage Unjamwesis und Ussumbwas', *Koloniale Rundschau* 705–728.

Bursian, A. (1910), 'Die Hauser und Hüttensteuer in Deutsch-Ostafrika', Jena: Abhandlungen des Staatswissenschaftlichen Seminars zu Jena.

Bursell, E. (1955), 'Experiments in Tsetse Control in Southern Tanganyika', *Bulletin of Entomological Research* XLVI:589–597.

Burton, R. F. (1859), 'The Lake Regions of Central Equatorial Africa', *Journal of the Royal Geographical Society* XXIX:1–454.

—— (1860), *The Lake Regions of Central Africa,* 2 vols. London: Longmans.

—— (1872), *Zanzibar City, Island and Coast,* 2 vols., London: J. Murray.

Burtt, B. D. (1937), 'Report on Uzinza', *TNA* 25102.

Busse, W. (1902), *Bericht über eine im Auftrage des Kaiserlichen Gouvernements von Deutsch-Ostafrika ausgeführte Forschungereise nach dem südlichen Teile dieser Kolonie*, Berlin: Mittler & Sohn.

—— (1908), 'Die periodischen Grassbrände im tropischen Afrika, ihre Einfluss auf die Vegetation und ihre Bedeutung für die Landeskultur', *MDS* XXI:113–139.

Büttner, C. (1909), 'Wakimbu, Bezirk Tabora (Deutsch Ostafrika)', in Kohler, J. (ed.) (1909).

—— (n.d.), *Der Aufstand in Deutsch-Ostafrika und seine Folgen*, Stuttgart: J. F. Steinkopf.

Cameron, V. L. (1877), *Across Africa*, 2 vols., London: Daldy, Isbister & Co.

Capus, Pater, (1898), 'Eine Missionsreise nach Uha und Urundi', *Petermanns Geographische Mittheilungen* XLIV:182–185.

Carr, E. H. (1961), *What is History?*, Harmondsworth: Penguin Books.

Casati, G. (1891), *Ten Years in Equatoria and the Return with Emin Pasha*, (2 vols.) London and New York: F. Warne.

Chittick, N. (1966), 'Kilwa; A Preliminary Report', *Azania*, I:1–36.

—— (1967), 'Discoveries in the Lamu Archipelago', *Azania* II:37–67.

Christie, J. (1876), *Cholera Epidemics in East Africa*, London: MacMillan and Co.

Claeson, C. E. and Egeroe, B. (1971), 'Population Movement in Tanzania', University of Dar es Salaam: BRALUP, Research Note No. 11.

Clark, J. D. (ed.) (1957), *Third Pan African Congress on Prehistory, Livingstone, 1955*, London: Chatto and Windus.

Cliffe, L. and Saul, J. S. (eds.) (1972), *Socialism in Tanzania*, 2 vols., Nairobi: East African Publishing House.

Cline, W. (1937), *Mining and Metallurgy in Negro Africa*, Manasha, Wisconsin: George Banta Publishing Co.

Collyer, J. J. (1939), *The South Africans with General Smuts in German East Africa*, Pretoria: Government Printer.

Cooley, W. D. (1845), 'The Geography of N'yassi, or the Great Lake of Southern Africa, investigated', *Journal of the Royal Geographical Society* XV:185–235.

Copley, H., and Mayer, R. F. (1934), *The East African Sportsman's Handbook*, Nairobi: The East African Standard Ltd.

Corson, J. F. (1935), 'Experimental Transmission of *Trypanosoma rhodesiense* through Antelopes and *Glossina morsitans* to Man', *Journal of Tropical Medicine and Hygiene* XXXVIII:9–11.

Coupland, R. (1938), *East Africa and its Invaders*, Oxford: The Clarendon Press.

—— (1939), *The Exploitation of East Africa*, London: Faber and Faber.

Cox, P. R. (1959), *Demography*, Cambridge: Cambridge University Press.

Croce, B. (1941), *History as the Story of Liberty*, London: Allen and Unwin.

Crosse-Upcott, A. R. W. (1956), 'The Social Structure of the Kingindo-Speaking Peoples', Ph.D. Dissertation, Cape Town: University of Cape Town.

Culwick, A. T. (1938), 'The Population Problem in the Bukoba District', Typewritten Manuscript in the Cory Files (File No. 239), University of Dar es Salaam, East Africana Collection.

Dantz, Dr. (1900), 'Ergebnisse der geologischen Expedition des Bergassessors', *MDS* XIII:39–44.

—— (1902), 'Die Reisen des Dr. Dantz', *MDS* XV:34–89, 139–165, 189–242.

—— (1903), 'Die Reisen des Dr. Dantz', *MDS* XVI:108–46, 183–204.

Darby, H. C. (1956), 'The Clearing of the Woodland in Europe', pp. 183–216 in Thomas, W. L. (ed.) (1956).

Datoo, B. A. (1970), 'Misconceptions about Use of Monsoons by Dhows in East African Waters', *East African Geographical Review* VIII : 1–10.

Davey, J. B. (1924), 'The Outbreak of Human Trypanosomiasis (*Trypanosoma Rhodesiense* Infection) in Mwanza District, Tanganyika Territory', *Transactions of the Royal Society of Tropical Medicine and Hygiene* XVII : 474–481.

Davies, J. N. P. (1959), 'James Christie and the Cholera Epidemics of East Africa', *East African Medical Journal* XXXVI : 1–6.

Decken, Baron C. C. von der (Kersten, O. ed.) (1869), *Baron Carl Claus von der Decken's Reisen in Ost-Afrika in den Jahren 1859 bis 1861*, 3 vols., Leipzig and Heidelberg: Winter'sche Verlagshandlung.

Denoon, D. and Kuper, A. (1970), 'Nationalist Historians in Search of a Nation; "The New Historiography" in Dar es Salaam', *African Affairs* LXX : 329–49.

Der Tropenpflanzer, Berlin: Kolonial-Wirtschaftliches Komite.

Desart, the Earl of (Chairman) (1914), 'Report of the Interdepartmental Committee on Sleeping Sickness', Cd. 7349; 'Minutes of Evidence', Cd. 7350, London: HMSO.

DKB—Deutsches Kolonialblatt, Berlin: Mittler und Sohn (published for the Kolonial-Abtheilung des Auswärtigen Amts).

DKZ—Deutsche Kolonialzeitung, Berlin: Verlag des Deutschen Kolonialvereins.

DOZ—Deutsche-Ostafrikanische Zeitung (1912), *Jagdhandbuch für Deutsch-Ostafrika*, Dar es Salaam: Deutsch-Ostafrikanische Zeitung.

Devereux, W. G. (1869), *A Cruise on the 'Gorgon'*, London: Bell and Daldy.

DDS—Die Deutschen Schutzgebiete in Afrika und der Südsee, Berlin: Mittler und Sohn (published for the Reichs-Kolonialamt).

Die Landes-Gesetzgebung des Deutsch-Ostafrikanischen Schutzgebiets (1911) 2 vols., Dar es Salaam: Kaiserliches Gouvernement von Deutsch-Ostafrika.

Diesing, E. (1909), 'Eine Reise in Ukonongo', *Globus* XLV : 309–212, 325–328.

Dixon, C. W. (1962), *Smallpox*, London: J. & A. Churchill Ltd.

EAAJ—East African Agricultural Journal, Nairobi: Government Printer.

East African Agricultural Journal (1939), 'Rinderpest', V : 57–60.

Eberle, R. F. (1960), 'The German Achievement in East Africa', *TNR* No. 55 : 181–214.

Ebner, E. (1959), 'History of the Wangoni', Peramiho Catholic Mission (mimeographed).

Eichhorn, A. (1911), 'Beiträge zur Kenntnis der Waschambaa' (Part 1) *Baessler-Archiv* I : 155–221.

—— (1913), 'Beiträge zur Kenntnis der Waschambaa' (Part 2) *Baessler-Archiv* III : 69–131.

—— (1918–22), 'Beiträge zur Kenntnis der Waschambaa' (Part 3) VII : 56–98.

Einseidel, Hauptmann (1913), 'Der Militärbezirk Mahenge', *DKB* XXIV : 802–5.

Eliot, Sir Charles (1903), 'Report by His Majesty's Commissioner on the East Africa Protectorate, dated 18th April 1903', Africa No. 6 (1903), Cd. 1626, London : HMSO.

—— (1905), *The East Africa Protectorate*, London: E. Arnold.

Eliot, C. N. E. (1904), 'British East Africa: From the Ravine Station, Fort Nandi', *Geographical Journal* XXIII : 97–100.

Elmslie, W. A. (1899), *Among the Wild Ngoni*, London: Frank Cass.

Elpons, Bezirksamtmann (1896), 'Uhehe', *MDS* IX:75–77.

—— (1898), 'Reise zum Rickwa-see', *DKB* IX:81–82.

Elton, J. F. (Cotterill, H. B. ed.) (1879), *Travels and Researches among the Lakes and Mountains of Eastern and Central Africa*, London: J. Murray.

Engelhardt, B. M. (1895), 'Über die Befestigung von Kuirenga', *DKB* VI:108–109.

Engler, A. (ed.) (1895), *Die Pflanzenwelt Ost-Afrikas u.d. Nachbargebiete*, 5 vols., Berlin: D. Reimer.

Fagan, B. M. (1961), 'Pre-European Ironworking in Central Africa', *Journal of African History* II:199–210.

—— (1965), *Southern Africa during the Iron Age*, London: Thames & Hudson.

—— (1970), 'Early Trade and Raw Materials in South Central Africa', pp. 24–38 in Gray and Birmingham (eds.) (1970).

—— and Yellen, J. E. (1968), 'Ivuna; Ancient Salt-Working in Southern Tanzania', *Azania* III:1–45.

—— *et al.* (1969), *Iron Age Cultures in Zambia*, 2 vols., London: Chatto and Windus.

Fairbairn, H. (1943), 'The Agricultural Problems Posed by Sleeping Sickness Settlements', *EAAJ* IX:17–22.

—— (1948), 'Sleeping Sickness in Tanganyika Territory, 1922–1946', *Tropical Diseases Bulletin* XLV:1–17.

Farler, J. P. (1882), 'Native Routes in East Africa from Pangani to the Masai Country and the Victoria Nyanza', *Proceedings of the Royal Geographical Society* IV (New Series): 730–747.

Feierman, S. (1970), 'The Shambaa Kingdom; a History', Ph.D. dissertation, Evanston, Illinois: Northwestern University.

Felkin, R. W. (1886), 'Notes on the Waganda Tribe of Central Africa', *Proceedings of the Royal Society of Edinburgh* XIII:699–770.

Fendall, C. P. (1921), *The East African Force 1915–1919*, London: Witherby.

Fischer, G. A. (1884), 'Bericht über die im Auftrage der Geographischen Gesellschaft in Hamburg unternommene Reise in das Massai-land', *Mittheilungen der Geographischen Gesellschaft in Hamburg 1882–83*:36–99, 189–237.

Fiske, W. F. (1927), 'History of Sleeping Sickness and Reclamation in Uganda', Entebbe (Confidential typewritten report to the Uganda Government).

Fitzgerald, W. W. A. (1898), *Travels in the Coastlands of British East Africa and the Islands of Zanzibar and Pemba*, London: Chapman & Hall.

Fonck, H. (1897), 'Ueber eine Erforschung des Malagarassiflusses', *DKB* VIII:98–100.

—— (1908), 'Bericht über die wirtschaftlichen Verhältnisse in der Ulangaebene und ihren Nachbargebieten', *DZA* (Potsdam) R. Kol. A. No. 278.

—— (1910), *Deutsch-Ostafrika. Eine Schilderung deutscher Tropen nach zehn Wanderjahren*, Berlin: Vossische Buchhandlung.

FAO (1962), Africa Survey; 'Report on the Possibilities of African Rural Development in Relation to Economic and Social Growth', Rome: FAO.

Ford, J. (1960), 'The Influence of Tsetse Flies on the Distribution of African Cattle', in *Proceedings of the First Federal Science Congress*, Salisbury.

—— (1971), *The Role of the Trypanosomiases in African Ecology*, Oxford: The Clarendon Press.

—— and Hall, R. de Z. (1947), 'The History of Karagwe, Bukoba District', *TNR* No. 24:3–27.

Fosbrooke, H. A. (1934), 'Some Aspects of the Kimwani Fishing Culture', *Journal of the Anthropological Institute* LXIV:1–22.

—— (1954), 'Further Light on Rock Engravings in Northern Tanganyika', *Man,* pp. 101–102.

—— (1957), 'Early Iron Age Sites in Tanganyika relative to Traditional History', pp. 318–325 in Clark, J. D. (ed.) (1957).

—— (1957a), 'Prehistoric Wells, Rain Ponds and Associated Burials in Northern Tanganyika', pp. 325–335 in Clark, J. D. (ed.) (1957).

French, M. H. (1938), 'The Conservation of Green Fodder for the Dry Season Feeding of Stock', *EAAJ* IV : 206–210.

Fröhlich, W. (1940), 'Das Afrikanische Marktwesen', *Zeitschrift für Ethnologie* LXXII : 234–328.

Fromm, P. (1912), 'Ufipa—Land und Leute: Ergebnisse einer in den Jahren 1908 und 1909 ausgeführten Forschungsreise', *MDS* XXV : 79–102.

Fuchs, P. (1905), 'Die wirtschaftliche Erkundung einer ostafrikanischen Südbahn', *Beiheft zum Tropenpflanzer.*

—— (1907), 'Wirtschaftliche Eisenbahn-Erkundungen im mittleren und nördlichen Deutsch-Ostafrika', *Beiheft zum Tropenpflanzer.*

Fuggles-Couchman, N. R. (1937), 'Green Manurial and Cultivation Trials', *EAAJ* V : 208–210.

Fülleborn, F. (1906), *Das Deutsche Njassa—und Ruwuma-Gebiet,* Berlin: D. Reimer.

—— and Glauning (1900), 'Die Fortschritte der Pendelexpedition', *MDS* XIII : 18–39.

Gillman, C. (1936), *A Population Map of Tanganyika Territory,* Dar es Salaam: Government Printer.

—— (1943), *The Geography and Hydrography of the Tanganyika Territory Part of the Ruvuma Basin,* Dar es Salaam: Government Printer.

—— (1954), 'Population Problems of Tanganyika Territory', *EAAJ* XI, 86–93.

Gillman, H. (1945), 'Bush Fallowing on the Makonde Plateau', *TNR* No. 19 : 34–44.

Giraud, V. (1890), *Les Lacs de l'Afrique équatoriale,* Paris: Hachette.

Good, C. M. (1970), *Rural Markets and Trade in East Africa; A Study of the Functions and Development of Exchange Institutions in Ankole, Uganda* (Research Paper No. 128) Chicago, Ill., University of Chicago, Department of Geography.

—— (1972), 'Salt, Trade and Disease: Aspects of Development in Africa's Northern Great Lakes Region', *International Journal of African Historical Studies* V : 543–586.

—— (1973), 'Markets in Africa: A Review of Research Themes and the Question of Market Origins', *Cahiers d'Études Africaines* XIII : 760–780.

Götzen, G. A. Graf von (1895), *Durch Afrika von Ost nach West,* Berlin: D. Reimer.

—— (1909), *Deutsch-Ostafrika im Aufstand, 1905–06,* Berlin: D. Reimer.

Gourou, P. (1961), *The Tropical World : its Social and Economic Conditions and its Future Status,* London: Longmans.

Grant, D. K. S. (1939), 'Mangrove Woods of Tanganyika Territory', *TNR* No. 5 : 5–16.

Grant, C. H. B. (1925), 'Uha in Tanganyika Territory', *Geographical Journal* LXVI : 411–422.

Grant, J. A. (1864), *A Walk Across Africa,* Edinburgh: Blackwood.

Grantham, D. R. (1932), 'Lupa Goldfields', *Geological Survey of Tanganyika* (Bulletin No. 3), Dar es Salaam: Government Printer.

Gray, A. and Birmingham, D. (eds.) (1970), *Pre-Colonial African Trade,* London: Oxford University Press.

Gray, E. (1945), 'Notes on the Salt-making Industry of the Nyanza People near Lake Shirwa', *South African Journal of Science* XLI : 465–475.

Gray, R. F. (1955), 'The Mbugwe Tribe: Origin and Development', *TNR* No. 38:39–50.

Gregory, J. W. (1896), *The Great Rift Valley*, London: J. Murray.

Greig, R. C. H. (1937), 'Iron Smelting in Fipa', *TNR* No. 4:77–81.

—— (1937a), 'Iron Smelting in Uha', *Kasulu District Book*.

Griffiths, J. E. S. (1936), 'The Aba-Ha of the Tanganyika Territory—Some Aspects of their Tribal Organization and Sleeping Sickness Concentrations', *TNR* No. 2:72–76.

Gunn, B. (1962), 'Locusts Ascending', *TNR* Nos. 58–59:162–171.

Gunn, D. L. (1956), 'A History of Lake Rukwa and the Red Locust', *TNR* No. 42:1–18.

Gutmann, B. (1912), 'Der Schmied und seine Kunst in animistischen Denken', *Zeitschrift für Ethnologie* XLIV:81–93.

—— (1926), *Das Recht der Dschagga*, München: Beck.

Gwassa, G. C. K. and Iliffe, J. (eds.) (1968), *Records of the Maji Maji Rising*, Nairobi: East African Publishing House.

Häfliger, P. J. (1952), 'Angaben über meinen Africanischen Lebenslauf', Peramiho Catholic Mission (Typescript).

Hailey, W. M. (1938), *An African Survey; a Study of Problems Arising in Africa South of the Sahara*, Oxford: Oxford University Press.

Haldemann, E. G. (1958), 'Geological Aspects of Further Development Possibilities of Brine at Uvinza, Western Tanganyika', *Geological Survey of Tanganyika*, Dar es Salaam: Government Printer.

Harlow, V. and Chilver, E. M. (eds.) (1965), *History of East Africa*, Oxford: Clarendon Press.

Harris, J. H. (1951), 'Lake Manyara', *TNR* No. 30:6–14.

Hartley, B. J. (1938), 'An Indigenous System of Soil Protection', *EAAJ* IV:63–66.

Hartnoll, A. V. and Fuggles-Couchman, N. R. (1937), 'The "Mashokora" Cultivation of the Coast', *TNR* No. 3:34–39.

Hatchell, C. W. (1949), An Early Sleeping Sickness Settlement', *TNR* No. 27:60–64.

Heichelheim, F. M. (1956), 'Effects of Classical Antiquity on the Land', pp. 165–182 in Thomas, W. L. *et al.* (eds.) (1956).

Henderson, W. O. (1943), 'The War Economy of German East Africa, 1914–1917', *Economic History Review* XIII:104–110.

Herrmann, C. (1892), 'Ugogo, das Land und seine Bewohner', *MDS* V:191–203.

—— (1893), 'Die Handlsverhältnisse am Victoria-Nyansa', *DKB* IV:81–82.

—— (1894), 'Die Wasiba und ihr Land', *MDS* VII:43–59.

—— (1900), 'Bercht über Land und Leute längs der deutschenglischen Grenze', *MDS* XIII:344–346.

—— (1908), 'Uber Salzgewinnung in Unyamwezi', *DKB* XIX:21.

Herskovits, M. J. (1926), 'The Cattle Complex in East Africa', *American Anthropologist* XXVIII:230–72, 361–88, 494–528, 633–64.

Hespers, K. (ed.), (1872) *Pater Schynses Letzte Reisen, Briefe und Tagebuch-blätter*, Köln: J. P. Bachem.

Hesse, P. (1899), 'Die Ausbreitung des Sandflohs in Afrika', *Geographisches Zeitschrift* V:522–530.

Hill, J. F. R. and Moffett, J. P. (1955), *Tanganyika; a Review of its Resources and their Development*, Dar es Salaam: Government Printer.

Hill, M. F. (1957), *Permanent Way*, 2 vols., Nairobi: East African Railroads and Harbours.

Hill, P. (1963), 'Markets in Africa', *Journal of Modern African Studies* I:441–453.

Hirschberg, W. (1929), 'Die Viertägige Marktwoche in Afrika', *Anthropos* XXIV:613–619.

Hoare, C. A. (1972), *The Trypanosomes of Mammals: a Zoological Monograph*, Oxford: Blackwell.

Hobley, C. W. (1894), 'Peoples, Places, and Prospects in British East Africa', *Geographical Journal* IV:97–123.

―― (1898), 'Kavirondo', *Geographical Journal* XII:361–372.

―― (1902), *Eastern Uganda; an Ethnographical Survey*, London: Anthropological Institute, Occasional Papers No. 1.

Hobson, J. A. (1938, first published 1902), *Imperialism: a Study*, London: Allen & Unwin.

Hodder, B. W. (1965), 'Some Comments on the Origins of Traditional Markets in Africa South of the Sahara', *Transactions and Papers, Institute of British Geographers* XXXVI:978–1005.

―― and Ukwu, U. I. (1969), *Markets in West Africa*, Ibadan: Ibadan University Press.

Hollis, A. G. (1905), *The Masai, their Language and Folklore*, Oxford: The Clarendon Press.

Holst, C. (1893), 'Die Kulturen der Waschambaa', *Deutsche Kolonialzeitung* VI:23–24.

―― (1893a), 'Der Landbau der Eingeborenen von Usambara', *Deutsche Kolonialzeitung* VI:113–114, 128–130.

Hore, E. C. (1892), *Tanganyika: Eleven Years in Central Africa*, 2nd ed. London: E. Stanford.

Hornby, H. E. (1952), *Animal Trypanosomiasis in Eastern Africa*, London: HMSO.

―― (1935), 'Overstocking in Tanganyika Territory', *EAAJ* I:353–60.

Hutchins, E. E. (n.d.), 'The Nguru and Zigua Tribe', *Morogoro District Book*.

Iliffe, J. (1967), 'The Organization of the Maji Maji Rebellion', *Journal of African History* VIII:495–512.

―― (1969), *Tanganyika under German Rule, 1905–1912*, Cambridge: Cambridge University Press.

―― (1971), *Agricultural Change in Modern Tanganyika*, Nairobi: East African Publishing House.

Ingham, K. (1962), *A History of East Africa*, London: Longmans.

Jackson, C. H. N. (1955), 'The Natural Reservoir of Trypanosoma rhodesiense', Transactions of the Royal Society of Tropical Medicine and Hygiene XLIX:582–587.

Jacobs, A. H. (1965), 'The Traditional Political System of the Pastoral Masai', Ph.D. Dissertation, Oxford: Nuffield College.

―― (1968), 'A Chronology of the Pastoral Masai', *Hadith* I:10–31.

Jäger, F. (1910), 'Der Gegensatz von Kulturland und Wildnis und die allgemeinen Züge ihrer Verteilung in Ost-Afrika', *Geographisches Zeitschrift* XVI:121–33.

―― (1913), 'Das Hochland der Riesenkrater und die umliegenden Hochländer Deutsch-Ostafrikas', *MDS* Erganzungsheft Nos. 4 and 8.

Jätzold, R. (1968), *The Kilombero Valley*, München: Afrika Studien, Weltforum Verlag.

Jahresbericht—Jahresbericht über die Entwicklung der Deutschen Schutzgebiete in Afrika und der Südsee (Beilage zum Deutschen Kolonialblatt), Berlin: Mittler und Sohn.

Johnston, H. H. (1886), *The Kilima-Njaro Expedition*, London: Kegan Paul.

—— (1890), 'Journey North to Lake Nyassa and Visit to Lake Leopold', *Proceedings of the Royal Geographical Society,* XII : 225.

—— (1897), *British Central Africa,* London: Methuen.

Kälin, S. (1945), *Die Töpferei in Ostafrika,* Dissertation, Göttingen: University of Göttingen.

Kanneberg, Hauptmann (1900), 'Durch die Marenga Makali', *MDS* XIII : 3–17.

—— (1900a), 'Reise durch die Hamitischen Sprachengebiete um Kondoa', *MDS* XIII : 144–172.

Katoke, I. K. (1969), 'A History of Karagwe: Northwest Tanzania from c. 1400–1915 A.D.', Ph.D. Dissertation, Boston: Boston University.

Katte, U. von (1908), 'Die Wirtschaftlichen Verhältnisse am Victoriasee', *Der Tropenpflanzer* 457–464, 507–519.

Kerr-Cross, D. (1890), 'Geographical Notes on the Country between Lakes Nyassa, Rukwa and Tanganyika', *Scottish Geographical Magazine* VI : 281–293.

—— (1891), 'Notes on the Country Lying between Lakes Nyassa and Tanganyika', *Proceedings of the Royal Geographical Society* XIII : 86–99.

—— (1895), 'Crater Lakes north of Lake Nyassa', *Geographical Journal* V : 112–124.

Kersten, O. (ed.) (1869), *Baron Carl Claus von der Decken's Reisen in Ost-Afrika in den Jahren 1859 bis 1861,* 3 vols., Leipzig and Heidelberg: Winter'sche Verlagshandlung.

Kimambo, I. N. (1969), *A Political History of the Pare of Tanzania,* Nairobi: East African Publishing House.

—— and Temu, A. J. (eds.) (1969), *A History of Tanzania,* Nairobi: East African Publishing House.

Kimwani, E. G. (1951), 'A Pictorial Description of the Manufacture of Barkcloth in the Bukoba District', *TNR* No. 30 : 85–98.

Kirk, Sir John (1865), 'On the "Tsetse" Fly of Tropical Africa', *The Journal of the Linnean Society* VIII : 15–56.

Kirkpatrick, T. W. (1936), 'East Africa and the Tsetse Fly', *EAAJ* II : 411–415.

Knight, C. G. (1971), 'The Ecology of African Sleeping Sickness', *Annals of the American Association of Geographers* LXI : 23–44.

Kohler, J. (1897), 'Fragebogen zur Erforschung der Rechtsverhältnisse der sogenannten Naturvölker, namentlich in den deutschen Kolonialländern', *Zeitschrift für Vergleichende Rechtswissenschaft* XII : 427–440.

—— (ed.) (1909), *Beantwortung des Fragebogens über die Rechte der Eingeborenen in den deutschen Kolonien,* Berlin: D. Reimer.

Kollmann, P. (1899), *The Victoria Nyanza,* London: Swann.

Koloniale Rundschau, Berlin: D. Reimer (Published by Vohsen, E. and Westermann, D.).

Koloniale Rundschau (1910), 'Der Gegenwärtige Stand der Arbeiterverhältnisse in Deutsch-Ostafrika', pp. 706–708.

König, D. B. von (1910), 'Die Eingeborenen-Besteuerung in unseren Kolonien', pp. 424–436, in *Verhandlungen des Deutschen Kolonial-Kongresses, 1910,* Berlin:D. Reimer.

Kozak, I. G. (1968), 'Two Rebellions in German East Africa and their Study in Microcosm', Ph.D. Dissertation, Washington D.C.: Howard University.

Krapf, J. L. (1860), *Travels, Researches, and Missionary Labours,* London: Trubner.

Kuczynski, R. R. (1949), *Demographic Survey of the British Colonial Empire,* 2 vols., London: Oxford University Press.

Langheld, W. (1897), 'Bericht des Hauptmanns Langheld über seine Expedition nach Unyamwezi', *DKB* VIII :511–512.

—— (1909), *Zwanzig Jahre in deutschen Kolonien*, Berlin: W. Weicher.

Langlands, B. W. (1966), *Bibliography on the Distribution of Disease in East Africa*, Kampala: Makerere University College Library.

—— (1967), 'The Sleeping Sickness Epidemic in Uganda, 1900–1920: a Study in Historical Geography', Kampala: Department of Geography, Makerere University.

Last, J. T. (1882), 'A Journey into the Nguru Country from Mamboya, East Central Africa', *Proceedings of the Royal Geographical Society* IV (New Series): 148–157.

—— (1883), 'A Visit to the Waitumba Iron-Workers and the Mangaheri, near Mamboya, in East Central Africa', *Proceedings of the Royal Geographical Society* V (New Series): 581–592.

Lechaptois, G. (1913), *Aux Rives du Tanganyika*, Alger (Algiers): Maison-Carree.

Lenin, V. I. (n.d. first published in 1913), *Imperialism, the Highest Stage of Capitalism. A Popular Outline*, Moscow: Foreign Languages Publishing House.

Lettow-Vorbeck, General P. von (1920), *My Reminiscences of East Africa*, London: Hurst and Blackett.

Leue, A. (1901), 'Ein Marsch durch Uwinsa', *Globus*, LXXX (4): 60–64.

—— (1903), 'Ungoni', *Deutsche Kolonialzeitung*.

Lichtenheld, G. (1913), 'Ueber Rinderrassen, Rinderzucht und ihre wirtschaftliche Bedeutung in Deutsch-Ostafrika', *Der Pflanzer*, IX :261–279.

—— (1913a), 'Über Rinderrassen, Rinderzucht und ihre wirtschaftliche Bedeutung in Deutsch-Ostafrika', *Der Tropenpflanzer* XVII :405–430.

Liebert, Generalmajor/Governor (1898), *Neunzig Tage im Zelt; meine Reise nach Uhehe*, Berlin: Mittler und Sohn.

Lieder, G. (1894), 'Beobachtungen auf der Ubena–Nyasa–Expedition', *MDS* VII :271–276.

—— (1894a), 'Zur Kenntnis der Karawanenwege in südlichen Theile des Schutzgebietes', *MDS* VII :277.

—— (1897), 'Reise von Mbampa-Bai nach Kisswere', *MDS* X :95–142.

Ling Roth, H. (1934), *Studies in Primitive Looms*, Halifax: F. King & Sons.

Livingstone, D. (1857), *Missionary Travels and Researches in South Africa*, London: J. Murray.

—— (Waller, H. ed.) (1874), *The Last Journals of David Livingstone*, 2 vols, London: J. Murray.

—— and Livingstone, C. (1865), *Narrative of an Expedition to the Zambezi and its Tributaries*, London: J. Murray.

Löbner, M. H. (1914), 'Zur Entvölkerungsfrage Unyamwesis', *Koloniale Rundschau*, 267–70.

Ludwig, H. D. (1968), 'Permanent Farming on Ukara', pp. 87–136 in Ruthenberg, H. (ed.) (1968).

Lugard, F. D. (1892), 'Travels from the East Coast to Uganda, Lake Albert Edward, and Lake Albert', *Proceedings of the Royal Geographical Society* XIV (New Series): 817–841.

—— (1893), *The Rise of our East African Empire*, 2 vols., Edinburgh: Blackwood.

Lunan, M. (1950), 'Mound Cultivation in Ufipa, Tanganyika', *EAAJ* XVI :88–89.

—— and Brewin, D. (1956), 'The Agriculture of Ukara Island', *The Empire Cotton Growing Review*.

McHenry, D. E. jr. (1974), 'Gaining Peasant Compliance', *Proceedings of the Universities of East Africa Social Science Conference*, Kampala.

Mackenzie, D. R. (1925), *The Spirit-Ridden Konde,* London: Seeley, Service & Co.

Maclean, G. (1929), 'The Relationship between Economic Development and Rhodesian Sleeping Sickness in Tanganyika Territory', *Annals of Tropical Medicine and Parasitology* XXIII : 37–46.

—— (1930), 'Sleeping Sickness Measures in Tanganyika Territory', *Kenya and East Africa Medical Journal* 120–126.

McMaster, D. N. (1962), 'Change of Regional Balance in the Bukoba District of Tanganyika', *TNR* Nos. 58–59:79–92.

Malcolm, D. W. (1953), *Sukumaland; An African People and their Country,* London: Oxford University Press.

Marsh, Z. and Kingsnorth, G. W. (1957), *An Introduction to the History of East Africa,* Cambridge: Cambridge University Press.

Marsland, H. (1938), '*Mlau* Cultivation in the Rufiji Valley', *TNR* No. 5:56–59.

Masao, F. T. (1974), 'The Irrigation System in Uchagga: An Ethno-Historical Approach', *TNR* No. 75:1–8.

Matzke, G. E. (1972) 'Settlement Reorganization for the Production of African Wildlife in Miombo Forest Lands: a Spatial Analysis', *Rocky Mountains Social Science Journal* IX (3):21–33.

Medizinal-Berichte über die Deutschen Schutzgebiete, Berlin: Mittler und Sohn (Published by Reichs-Kolonialamt).

Meillassoux, C. (1960), 'Essai d'interprétation du phénomène économique dans less societies traditionnelles d'auto-subsistance', *Cahiers d'études africaines* IV:38–67.

Merensky, A. (1894), *Deutsche Arbeit am Njassa; Deutsch-Ostafrika,* Berlin: Buchhandlung der Berliner evangelischen Missionsgesellschaft.

Merker, M. (1904), *Die Masai,* Berlin: D. Reimer.

Mettam, R. W. M. (1937), 'A Short History of Rinderpest with special Reference to Africa', *Uganda Journal* V :22–26.

Meyer, H. (1900), *Der Kilimandjaro,* Berlin: D. Reimer.

—— (1909), *Das deutsche Kolonialreich; Eine Länderkunde der deutschen Schutzgebiete,* 2 vols., Leipzig and Wien: Verlag des Bibliographischen Instituts.

—— (1911), 'Reiseberichte', *MDS* XXIV:342–359.

—— (1913), 'Ergebnisse einer Reise durch das Zwischenseegebiet Ostafrikas 1911', *MDS* Erganzungsheft No. 6.

—— (1916), *Die Barundi,* Leipzig: O⁻. Spamer.

Meyer, T. (1901), 'Von Utengule nach Kipembambwe, Mwendo, Ibungu, Inyika, und zerück', *MDS* XIV :172–183 (map).

Milne, G. (1938), 'Bukoba: High and Low Fertility on a Laterized Soil', *EAAJ* IV:13–24.

Miracle, M. P. (1961), 'Seasonal Hunger: A Vague Concept and an Unexplored Problem', *Bulletin Institut Français d'Afrique Noire* XXIII (Serié B): 273–283.

MDS—Mittheilungen (von Forschungsreisenden und Gelehrten) aus den Deutschen Schutzgebieten, Berlin: Mittler und Sohn.

Moffett, J. P. (1939), 'A Strategic Retreat from Tsetse Fly; Uyowa and Bugoma Concentrations 1937', *TNR* No. 7:35–38.

—— (1958), *Handbook of Tanganyika,* Dar es Salaam: The Government Printer.

Money, R. I. and Kellett Smith, S. (1897), 'Explorations in the Country West of Lake Nyasa', *Geographical Journal* X :146–170.

Moore, J. E. (1971), 'Traditional Rural Settlement', pp. 124–7 in Berry, L. (ed.) (1971).

Moore, R. J. (1937), 'Industry and Trade on the Shores of Lake Mweru', *Africa* X:137–158.

Morgan, D. R. (1974), 'Salt-Production in Tanzania: Past and Present', *TNR* No. 74:31–37.

Morris, K. R. S. (1951), 'The Ecology of Endemic Sleeping Sickness', Bulletin of Entomological Research XLII:427–443.

—— (1963), 'The Movement of Sleeping Sickness across Africa', *Journal of Tropical Medicine and Hygiene* XLVI:59–76.

Müller, F. F. (1959), *Deutschland–Zanzibar–Ostafrika: Geschichte einer deutschen Kolonialeroberung 1884–1890*, Berlin: Rütter und Leoning.

Mullens, Rev. J. (1877), 'A New Route and New Method of Travelling into Central Africa Adopted by the Rev. Robert Price in 1876', *Proceedings of the Royal Geographical Society* XXI:241.

Mulligan, H. W. (ed.) (1970), *The African Trypanosomiases*, London: Allen & Unwin.

Napier Bax, S. (1943), 'A Practical Policy for Tsetse Reclamation and Field Experiment', *EAAJ* IX:2–13, 83–87, 157–162.

—— (1943a), 'Notes on the Presence of Tsetse Fly, between 1857 and 1915, in the Dar es Salaam Area', *TNR* No. 16:33–49.

Nash, T. A. M. (1969), *Africa's Bane: the Tsetse Fly*, London: Collins.

Neumann, O. (1894), 'Von der wissenschaftlichen Expedition Oscar Neumanns', *DKB* V:421–424.

Nicholls, C. S. (1972), *The Swahili Coast; Politics, Diplomacy and Trade on the East Africa Littoral, 1798–1856*, London: Allen & Unwin.

Nicholson, B. D. (1969), 'The Selous Game Reserve', Dar es Salaam:Ministry of National Resources, Game Department (Typescript).

Nigmann, E. (1907), *Die Wahehe*, Berlin: Mittler.

—— (1911), *Geschichte der Kaiserlichen Schutztruppe für Deutsch-Ostafrika*, Berlin: Mittler.

Nyerere, J. K. (1973), *Freedom and Development*, Dar es Salaam: Oxford University Press.

Oliver, R. and Mathew, G. (eds.) (1963), *History of East Africa*, Oxford: The Clarendon Press.

Omer-Cooper, J. D. (1966), *The Zulu Aftermath, A Nineteenth Century Revolution in Bantu Africa*, London: Longmans.

Ormerod, W. E. (1961), 'The Epidemic Spread of Rhodesian Sleeping Sickness, 1908–1960', *Transactions of the Royal Society of Tropical Medicine and Hygiene* LV:525–538.

Ormsby-Gore, W. (Chairman) (1925), 'Report of the East African Commission', Cmd. 2387. London: HMSO.

Orr, D. and Grantham, D. R. (1931), 'Some Salt Lakes of the Northern Rift Zone', *Geological Survey of Tanganyika,* Dar es Salaam: Government Printer.

Patterson, R. L. (1956), 'Ukara Island', *TNR* No. 44:54–62.

Pechuel-Loesche, E. *et al.* (1882), *Die Loango Expedition,* Leipzig: P. Frohberg.

Peiper, O. (1920), 'Der Bevölkerungs-rückgang in den tropischen Kolonien Afrikas und der Südsee—seine Ursache und seine Bekämpfung', *Veröffentlichungen aus dem Gebiete der Medizinalverwaltung* XI:7.

—— (1926), 'Ethnographische Beobachtungen aus dem Bezirke Kilwa, Deutsch-Ostafrika', *Baessler-Archiv* X:16–36.

Percival, A. B. (1918), 'Game and Disease', *Journal of East African and Uganda Natural History Society* XIII:302.

Peters, K. (1891), *New Light on Dark Africa*, London: Ward, Lock & Co.

Picarda, Fr. (1886), 'Autour du Mandera: Notes sur l'Ouzigoua, l'Oukwere, ét l'Oudi', *Les Missions Catholique* XVIII:184–189, 197–201, 208–211, 234–237, 246–249, 258–261, 269–274, 281–285, 294–297, 322–324, 332–336, and 356–357.

Pike, A. H. (1938), 'Soil Conservation amongst the Matengo Tribe', *TNR* No. 6:79–81, No. 7:117–118.

Popplewell, G. D. (1939), 'Salt Production among the Wasambaa', *TNR* No. 8:102–103.

Portal, Sir Gerald (Rodd, R. ed.) (1894), *The British Mission to Uganda in 1893*, London: L. Arnold.

Porter, Ph.W. (1966), 'East Africa—Population Distribution', *Annals of the Association of American Geographers*, LVI (map supplement).

Potts, W. H. (1937), 'The Distribution of Tsetse Flies in Tanganyika Territory', *Bulletin of Entomological Research* XXVIII:129–148 (with map).

—— and Jackson, C. H. N. (1952), 'The Shinyanga Game Destruction Experiment', *Bulletin of Entomological Research* XLIII:365–374.

Prince, T. von (1894), 'Geschichte der Magwangwara', *MDS* VII:213–224.

—— (1899), 'Über eine Bereisung des Merere-Reiches', *DKB* X:732–734.

—— (1914), *Gegen Araber und Wahehe*, Berlin: Mittler und Sohn.

Prittwitz and Gaffron (1910), 'Das Massaireservat südlich des Kilimanjaro', *MDS* XXIII (map).

Prothero, R. M. (ed.) (1972), *People and Land in Africa South of the Sahara*, London and New York: Oxford University Press.

PCAR—Provincial Commissioners' Annual Report, Dar es Salaam: Government Printer.

Quiggin, A. H. (1949), *Trade Routes, Trade and Currency in East Africa*, Livingstone: Rhodes-Livingstone Museum.

Ramsay, Hauptmann (1896), 'Bericht über seine Ankunft am Tanganyika', *DKB* VII:770–773.

—— (1897), 'Bericht des Kompagnieführers Ramsay', *DKB* VIII:286–287.

Ranger, T. O. (1968), 'Connections between "Primary Resistance" Movements and Modern Mass Nationalism in East and Central Africa', *Journal of African History*, IX:437–453, 631–641.

—— (ed.) (1968a), *Emerging Themes of African History; Proceedings of the International Congress of African Historians, October, 1965*, Nairobi: East African Publishing House.

—— (1969), 'The Recovery of African Initiative in Tanzanian History', Dar es Salaam: University College.

—— and Kimambo, I. (eds.) (1972), *The Historical Study of African Religions*, Berkeley: University of California Press.

Raum, O. F. (1965), 'Changes in African Life Under German Administration, 1892–1914', pp. 193–207 in Harlow and Chilver (eds.) (1965).

Reche, O. (1914), 'Zur Ethnographie des Abflusslosen Gebietes Deutsch-Ost-Afrikas', Abhandlung, Hamburg: Hamburgischen Kolonialinstituts.

Reckling, W. (1942), 'Handwerk und Kunst der Wasaramo', *Koloniale Rundschau* 31–37.

Redmond, P. M. (1972), 'A History of the Songea Ngoni', Ph.D. Dissertation, London: University of London.

Rehse, H. (1910), *Kiziba; Land und Leute,* Stuttgart: Strecker und Schröder.

Reichard, P. (1892), *Deutsch Ostafrika; das Land und seine Bewohner,* Leipzig: O. Spamer.

Reining, P. C. (1967), 'The Haya: the Agricultural System of a Sedentary People', Ph.D. Dissertation, Chicago: University of Chicago.

Richter, Hauptmann (1899), 'Der Bezirk Bukoba', *MDS* XII :67–105.

—— (1900), 'Einige weitere ethnographische Notizen über den Bezirk Bukoba', *MDS* XIII :61–75.

—— (1900a), 'Notitzen über Lebensweise, Zeitrechnung, Industrie und Handwerk der Bewohner des Bezirk Bukoba', *MDS* XIII :115–126.

Robert, R. P. J. M. (1949), *Croyance et Coutumes Magico-Religieuses des Fipa Paiens,* Kipalapala, Tabora: Tanganyika Mission Press.

Roberts, A. D. (ed.) (1968), *Tanzania Before 1900: Seven Area Histories,* Nairobi: East African Publishing House.

—— (1970), 'Nyamwezi Trade', pp. 39–74 in Gray and Birmingham (eds.) (1970).

Robertson, J. K. (1941), 'Mixed or Multiple Cropping in Native Agricultural Practice', *EAAJ* VI :228–232.

Robinson, R. and Gallagher, J. (1961), *Africa and the Victorians; the Climax of Imperialism in the Dark Continent,* London: Macmillan.

Rodney, W. (1972), *How Europe Underdeveloped Africa,* London: Bogle-l'Ouverture Publications.

Rosemond, C. C. de (1943), 'Iron Smelting in the Kahama District', *TNR* No. 16:73–84.

Rounce, N. V. (1936), 'The Unsuitability of Certain Virgin Soils to the Growth of Grain Crops', *EAAJ* II :145–148.

—— (1939), 'Ingereza Ng'wana Sweya: His own Story and his Agricultural Practices', *EAAJ* V :211–215.

—— (1949), *The Agriculture of the Cultivation Steppe,* Cape Town: Longmans, Green & Co.

—— and Thornton, D. (1936), 'Ukara Island and the Agricultural Practices of the Wakara', *TNR* No. 1 :25–32.

—— and Thornton, D. (1939), 'The Ridge in Native Cultivation, with Special Reference to the Mwanza District', *EAAJ* IV :352–355.

Routledge, W. S. (1910), *With A Prehistoric People; the Akikuyu of British East Africa,* London: E. Arnold.

Ruthenberg, H. (ed.) (1968), *Smallholder Farming and Smallholder Development in Tanzania, Ten Case Studies,* London: Hurst.

—— (1971), *Farming Systems in the Tropics,* Oxford: Clarendon Press.

St. John, C. (1970), 'Kazembe and the Tanganyika-Nyasa Corridor, 1800–1890', pp. 202–230 in Gray and Birmingham (eds.) (1970).

Sander, L. (1893), 'Einem Vortrage über die Viehseuchen in Afrika', *DKB* IV :542–545.

—— (1902), *Die Wanderhauschrecken und ihre Bekämpfung in unsere Ostafrikanischen Kolonien,* Berlin: D. Reimer.

Saul, J. S. (1972), 'Nationalism, Socialism and Tanzanian History', pp. 65–79 in Cliffe, L. and Saul, J. S. (eds.) (1972).

Savage, D. C. and Munro, J. F. (1966), 'Carrier Corps Recruitment in the British East African Protectorate, 1914–1918', *Journal of African History* VII :313–42.

Schaele, Dr. (1913), 'Die Rinder des Muansa-und Tabora Bezirkes', *Der Pflanzer* IX :117–130.

Scheerer, J. H. (1959), 'The Ha of Tanganyika', *Anthropos* LIV : 841–904.

Schele, Freiherr von (1894), 'Bericht über die Expedition des Gouverneurs in das Gebiet des Rufidji und Ulanga, am Nyassassee und in das Hinterland von Kilwa', *DKB* V : 224–230.

—— (1896), 'Uhehe', *MDS* IX : 67–74.

Schmidt, P. R. (1974), 'An Investigation of Early and Late Iron Age Cultures though Oral Tradition and Archaeology; an Interdisciplinary Case Study in Buhaya, Tanzania', Ph.D. dissertation, Evanston: Northwestern University.

Schmidt, R. (1892), *Geschichte des Araberaufstandes in Ostafrika*, Frankfurt a.d. Oder: Trowitzsch.

Schnee, H. (1913), 'Zur Frage der Besiedelung Deutsch-Ostafrikas', *DKB* XXIV : 260–269.

—— (1919), *Deutsch-Ostafrika im Weltkriege*, Leipzig: Quelle & Meyer.

—— (ed.) (1919–1920), *Deutsches Kolonial-Lexicon*, 3 vols., Leipzig: Quelle & Meyer.

Scholz, Dr. (1913), 'Ueber Sälzvorkommen und Salzgewinnung in Deutsch-Ostafrika', *Der Pflanzer*, IX : 226–232.

Schurtz, H. (1900), *Das Afrikanische Gewerbe*, Leipzig: B. G. Teubner.

Schynse, A. (Hespers, K. ed.) (1892), *Pater Schynse's letzte Reisen, Briefe und Tagebuchblätter*, Köln: J. P. Bachem.

Senior, H. S. (1938), 'Sukuma Salt Caravans to Lake Eyasi', *TNR* No. 6 : 87–90.

Sharpe, A. (1893), 'A Journey from the Shire River to Lake Mweru and the Upper Luapula', *Geographical Journal* I : 524–533.

—— (1896), 'The Geography and Resources of British Central Africa', *Geographical Journal* VII : 366–387.

Sheriff, A. M. H. (1971), 'The Rise of a Commercial Empire; An Aspect of the History of Zanzibar from 1770 to 1873', Ph.D. Thesis, London: University of London.

—— (forthcoming), 'Trade and Underdevelopment. The Role of International Trade in the Economic History of the East African Coast before the 16th Century', *Hadith* (Nairobi).

Shinnie, P. L. (ed.) (1971), *The African Iron Age*, Oxford: Clarendon Press.

Shorter, A. E. M. (1972), *Chiefship in Western Tanzania; A Political History of the Kimbu*, Oxford: Clarendon Press.

Sigl, Leutnant (1892), 'Bericht über den Handelsverkehr von Tabora', *DKB* III : 164–166.

—— (1894), 'Bericht des Leutnant Sigl, Tabora', *DKB* V : 6–13.

Smith, A. (1963), 'The Southern Section of the Interior, 1840–1884', pp. 253–296 in Oliver and Mathew (eds.) (1963).

Smith, Consul G. S. (1887), 'Explorations in Zanzibar Dominions', *Supplementary Papers, Royal Geographical Society* II (1) : 99–125.

Smith, H. C. (1938), 'The Sukuma System of Grazing Rights', *EAAJ* IV : 129–30.

Sommerfeld, Dr. (1912), 'Einiges über Haltung und Zucht des Zeburindes und seiner Kreuzungen durch den Eingeborenen', *Der Pflanzer* VIII : 316–23.

—— (1912a), 'Verwendung von Düngemittel durch ackerbautreibende Eingeborenenstämme in Deutsch-Ostafrika', *Der Pflanzer* VIII : 91–93.

Soper, R. (1967), 'Kwale: An Early Iron Age Site in South Eastern Kenya', *Azania* II : 1–17.

—— (1971), 'A General Review of the Early Iron Age of the Southern Half of Africa', *Azania* VI : 5–37.

Speke, J. H. (1863), *Journal of the Discovery of the Source of the Nile*, Edinburgh: Blackwood.

—— (1864), *What led to the Discovery of the Source of the Nile*, Edinburgh: Blackwood.

Spence, J. (1957), 'The Geology and Archaeology of the Ivuna Salt Pans', *Records of the Geological Survey of Tanganyika*, III : 21–28, Dar es Salaam: Government Printer.

Spengler, J. J. and Duncan, O. D. (1956), *Demographic Analysis*, Glencoe: The Free Press.

Spreiter (1908), Letter to Fuchs, 2 September, 1908 (MDI/10), (Missionary Diocese, Iringa).

Springer, A. (1918), 'Die Salzversorgung der Eingeborenen Afrikas vor der neuzeitlichen europäischen Kolonisation', Inaugural Dissertation, Jena: Universitat von Jena.

Stadlbaur, Leutenant (1897), 'Turu', *MDS* X : 169–179.

Stanley, H. M. (1872), *How I found Livingstone in Central Africa*, London: Sampson, Low.

—— (1880), *Through the Dark Continent*, London: Sampson, Low.

—— (1890), *In Darkest Africa*, 2 vols., London: Sampson, Low.

Stenhouse, A. S. (1944), 'Agriculture in the Matengo Highlands', *EAAJ* X : 22–24.

Stern, R. (1910), 'Die Gewinnung des Eisens (Nyamwezi)', pp. 152–163 in Stuhlmann, Fr. (1910).

Steudel, E. (1928), 'Die Schlafkrankheit in Deutsch-Ostafrika vom Beginn bis zur Gegenwart', *MDS* XXXVI : 61–79.

Stevenson, R. F. (1968), *Population and Political Systems in Tropical Africa*, New York: Columbia University Press.

Stolowsky, Dr. (1903), 'Erkundigung der Wegverhältnisse zwischen der Station Mahenge und Kungulio am Ulanga', *MDS* XVI : 253–263.

Strandes, J. (1899), *Die Portugiesenzeit von Deutsch-und Englisch Ostafrika*, Berlin: D. Reimer.

Stuhlmann, Fr. (1892), 'Rückreise vom Victoria-Nyansa nach Bagamoyo', *MDS* V : 185–188.

—— (1894), *Deutsch-Ostafrika; mit Emin Pascha ins Herz von Afrika*, Berlin: D. Reimer.

—— (1894a), 'Forschungsreise in Usaramo', *MDS* VII : 225–232.

—— (1895), 'Über die Uluguruberge in Deutsch-Ostafrika', *MDS* VIII : 209–226.

—— (1897), 'Bericht über das deutsch-portugiesische Grenzgebiet am Ruvuma', *MDS* X : 182–188.

—— (1898), *Die wirtschaftliche Entwicklung Deutsch-Ostafrikas*, Berlin: D. Reimer.

—— (1902), 'Notizen über die Tsetsefliege (*Glossina Morsitans*, Westw.) und die durch sie übertragene Surrankrankheit in Deutsch-Ostafrika', *Berichte über Land- und Forstwirtschaft in Deutsch-Ostafrika* I : 137–153.

—— (1909), *Beiträge zur Kulturgeschichte von Ostafrika*, Berlin: D. Reimer.

—— (1910), *Handwerk und Industri in Ostafrika*, Hamburg: Friederichsen.

Sturdy, D. (1939), 'Leguminous Crops in Native Agricultural Practice', *EAAJ* V : 31–33.

Sulivan, G. L. (1873), *Dhow Chasing in Zanzibar Waters on the East Coast of Africa*, London: Low & Searle.

Supan, A. (1904), 'Die Bevölkerung der Erde', *Petermanns Geographische Mittheilungen*, Erganzungsheft No. 146.

Survey Division, Department of Lands and Mines (1948), *Atlas of the Tanganyika Territory* (2nd ed.) Dar es Salaam: Government Printer.
—— (1956), *Atlas of Tanganyika, East Africa* (3rd ed.) Dar es Salaam: Government Printer.
Sutton, J. E. G. (1969), 'Ancient Civilizations and Modern Agricultural Systems in the Southern Highlands of Tanzania', *Azania* IV : 1–13.
—— (1973), 'The Ancient Dams of Tanganyika Masailand', *Azania* VIII : 105–114.
—— (1973a), *Early Trade in Eastern Africa,* Nairobi: East African Publishing House.
—— and Roberts, A. D. (1968), 'Uvinza and its Salt Industry', *Azania* III : 45–86.
Swynnerton, C. F. M. (1921), 'An Examination of the Tsetse Problem in North Mossurise, Portuguese East Africa', *Bulletin of Entomological Research* XI : 315–385.
—— (1923), 'A Critical Summary of the Preliminary Observations of the Sleeping Sickness Outbreak near Mwanza', *Transactions of the Royal Society of Tropical Medicine and Hygiene* XVII : 142–150.
—— (1923a), 'The Entomological Aspects of an Outbreak of Sleeping Sickness near Mwanza, Tanganyika Territory', *Bulletin of Entomological Research* XVII : 317–372.
—— (1923b), 'The Relations of some East African Tsetse Flies to the Flora and the Fauna', *Transactions of the Royal Society of Tropical Medicine and Hygiene* XVII : 128–140.
—— (1936), 'The Tsetse Flies of East Africa', *Transactions of the Royal Entomological Society of London* LXXXIV (Special Issue).
Swynnerton, R. J. M. (1939), '*Vernonia Subuligera* as a Green Manure', *EAAJ* IV : 378.
TNA—Tanganyika/Tanzania National Archives.
—— No. 2702 'Tsetse Fly' (4 vols.).
—— No. 3517 'Administration of Kigoma District'.
—— No. 11234 'Game Reserves'.
—— No. 11341 'Effects of Tsetse Operations'.
—— No. 11825 'Games Policy in Relation to Tsetse Fly'.
—— No. 20853 'Development of Game Reserves'.
—— No. 21210 'Lake Rukwa Game Reserve'.
—— No. 21709 'Sleeping Sickness Concentration Committee'.
—— No. 22856 'Development of Game Reserves'.
—— No. 23892 'Sleeping Sickness Settlements: Kigoma', (2 vols.).
—— No. 25102 'Report on Uzinza by Mr. B. D. Burtt'.
—— No. 26899 'Selous Game Reserve'.
—— No. 28446 'Sleeping Sickness Concentrations in Ulanga'.
—— No. 30600 'Sleeping Sickness Concentration: Singida District'.
—— No. 31317 'Chimpanzee Sanctuary'.
—— No. 31351 'Compulsory Resettlement of Africans'.
—— No. 31756 'Matandu River Game Reserve'.
—— No. 31796 'Administration of Liwale District' (2 vols.).
Tanner, R. E. S. (1966) 'Cattle Theft in Musoma 1958–1959', *TNR* No. 65 : 31–42.
TNP—Tanzania National Parks (1970), 'Lake Manyara National Park; A Guide', Arusha: Tanzania Litho.
Tetzlaff, R. (1970), *Koloniale Entwicklung und Ausbeutung,* Berlin: Dunker & Humbolt.
Thomas, D. K. (1963), 'Illegal Hunting in Tanganyika', *TNR* No. 61 : 190–194.
Thomas, W. L. (ed.) (1956), *Man's Role in Changing the Face of the Earth,* Chicago: University of Chicago Press.

Thomson, J. (1881), *To the Central African Lakes and Back*, 2 vols., London: Low, Marston, Searle.

—— (1882), 'Notes on the Basin of the River Ruvuma', *Proceedings of the Royal Geographical Society*, IV.

—— (1885), *Through Masailand*, London: Low, Marston, Searle.

Thornton, D. and Rounce, N. V. (1933), *Ukara Island and the Agricultural Practices of the Wakara*, Nairobi: Government Printer.

Thwaites, D. H. (1943), 'Wanyakyusa Agriculture', *EAAJ* IX :236–239.

Tiller, Oberleutnant (1913), 'Süd-Ussagara', pp. 51–57 in Meyer (1913).

Tornau, F. (1904), 'Die Geologischen and Hydrographischen Verhältnisse an der Karawanenstrasse Kilwa-Songea', *Berichte über Land- und Forstwirtschaft in Deutsch-Ostafrika* II : 128–142.

Tosh, J. (1970), 'The Northern Interlacustrine Region', pp. 103–118 in Gray and Birmingham (eds.) (1970).

Trapnell, G. G. (1937), *Ecological Methods in the Study of Native Agriculture in Northern Rhodesia*, Kew: Royal Botanical Gardens, Bulletin of Miscellaneous Information, No. 1.

—— (1943), *The Soils, Vegetation and Agricultural Systems of North Eastern Rhodesia*, Lusaka: Government Printer.

Trigger, B. G. (1969), 'The Myth of Meroe and the African Iron Age', *African Historical Studies* II. 23–50.

Tylecote, R. F. (1965), 'Iron Smelting in Pre-industrial Communities', *Journal of Iron and Steel Institute* 203 :340–348.

Udo, R. K. (1963), 'Patterns of Population Distribution and Settlement in Eastern Nigeria', *Nigerian Geographical Journal* VI : 73–88.

Uhlig, C. (1904), *Wirtschaftskarte von Deutsch-Ostafrika*, Berlin: D. Reimer.

Unomah, A. C. (1972), 'Economic Expansion and Political Change in Unyanyembe', Ph.D. Dissertation, Ibadan: University of Ibadan.

Uzoigwe, G. N. (1970), 'Precolonial Markets in Bunyoro-Kitara', Proceedings of the Universities of East Africa Social Science Conference, Dar es Salaam.

Vansina, J. (1962), 'Long-distance Trade-routes in Central Africa', *Journal of African History* III : 375–390.

Vaegler, P. (1912), 'Ugogo', *Beihefte zum Tropenpflanzer*.

Verhandlungen des Deutschen Kolonialkongresses 1910 (1910), Berlin: D. Reimer.

Vesey-FitzGerald, L. D. E. F. (1964), 'Mammals of the Rukwa Valley', *TNR* No. 62 :61–72.

Volkens, G. (1897), *Der Kilimandscharo*, Berlin: D. Reimer.

Wallace, L. A. (1899), 'The Nyasa-Tanganyika Plateau', *Geographical Journal* XIII : 595–621.

Warburg, O. (1894), 'Die Kulturpflanzen Usambaras', *MDS* VII : 131–198.

Watermeyer, A. M. and Elliott, H. F. I. (1943), 'Lake Manyara', *TNR* No. 15 :58–71.

Weitz, B. (1963), 'The Feeding Habits of *Glossina*', *Bulletin of the World Health Organization* XXVIII : 711–729.

—— and Glasgow, J. P. (1956), 'The Natural Hosts of Some Species of *Glossina* in East Africa', *Transactions of the Royal Society of Tropical Medicine and Hygiene* L : 593–612.

Werther, C. W. (1896), *Zum Victoria Nyanza*, Berlin: H. Paetel.

—— et al. (1898), *Die Mittleren Hochländer des nordlichen Deutsch-Ost-Afrika*, Berlin: H. Paetel.

Weule, K. (1908), 'Ethnographische Forschungsreise in den Südosten Deutsch

Ostafrikas', MDS Erganzungsheft.

— (1909), *Native Life in East Africa*, London: Pitman.

Widenmann, A. (1895), 'Bericht iber die klimatischen und gcsundheitlichen Verhältnisse von Moshi am Kilimanjaro', *MDS* V111:283–309.

— (1899), 'Die Kilimandscharo-Bevölkerung, *Petermanns Geographische Mittheilungen*, Erganzungsheft No. 129.

Wilcox, W. F. (1940), *Studies in American Demography*, Ithacha: Cornell University Press.

Winan's, E. V. (1965), 'The Political Context of Economic Adaptation in the Southern Highlands of Tanganyika', *American Anthropologist* LXVII :435–441.

Wise, R. (1958), 'Iron Smelting in Ufipa', *TNR*, No. 50 :106–111.

Wissmann, H. von (1891), *My Second Journey through Equatorial Africa*, London: Chatto & Windus.

Wolfel,K.(1911), 'Beiträgezur Kenntnis der Tsetse und der Trypanosomiases', *Der Pflanzer* VII :397–406.

—— (1991a), 'Viehhaltung im Tabora Bezirk', *Der Pflanzer* Vl 1: 77–85 .

Wood, L.J. (1974), 'Market Origins and Development in EastAfrica', Kampala: Department of Geography,University o fMakerere, Occasional Paper No.57.

Wrigley, C. C. (1965), 'Kenya: the Patterns of Economic Lifc, 1902–1945', pp. 209–264 in Harlow and Chilver (eds.) (1965).

Wyckaert, R. P. (1914), 'Forgerons paiens et forgerons chrétiens au Tanganyika', *Anthropos* IX: 371–380.

Young, D. D. (1957), 'Commentary to Livingstone's Last Journal', *Sumbawanga (Ufipa) District Book.*

Young, R. and Fosbrooke, H. (1960), *Land and Politics among the Luguru of Tanganyika*, London: Routledge.

Ziegenhorn (1890), 'Das Rufiji Delta', *MDS* IX:78–85.

Additional Bibliography 1977–1995

Abrahams, R.G. (1981), *The Nyamwezi Today*, New York: Cambridge University Press.

—— (ed.) (1985), *Villagers, Villages, and the State in Modern Tanzania*, Cambridge: Cambridge University, African Studies Centre.

Ambler, Charles (1978), 'The Great Famine in East Central Kenya, 1897–1900, a Regional View', Historical Association of Kenya, Annual Conference (mimeographed).

—— (1988), *Kenyan Communities in the Age of Imperialism: The Central Region in the Late Nineteenth Century*, New Haven: Yale University Press.

Anderson, David M. (1988), 'Cultivating Pastoralists: Ecology and Economy Among the Il Chamus of Baringo, 1840–1980', in Johnson, Douglas H. and David M. Anderson (eds.).

—— (forthcoming) *Eroding the Commons: Politics and Ecology in Baringo, Kenya*, London: James Currey.

Anderson, David M. and R. Grove (eds.) (1987) *Conservation in Africa: Peoples,*

Policies and Practice, Cambridge: Cambridge University Press.

Arnold, David (ed.) (1988), *Imperial Medicine and Indigenous Societies*, Manchester: Manchester University Press.

Austen, Ralph (1987), *African Economic History: Internal Development and External Dependency*, London: James Currey; Portsmouth NH: Heinemann.

Århem, Kaj (1985), *Pastoral Man in the Garden of Eden. The Maasai of the Ngorongoro Conservation Area, Tanzania*, Uppsala: University of Uppsala and Scandinavian Institute of African Studies.

Beck, Ann (1977), *Medicine and Society in Tanganyika, 1890–1930: A Historical Inquiry*, Philadelphia: The American Philosophical Society.

Bennett, Norman R. (1971), *Mirambo of Tanzania, 1840?–1884*, New York: Oxford University Press.

Bernstein, Henry (1981), 'Notes on State and Peasantry: the Tanzanian Case', *Review of African Political Economy*, 21:44–62.

Berthelot, B. (1987), *Maîtrise de l'eau en Afrique de l'Est: des systèmes d'irrigation au Kenya et en Tanzanie*, Paris.

Boesen, Jannik *et al.* (1978), *Ujamaa – Socialism from Above*, New York: Africana Publishing Co.

Brokensha, D.W., D.M. Warren, and O. Werner (eds.) (1980), *Indigenous Knowledge and Development*, Washington, DC: University Press of America.

Bujra, Janet (1990), 'Taxing Development in Tanzania: Why Must People Pay?', *Review of African Political Economy*, 47:44–63.

Cambridge History of Africa (1977–1986), Vols. I–VIII, Cambridge: Cambridge University Press.

Chrétien, Jean-Pierre (1986) 'L'Afrique des grands lacs existe-elle?' *Revue Tiers Monde* XXVII, 106: 253–270.

Clarke, J. I. *et al.* (eds.) (1985), *Population and Development Projects in Africa*, Cambridge: Cambridge University Press.

Clyde, David F. (1962), *History of the Medical Services of Tanganyika*, Dar es Salaam: Government Printer.

—— (1967), *Malaria in Tanzania*, London: Oxford University Press.

Cohen, David William (1983) 'Food Production and Food Exchange in the Precolonial Lakes Plateau Region', in Rotberg, R.I. (ed.) (1983).

Collier, Paul, Samir Radwan and Samuel Wangwe (1990), *Labour and Poverty in Rural Tanzania: Ujamaa and Rural Development in the United Republic of Tanzania*, Oxford: Clarendon Press.

Cooper, Frederick (1977), *Plantation Slavery on the East Coast of Africa*, New Haven: Yale University Press.

—— (1980), *From Slaves to Squatters: Plantation Labor and Agriculture in Zanzibar and Coastal Kenya, 1890–1925*, New Haven: Yale University Press.

—— (1993), 'Africa and the World Economy', in Cooper, Frederick *et al.* (1993).

Cooper, Fredrick *et al.* (1993) *Confronting Historical Paradigms*, Madison, Wis.: University of Wisconsin Press.

Cordell, Dennis D., Joel W. Gregory and Victor Piche (1987), 'African Historical Demography: The Search for a Theoretical Framework', in Cordell, Dennis D. and Joel W. Gregory (eds.) (1987).

Cordell, Dennis D. and Joel W. Gregory (eds.) (1987), *African Population and Capitalism: Historical Perspectives*, Boulder, Col.: Westview Press, 1987.

Coulson, Andrew (ed.) (1979), *African Socialism in Practice: the Tanzanian Experience*, Nottingham: Review of African Political Economy.

—— (1982), *Tanzania: A Political Economy*, Oxford: Clarendon Press.

Crosby, A. (1986), *Ecological Imperialism: The Biological Expansion of Europe 900 –1900*, Cambridge: Cambridge University Press.

Dawson, Marc H. (1979), 'Smallpox in Kenya, 1880–1920', *Social Science and Medicine* 13B:245–250.

Ellis, F. (1983), 'Agricultural Marketing and Peasant–State Transfers in Tanzania', *Journal of Peasant Studies* 10, 4:214–242.

Eriksen, Tore Linné (1979), 'Modern African History: Some Historiographical Observations', *Scandinavian Journal of History* 4:75–97.

Feierman, Steven (1990), *Peasant Intellectuals: Anthropology and History in Tanzania*, Madison, Wis.: University of Wisconsin Press.

Ferguson, D. E. (1980), 'The Political Economy of Health and Medicine in Tanganyika', in Kaniki, M.H.Y. (ed.) (1980).

Ford, John (1979), 'Ideas which have influenced attempts to solve the problems of African Trypanosomiasis', *Social Science and Medicine* 13B:269–275.

Freyhold, Michaela von (1979), *Ujamaa Villages in Tanzania*, London: Heinemann.

Fyfe, Christopher and David McMaster (eds.) (1977), *African Historical Demography* (Proceedings of a Seminar), Edinburgh: University of Edinburgh, Centre of African Studies.

—— (1981), *African Historical Demography*, Edinburgh: University of Edinburgh, Centre of African Studies.

Ghai, D. *et al.* (eds.) (1979), *Agrarian Systems and Rural Development*, London: Macmillan.

Giblin, James (1990), 'Trypanosomiasis Control in African History: An Evaded Issue?' *Journal of African History* 31, 1: 59–80.

—— (1993), *The Politics of Environmental Control in Northeastern Tanzania, 1840 –1940*, Philadelphia: University of Pennsylvania Press.

Glass, D.V. (1948), 'Bibliography of the demographic studies of Dr. R.R. Kuczynski', *Population Studies* 2,1:125–126.

Glassman, Jonathon Philip (1991), 'The Bondsman's New Clothes: The Contradictory Consciousness of Slave Resistance on the Swahili Coast', *Journal of African History* 32, 2:277–312.

Gregory, Joel W., Dennis D. Cordell and Raymond Gervais (1984), *African Historical Demography: A Multidisciplinary Bibliography*, Los Angeles, Cal.: Crossroads Press.

Hartwig, Gerald W. (1970), 'The Victoria Nyanza as a Trade Route in the Nineteenth Century', *Journal of African History* 11:535–552.

—— (1976), *The Art of Survival in East Africa: the Kerebe and Long-distance Trade, 1800 –1895*, New York: Africana Publishing.

—— (1979), 'Demographic Considerations in East Africa During the Nineteenth Century', *International Journal of African Historical Studies* 12, 4:653–672.

Hartwig, Gerald W. and K. David Patterson (eds.) (1978), *Disease in African History: An Introductory Survey and Case Studies*, Durham, NC: Duke University Press.

Homewood, K.M. and W.A. Rodgers (1991), *Maasailand Ecology*, Cambridge: Cambridge University Press.

Hopkins, A. G. (1973), *An Economic History of West Africa*, London: Longman.

Hyden, Göran (1980), *Beyond Ujamaa in Tanzania: Underdevelopment and an Uncaptured Peasantry*, Berkeley, Cal.: University of California Press.

Iliffe, John (1979), *A Modern History of Tanganyika*, Cambridge: Cambridge University Press.

—— (1990), *Famine in Zimbabwe, 1890–1960*, Gweru: Mambo Press.

Ishumi, Abel G.M. (1980), *Kiziba: The Cultural Heritage of an Old African Kingdom*, Syracuse, NY: Syracuse University.

Jewsiewicki, B. and David Newbury (eds.) (1986), *African Historiographies: What History for Which Africa?* Beverly Hills, Cal.: Sage Publications.

Johnson, Douglas H. and David M. Anderson (eds.) (1988), *The Ecology of Survival: Case Studies from Northeast African History*, Boulder, Col.: Westview Press.

Junker, Wilh. (1891), *Dr. Wilh. Junkers Reisen in Afrika, 1875–1886*, Wien: Eduard Hölzel.

Kaniki, M.H.Y. (ed.) (1980), *Tanzania Under Colonial Rule*, London: Longman.

Kanogo, Tabitha (1992) 'Women and Environment in History', in Khasiani, S.A. (ed.) (1992).

Katoke, Israel K. (1975), *The Karagwe Kingdom: A History of the Abanyambo of North Western Tanzania c. 1400–1915*, Nairobi: East African Publishing House.

Kenny, Michael G. (1979), 'Pre-Colonial Trade in Eastern Lake Victoria', *Azania* 14:97–107.

Khasiani, Shanyisa A. (ed.) (1992), *Groundwork. African Women as Environmental Managers*, Nairobi: ACTS Press.

Kimambo, I. N. (1991), *Penetration and Protest in Tanzania: The Impact of the World Economy on the Pare, 1860–1960*, London: James Currey.

Kjekshus, Helge (1974), 'Ecological Control and Economic Development', Dar es Salaam: University of Dar es Salaam, History Research Seminar Paper (mimeographed).

—— (1974a), 'Pre-colonial Industries. A Preliminary Survey', Dar es Salaam: University of Dar es Salaam, Department of Political Science (mimeographed).

—— (1977), 'The Population Trends of East African History: A Critical Review', in Fyfe and McMaster (eds.) (1977).

—— (1977a), 'The Tanzanian Villagization Policy: Implementational Lessons and Ecological Dimensions', *Canadian Journal of African Studies* 11, 2:269–282.

Klein, Martin A. (ed.) (1980), *Peasants in Africa: Historical and Contemporary Perspectives*, Beverly Hills, Cal.: Sage Publications.

Knight, C.G. (1974), *Ecology and Change: Rural Modernization in an African Community*, New York: Academic Press.

Koponen, Juhani (1988), *People and Production in Late Precolonial Tanzania: History and Structures*, Uppsala: Scandinavian Institute of African Studies.

Lamphear, John (1976), *The Traditional History of the Jie*, Oxford: Clarendon Press.

Larson, L.E. (1978), 'Book Review', *African Affairs* 77,1:129–130.

Lyons, Maryinez (1992), *The Colonial Disease: A Social History of Sleeping Sickness in Northern Zaire, 1900–1940*, Cambridge: Cambridge University Press.

MacLeod, Roy and Milton Lewis (eds.) (1988), *Disease, Medicine, and Empire: Perspectives on Western Medicine and the Experience of European Expansion*, London: Routledge.

Maddox, Gregory (1986), 'Njaa: Food Shortages and Famines in Tanzania Between the Wars', *International Journal of African Historical Studies* 19,1:17–34.

—— (1990), 'Mtunya: Famine in Central Tanzania, 1917–1920', *Journal of African History* 31, 2:181–98.

Maddox, Gregory, James L. Giblin, and I.N. Kimambo (eds.) (1996) *Custodians of the Land: Ecology and Culture in the History of Tanzania*, London: James Currey.

Mandala, Elias C. (1990), *Work and Control in a Peasant Economy: A History of the Lower Tchiri Valley in Malawi, 1859–1960*, Madison, Wis.: University of Wisconsin Press.

Marshall, Alfred (1938), *Principles of Economics*, 8th ed., New York: The Macmillan Company.

Mascarenhas, Ophelia and Marjorie Mbilinyi (1983), *Women in Tanzania. An Analytical Bibliography*, Uppsala: Scandinavian Institute of African Studies.

Matzke, Gordon (1983), 'A Reassessment of the Expected Development Consequences of Tsetse Control Efforts in Africa', *Social Science and Medicine* 17:531–537.

Mbilinyi, M. (1991), *Big Slavery: Agribusiness and the Crisis of Women's Employment in Tanzania*, Dar es Salaam: Dar es Salaam University Press.

McCall, Michael (1985), 'Environmental and Agricultural Impacts of Tanzania's Villagization Programme', in Clarke, J.I. *et al.* (eds.) (1985).

McCann, James C. (1991), 'Agriculture and African History', *Journal of African History* 32, 3:507–513.

McHenry, Dean (1979), *Tanzania's Ujamaa Villages: The Implementation of a Rural Development Strategy*, Berkeley: University of California, Institute of International Studies.

McNeill, William H. (1977), *Plague and Peoples*, Oxford: Basil Blackwell.

Mohiddin, Ahmed (1981), *African Socialism in Two Countries*, Totowa, NJ: Barnes and Noble Books.

Morton, Fred (1990), *The Children of Ham: Freed Slaves and Fugitive Slaves on the Kenya Coast, 1873 to 1907*, Boulder, Col.: Westview Press.

Muller, A.S. *et al.* (1988), *A Bibliography of Health and Disease in East Africa*, Amsterdam: Elsevier.

Mung'ong'o, Claude (1991), 'Sociological Processes and the Land Question in the Kondoa Irangi Hills, Tanzania', *Ambio* 20, 8:362–365.

Musere, Jonathan (1990), *African Sleeping Sickness: Political Ecology, Colonialism and Control in Uganda*, Lewiston, NY: Edwin Mellen Press.

Mwansasu, Bismarck U. and Cranford Pratt (eds.) (1979), *Towards Socialism in Tanzania*, Toronto: University of Toronto Press.

Neale, Catherine (1985), *Writing 'Independent' History: African Historiography, 1960–1980*, Westport, Conn.: Greenwood Press.

Newbury, David S. (1991), *Kings and Clans: Ijwi Island and the Lake Kivu Rift, 1780–1840*, Madison, Wis.: University of Wisconsin Press.

Ngaiza, Magdalene K. and Bertha Koda (eds.) (1991), *Unsung Heroines, Women's Life Histories from Tanzania*, Dar es Salaam: WRDP Publishers.

Ogot, Bethwell A. (ed.) (1979), *Ecology and History in East Africa*, Nairobi: Kenya Literature Bureau.

Palmer, Robin (1977), *Land and Racial Domination in Rhodesia*, London: Heinemann.

Paul, Jean-Luc (1993), 'Avant les paysans: agriculture et écologie dans une société agraire. L'exemple des Waluguru (Tanzanie)', *Revue Tiers Monde* 34,134:263–280.

Patterson, K. David (ed.) (1979), *Infectious Diseases in Twentieth-century Africa: A Bibliography of their Distribution and Consequences*, Waltham, Mass.: African Studies Association.

—— (1981), 'The Demographic Impact of the 1918–19 Influenza Pandemic in Sub-Saharan Africa: A Preliminary Assessment', in Fyfe and McMaster (eds.) (1981).

Peires, J. (ed.) (1981), *Before and After Shaka*, Grahamstown: Rhodes University, Institute of Social and Economic Research.

Ransford, Oliver (1983), *'Bid the Sickness Cease': Disease in the History of Black Africa*,

ECOLOGY CONTROL AND ECONOMIC DEVELOPMENT

London: Murray.

Redmond, Patric M. (1985), *The Politics of Power in Songea Ngoni Society*, Chicago: Adams Press.

Richards, Paul (1983), 'Ecological Change and the Politics of African Land Use', *African Studies Review* 26, 2: 1–72.

—— (1985), *Indigenous Agricultural Revolution. Ecology and Food Production in West Africa*, London: Hutchinson.

Rigby, Peter (1985), *Persistent Pastoralists: Nomadic Societies in Transition*, London: Zed Books.

Rotberg, Robert I. (ed.) (1983) *Imperialism, Colonialism and Hunger, East and Central Africa*, Lexington, Mass.: Lexington Books.

Schweinfurth, G. *et al.* (eds.) (1888), *Emin Pasha in Central Africa*, London: Georg Philip & Son.

Seavoy, Ronald E. (1989), *Famine in East Africa: Food Production and Food Policies*, New York: Greenwood Press.

Sender, John, and Sheila Smith (1990), *Poverty, Class and Gender in Rural Africa: A Tanzanian Case Study*, London: Routledge.

Sheriff, Abdul (1987), *Slaves, Spices and Ivory in Zanzibar*, London: James Currey.

Shields, Nwangana (1980), *Women in the Urban Labor Markets of Africa: the Case of Tanzania*, Washington, DC: World Bank.

Slater, Henry (1986), 'Dar es Salaam and the Postnationalist Historiography of Africa', in Jewsiewicki, B. and David Newbury (eds.) (1986).

Spear, T. and R. Waller (eds.) (1993), *Being Maasai. Ethnicity and Identity in East Africa*, London: James Currey.

Stirnmann, Hans (1976), *Existenzgrundlagen und traditionelles Handwerk der Pangwa von S.W.-Tanzania*, Freiburg, Switzerland: Universitätsverlag.

—— (1979), *Die Pangwa von SW-Tanzania: Soziale Organisation und Riten des Lebens*, Freiburg, Switzerland: Universitätsverlag.

Ström, G.W. (1978), *Development and Dependence in Lesotho, the Enclave of South Africa*, Uppsala: Scandinavian Institute of African Studies.

Sunseri, Thaddeus (1993), 'Slave Ransoming in German East Africa, 1885–1922', *International Journal of African Historical Studies* 26, 3:481–511.

Sutton, John (ed.) (1989), 'History of African Agricultural Technology and Field Systems', *Azania*, Vol. XXIV, Nairobi: British Institute in Eastern Africa.

Swantz, Maria Lisa (1985), *Women in Development: A Creative Role Denied? The Case of Tanzania*, London: Christopher Hurst.

Temu, Arnold, and Bonaventure Swai (1981), *Historians and Africanist History: A Critique*, London: Zed Books.

Theuws, Jaques (1992), 'Space, Travel and Ritual among the Luba', *Africana Gandensia*, 7, Gent: University of Gent.

Turshen, Meredeth (1984), *The Political Economy of Disease in Tanzania*, New Brunswick, NJ: Rutgers University Press.

UNESCO (1985–1989), *The UNESCO General History of Africa*, Vols. I–VII, Berkeley, Calif.: University of California Press; London: James Currey.

Vail, Leroy (1977), 'Ecology and History: the Example of Eastern Zambia', *Journal of Southern African Studies* 3, 2:129–155.

—— (1981), 'The Making of the "Dead North": A Study of the Ngoni Rule in Northern Malawi, 1855–1907', in Peires, J. (ed.).

Waller, Richard (1988), 'Emutai: Crisis and Response in Maasailand, 1883–1902', in Johnson, Douglas H. and David M. Anderson, (eds.) (1988).

Willis, Roy (1981), *A State in the Making: Myth, History, and Social Transformation in Pre-colonial Ufipa*, Bloomington: Indiana University Press.

Wollaston, A.F.R. (1908), *From Ruwenzori to the Congo, A Naturalist's Journey Across Africa*, London: John Murray.

World Commission on Environment and Development (The Brundtland Commission) (1987), *Our Common Future*, Oxford: Oxford University Press.

Wrigley, C.C. (1979), 'Population in African History', *Journal of African History* 20,1:127–131.

Young, E.D. (1877), *Nyassa, A Journal of Adventures Whilst Exploring Lake Nyassa, Central Africa*, London: John Murray.

AUTHOR INDEX

GENERAL INDEX

Africans, role of, against tsetse fly, 175–6
Agricultural systems, 26–48
  Bukoba, 44–6; coastal area, 29–30;
  Kilimanjaro, 34–6; river flood plains, 31–3;
  settlement patterns, 48–50; Ufipa, 41; Uhehe,
  38–40; Ukara, 44; Ukonde, 36–7; Umatengo,
  37–8; Ungoni, 40–1; Unyakyusa, 36–7;
  Unyamwezi, 42–3; Upare, 34–6; urbanism and
  trade, 30–1; Usagaras, 36; Usambaras, 33–4;
  summary, 46–8
Arms in war-time, 144–5; see also Firearms

Bananas, trading in, 119
Barter system, 116–17
Bibliography, 190–209; see also Author Index
Blacksmiths, prestige of, 81
Blood diets. human, 92
Border markets, 114
Bride wealth, 118
Bukoba
  agriculture, 44–6; district book, 19; iron-
  smelting, 83

Calcium, 92
Caravans, see Trade
Cattle
  ecological control through, 6
  19th cent. complex, 51–68
    coast and inland caravan routes, 56–9;
    Geita, 67–8; Karagwe, 67–8; Kilom-
    bero Valley, 60–1; pre-colonial entomology,
    52–6; Ruvuma Valley, 61–2; Sukumaland,
    67–8; Uha, 66–7; Ujiji, 66–7; Ukimbu, 64–6;
    Unyamwezi, 62–4;
  salt for, 93; trade patterns in, 118–19
Chagga markets, 114–15
Coastal belt
  agriculture, 29–30; cattle complex, 56–9
Coffee, trading in, 119
Colonial affairs
  effects on agriculture, 26; impact on trading
  patterns, 115; warfare, effects of, see under
  Ecological System; wars, table of actions during
  1889–1896, 186–90
Commodity trade, see Trade
Communal labour projects against tsetse fly, 174
Compost, 42
Conclusions (of this study), 180–5
Cotton weaving, 80, 105–9
Craftsmen (Fundis) emergence of, 117
Critical density (of population), 28
Cropping, frequency of, 28
Crop selection and rotation, 37, 47
Cultivation, see Agricultural systems

Death rate, effects of, on slave trading figures, 15

Demography, review of, 9–25
  maximum population disruption, 10–16
    internecine wars, 10–13; slave raiding,
    14–16
  minimum population disruption, 16–25
    internecine wars, 18–21; slave raiding, 21–4;
    a new hypothesis, 24–5
Depopulation
  effects, see Ecological system, breakdown of
  man-controlled trends, significance of, 9
Diseases
  among caravaners, 24; in population, see under
  Ecological system; see also Jiggers-plague;
  Sleeping sickness; Smallpox
District Books, quotations from
  Bukoba. 19; Geita, 68; Kasulu, 83–4;
  Morogoro, 58; Newala, 61; Old Liwale, 73;
  Songea, 62; Sumbawanga (Ufipa), 65, 109, 128
Donkeys, trading in, 119
Dry-season problems, 36

East Africa and Its Invaders, 14
Ecological matters
  collapse, results and remedies, 161–79
    periphery of colonial development, 168–79;
      concentration of sleeping sickness,
      168–73; local support, absence of,
      173–4; role of Africans, 175–6; wild life
      preservation, 176–8; development of
      periphery, 178–79
    sleeping sickness, 165–8; tsetse belts, 164–5;
    see also Breakdown of man-controlled (below)
  control measures, 3–5
  breakdown of man-controlled, 126–60
    colonial warfare, 143–53; arms, 144–5;
      scorched earth, 145–9; impact of
      pacification policy, 149–51; World War
      I, 151–3
    famine, 137–42
    labour recruitment, 154–60
      African, 154; impact on local economies,
      154–60
    procurations, 142–3; rinderpest, 126–32;
    sand-flea plague, 134–6; smallpox, 132–4;
    see also Collapse, results and remedies above
Economy
  development of, 3–5; ecological impact on
  local, 154–60
Ecosystem, Man's control of the, 3–4
Elephant hunters, prestige of, 117–18
Entomology, pre-colonial, 52–6
Erosion, problems of soil, 39, 47
Ethnicities of Tanganyika, map of, 11
Exploitation, The, of East Africa, 14
Exports from Rufiji, 32